CAMBRIDGE LIBRARY COLLECTION

Books of enduring scholarly value

Linguistics

From the earliest surviving glossaries and translations to nineteenth century academic philology and the growth of linguistics during the twentieth century, language has been the subject both of scholarly investigation and of practical handbooks produced for the upwardly mobile, as well as for travellers, traders, soldiers, missionaries and explorers. This collection will reissue a wide range of texts pertaining to language, including the work of Latin grammarians, groundbreaking early publications in Indo-European studies, accounts of indigenous languages, many of them now extinct, and texts by pioneering figures such as Jacob Grimm, Wilhelm von Humboldt and Ferdinand de Saussure.

A Compendium of the Comparative Grammar of the Indo-European, Sanskrit, Greek and Latin Languages

August Schleicher (1821–68) is often credited with being the first scholar to apply a 'family tree' model to language groups. He had published extensively on individual European languages before his groundbreaking comparative Indo-European *Compendium* (also reissued in this series) appeared in German in 1861–2. The book was derived from his lectures, and was intended to save his students note-taking and copying from the blackboard. Each section begins with his reconstruction of a Proto-Indo-European phonological or morphological feature, and then shows how this is reflected in a range of daughter languages. This abridged English translation, based on the German third edition, appeared in 1874–7. Produced for students of Greek and Latin philology, it focuses on the phonology and morphology of 'the original Indo-European language', Sanskrit, Greek and Latin, omitting Schleicher's extensive discussion of other languages and the comparative paradigms provided in the German edition. Volume 1 covers phonology.

T0371220

Cambridge University Press has long been a pioneer in the reissuing of out-of-print titles from its own backlist, producing digital reprints of books that are still sought after by scholars and students but could not be reprinted economically using traditional technology. The Cambridge Library Collection extends this activity to a wider range of books which are still of importance to researchers and professionals, either for the source material they contain, or as landmarks in the history of their academic discipline.

Drawing from the world-renowned collections in the Cambridge University Library and other partner libraries, and guided by the advice of experts in each subject area, Cambridge University Press is using state-of-the-art scanning machines in its own Printing House to capture the content of each book selected for inclusion. The files are processed to give a consistently clear, crisp image, and the books finished to the high quality standard for which the Press is recognised around the world. The latest print-on-demand technology ensures that the books will remain available indefinitely, and that orders for single or multiple copies can quickly be supplied.

The Cambridge Library Collection brings back to life books of enduring scholarly value (including out-of-copyright works originally issued by other publishers) across a wide range of disciplines in the humanities and social sciences and in science and technology.

A Compendium of the Comparative Grammar of the Indo-European, Sanskrit, Greek and Latin Languages

VOLUME 1

AUGUST SCHLEICHER

TRANSLATED BY HERBERT BENDALL

CAMBRIDGE
UNIVERSITY PRESS

CAMBRIDGE
UNIVERSITY PRESS

University Printing House, Cambridge, CB2 8BS, United Kingdom

Cambridge University Press is part of the University of Cambridge.
It furthers the University's mission by disseminating knowledge in the pursuit of
education, learning and research at the highest international levels of excellence.

www.cambridge.org
Information on this title: www.cambridge.org/9781108073707

© in this compilation Cambridge University Press 2014

This edition first published 1874
This digitally printed version 2014

ISBN 978-1-108-07370-7 Paperback

COMPARATIVE GRAMMAR.

A COMPENDIUM

OF THE

COMPARATIVE GRAMMAR

OF THE

INDO-EUROPEAN, SANSKRIT, GREEK AND LATIN LANGUAGES.

BY

AUGUST SCHLEICHER.

TRANSLATED FROM THE THIRD GERMAN EDITION

BY

HERBERT BENDALL, M.A.
CHR. COLL. CAMB.

PART I.

LONDON:
TRÜBNER & CO., 57 AND 59, LUDGATE HILL.

1874.

TRANSLATOR'S PREFACE.

THIS book is a translation of those parts of Schleicher's 'Compendium der vergleichenden Grammatik der Indo-germanischen sprachen' which treat directly of the Indo-European original language, Sanskrit, Greek, and Latin: it was undertaken for the use of students of Greek and Latin Philology, on the suggestion of Mr. Peile, M.A., of Christ's College, Cambridge, to whom I am indebted for several hints and corrections. My thanks are due to Herr Gustav Voigt also, for help kindly given.

I shall be glad if readers will point out any mistakes in the translation.

HERBERT BENDALL.

LIVERPOOL COLLEGE,
Oct. 1874.

PREFACE TO THE FIRST EDITION.

THIS work is meant to be an elementary handbook for lectures and self-instruction. The want of such a work has been hitherto widely felt. The state of Indo-European Philology is now such that it has become possible to write a compendium of the comparative grammar of the Indo-European languages. After we have discarded that part which is still doubtful, there remains a large store of knowledge, embracing the different sides which language offers to scientific treatment: this knowledge will, in my opinion, stand unshaken for all time. The chief object of a compendium of the Indo-European languages is to collect and arrange in a short and appropriate form, and yet in an intelligible manner, these results of Indo-European Philology. Where, however, it is impossible to avoid mentioning what is obscure and doubtful, it will be expressly characterized as such.

It is no slight task to compose a first handbook of this kind treating of the formation of the Indo-European languages: whether the writer of the present work has succeeded in temporarily satisfying the want, others must decide; but he begs them to take it into consideration that his book is a first essay in the direction pointed out.

The following account of the origin of my book may to some extent at least show that I have honestly encountered the difficulties of the task.

I have been Academical Professor for fifteen years, and have lectured on Indo-European grammar from the outset; partly sketching out grammars of particular Indo-European languages, from a philological point of view, partly writing a grammar of the languages which collectively form a speech-stem, *i.e.* a so-called Comparative Grammar. To infer from the number of hearers whom even these latter lectures attracted, and from the perseverance and attention with which I was listened to, they must have treated the subject in a manner intelligible to beginners. I have remodelled my notes more than once. It was a real pleasure to work for my hearers and pupils here: I am indebted to their encouragement and participation for the heartiness with which I undertook the complete re-arrangement of my treatise on Comparative Grammar of Indo-European languages, which I had delivered in two sets of half-yearly lectures.

In these lectures on Indo-European grammar I felt the want of a printed elementary treatise, which should offer in the most appropriate way the necessary examples and comparative tables. Dictating, and continually writing on the black board, is wearisome both to hearers and to the lecturer. Hence the thought first occurred to me of having my paper multiplied in MS. for the use of my pupils. And from this arose by degrees what I have now completed, the composition of a compendium especially for beginners. This book is therefore my notes repeatedly revised, and this is the point of view from which I desire it to be used and criticized.

It is to be understood that in my lectures I did not confine myself to the matter in the notes; what is printed here is merely that part which I used to dictate. Enlargements on particular points and excursus by the way I have never denied myself. Those who make use of this compendium will perhaps take this into consideration. The attempt to reduce the compass of the book to the narrowest limits possible made it a necessity to banish from it all discussions as regards different views. Generally I have attempted, whenever I could, to arrange the facts in such a way that they carried their proofs with them: moreover, the materials are so copious that even in the lectures it is difficult to find time for a controversial statement of details.

Circumstances unfortunately compelled me to finish the last preparation of the MS. for a printed compendium in a short time: but I hope that I have nevertheless written a useful book.

The design and execution of my work must speak for themselves; to discuss these points here would occupy too much space, and lengthen the compass of the preface to excess.

AUGUST SCHLEICHER.

JENA, *September*, 1861.

ABBREVIATIONS.

A.S.	Anglo-Saxon	mom.	momentary
acc. to	according to	N.H.G.	New High German
bef.	before	O.Bulg.	Old Bulgarian
bes.	beside	O.H.G.	Old High German
betw.	between	origl.	original Indo-European
caus.	causative		language
comb.	combination	partt.	particles
dial.	dialect	Pol.	Polish
diall.	dialects	√	root
ex.	example	Scl.	Sclavonic
exx.	examples	sf.	suffix
f.f.	fundamental form	sff.	suffixes
fm.	form	st.	stem
fmn.	formation	stt.	stems
inscrr.	inscriptions	termn.	termination
M.H.G.	Middle High German.	unacc.	unaccentuate

Asterisk * indicates that the form does not occur.

The other abbreviations explain themselves.

TABLE OF CONTENTS.

INTRODUCTION.

		PAGE
I.	SCIENCE OF LANGUAGE	1
	Grammar	1
II.	CHIEF FORMS OF LANGUAGES	2
	(*i.e.* the arrangement of languages according to their morphology, as Monosyllabic, Confixative, and In- flexive)	
III.	THE LIFE OF A LANGUAGE	4
	1. Its Development	4
	2. Its Decay	4
	Differentiation of Languages (Speech-stems, etc.) . . .	4
IV.	THE INDO-EUROPEAN LANGUAGES	5
	1. The Asiatic group.	5
	2. The S.W.-European group	5
	3. The N.-European group	
	The earliest divisions of the Indo-European Language . .	
	Plan of the original separations	

GRAMMAR.

I. PHONOLOGY.

A. VOWELS.

PAGE

§ 1. INDO-EUROPEAN ORIGINAL LANGUAGE 9

Table of Sounds 9

§ 2. Vowels 10

Examples—1. a-scale. 10

           2. i-scale 10

           3. u-scale 10

§ 3. Vowel Sound-laws. 12

§ 4. SANSKRIT 12

Table of Sounds 13

Pronunciation of Sounds 14

§ 5. Vowels 16

§ 6. Examples—1. a-scale 16

Loss of a before r, l ($r=ar$, $l=al$) 17

Weakening: $r=ra$ 17

Loss before other Consonants—

$u=va$, $i=ya$ 18

§ 7. Weakening of a, firstly, to i and u 18

$u=an$, am 19

Weakening of a, secondly, to $\bar{i}$ and $\bar{u}$ ($\bar{i}r$, $\bar{u}r=ar$) . . . 19

§ 8. Fundamental Vowel a 20

§ 9. Step-formation of a to $\bar{a}$ as root-vowel 21

Note.—The roots ending in a which are usually classed

with $\bar{a}$ 21

Step-formation of a in elements expressing relativity . . 22

PAGE

§ 10. 2. *i*-scale; fundamental vowel *i* 22
    Lengthening of *i* to *ī* 22
§ 11. First step-formation of *i* to *ē* 23
    Second step-formation of *i* to *āi* 23
§ 12. 3. *u*-scale; fundamental vowel *u* 24
    Lengthening of *u* to *ū* 24
§ 13. First step-formation of *u* to *ō* 24
    Second step-formation of *u* to *āu* 24
§ 14. **Vowel Sound-laws** 25
    1. Laws regulating the concourse of vowels 25
        a. Contraction 25
        b. Loss of *a* 26
        c. Splitting-up of *i* (*ī*) and *u* (*ū*) into *iy, uv* 26
        d. Change into corresponding semi-vowel 26
§ 15. 2. Vowel variations conditioned by neighbouring consonants 27
        a. Lengthening of vowels before *y* 27
        b. *iy, īy = y* 28
        c. Contraction of *yā* to *ī* (*ī* also as product of older
          contractions) 28
        d. Compensatory lengthening 29
        e. Dulling of *ā* to *ē* and *āu* 30
        f. Auxiliary vowel *i, ī* 31
§ 16. Greek. **Table of Sounds** 31
    Their pronunciation 32
§ 17. **Vowels.**
    Note.—Ambiguity of sounds 33
§ 18. Examples; 1. *a*-scale. Loss 34
    Weakening of *a* to *ι* 34
    Lengthening of this *ι* to *ῑ* 35
    Weakening of *a* to *υ* 35
§ 19. Fundamental vowel; *ε* = origl. *a* 36
    o = origl. *a* 37

PAGE

o beside *a* dialectically 37

a = origl. *a* 37

a beside ε 37

a = *a* + nasal. 38

§ 20. Step-formations of *a*. First step : 1. ε 38

raised to *o*. 2. *a* raised to *ā*, *η* 39

Second step, *ω* 40

§ 21. 2. *i*-scale; fundamental vowel *ι* 40

Lengthening of *ι* to *ῑ* 41

§ 22. Step-formations of *ι*. First step : *ι* raised to ει, αι . . 41

Second step. *ι* raised to οι 42

§ 23. *u*-scale. Fundamental vowel *υ*. Lengthening of *υ* to *ῡ*. 42

Note.— *ι* in place of *υ* 43

§ 24. Step-formations of *υ*. First step, *υ* raised to ευ, αυ . . 43

Second step: *υ* raised to ου 44

αυ, ωυ, ω as second steps of *υ* 44

Note.—Initial ου, ευ = origl. *va*. 45

§ 25. **Vowel Sound-laws**: general 45

§ 26 a. Insertion of *ι* in preceding syllable in case of termination -σι 46

§ 26 b. Vocalisation and transposition of *y*, *v*. 1. *y* becomes *ι*,
v becomes *υ* 46

2. ε = *y* 47

3. Transposition and assimilation of origl. *y* and *v* after
ν, *ζ*, *λ* 48

§ 27. Loss of *y*, *v*, *s*; consequent vowel-accumulations and contractions 49

§ 28. Compensatory lengthening. 1. Compensatory lengthening
after loss of *n* before *s* 50

2. Compensatory lengthening *in medio* after loss of *s* from
after *λ*, *μ*, *ν* 50

3. Compensatory lengthening in nom. sing. 50

PAGE

§ 29. 1. Vowel-insertion 51

2. Vowel-prefixure 52

§ 30. Latin. **Table of Sounds** 53

§ 31. **Vowels** 54

§ 32. Examples—1. *a*-scale. 1. Loss 55

2. Weakening of *a* to *i* 56

3. Weakening of *a* to *u*; decline of *a* to *o, u, ü, i* . . . 57

u for the *o* of the older language 57

o retained after *v, u* 58

§ 33. Fundamental vowel. 1. *a* = origl. *a* 58

2. *o* = origl. *a* 58

o after *v* 58

so = origl. *sva* 58

o before *v*; *o* in other combinations; *o*, later *u*, in final
stem- and word-formative elements 59

3. *e* = origl. *a* 59

§ 34. Step-formations of origl. *a*. 1. *e* raised to *o* 60

2. *ē* = origl. *ā* 61

3. *ā* = origl. *ā* 61

4. *ō* = origl. *ā* 62

5. *ū* = origl. *ā* 62

§ 35. 2. *i*-scale 63

Fundamental vowel *i* 63

Dulling of *i* to *e* 63

First step: *i* raised to *ei, ī, ē*; further to *ai, ae* 64

Second step: *i* raised to *oi, oe, ū* 65

§ 36. 3. *u*-scale 65

Fundamental vowel *u* 65

Weakening of *u* to *ü, i* 65

Note.—*ū* as a lengthening of *u* 66

First step: *u* raised to *eu*, for which occur *ou, ū* . . . 66

u raised to *au* 67

Second step: *u* raised to *ou, ū*, coinciding with First step . 67

PAGE

§ 37. **Vowel Sound-Laws** 68

Hiatus; contraction; *u* and *i*, *e* remain before vowels . . 68

§ 38. Assimilation: relationship of vowels to consonants . . . 68

o near *u, v*; *u* near labials, *m, l* 69

e in final syllables before nasals and two or more consonants;

o before *r* 70

Fluctuation of *e* and *u* before *nt, nd*; *i* before *n* 70

Dissimilation 70

§ 39. Final loss of consonants 70

1. Compensatory lengthening 71

2. Contraction 71

§ 40. Vowel-weakening 71

a weakened to *e, i,* to *u*; *ā* to *ē* 72

ae to *ī*; *au* to *ō, ū*: weakening and shortening of longer

vowels and diphthongs to *i* 72

Weakening of *o, u,* to *i* before secondary suffixes and in

compounds 72

§ 41. Shortening of vowels in unaccented final syllables . . . 72

§ 42. Loss of final vowels 73

Medial loss of vowels 73

§ 43. Auxiliary vowels 74

B. CONSONANTS.

§ 44. **Consonants of the Indo-European Original Language** . 76

§ 45. Momentary mute unaspirated Consonants . . . 77

1. *k,* 2. *t,* 3. *p* 77

§ 46. Momentary sonant unaspirated Consonants . . 78

1. *g,* 2. *d,* 3. *b* 78

Note.—On the original existence of *b* 78

§ 47. Momentary sonant aspirated Consonants . . . 78

1. *gh,* 2. *dh,* 3. *bh* 78

PAGE

§ 48. Spirants. 1. *y*, 2. *s*, 3. *v* 79

§ 49. Nasals. 1. *n*, 2. *m* 79

§ 50. *r* 80

§ 51. SANSKRIT. **Consonants** 80

§ 52. Original momentary mute unaspirated Consonants 80

1. Origl. *k*; Sk. *k* = origl. *k*; *k'* = origl. *k* 82

Sk. *kh* = origl. *sk*; Sk. *k'h* = origl. *sk* (a variation of Sk. *kh* 82

acc. to sound-laws); Sk. *ç* = origl. *k* and its interchange

with *k*, *š*, etc. 83

Sk. *p* = origl. *k* 83

2. Origl. *t*; Sk. *t* = origl. *t*; Sk. *th* = origl. *t* 84

Note.—ks for *kt* 84

3. Origl. *p*; Sk. *p* = origl. *p*; Sk. *ph* = origl. *p* 85

§ 53. Origl. momentary sonant unaspirated consonants:

1. Origl. *g* 85

Sk. *g* = origl. *g*; Sk. *g'* (and its representatives acc. to

sound-laws) = origl. *g* 85

Sk. *h* for origl. *g* 86

2. Origl. *d*; Sk. *d* = origl. *d* 86

d from *sd* 86

3. Sk. *b* 86

§ 54. Origl. momentary sonant aspirated consonants:

1. *gh*; Sk. *gh* = origl. *gh*; Sk. *h* = origl. *gh*; Sk. *g'h*. . . 86

2. *dh*; Sk. *dh* = origl. *dh*; Sk. *h* = origl. *dh* 87

3. *bh*; Sk. *bh* = origl. *bh*; Sk. *h* = origl. *bh* 87

Roots beginning or ending with origl. aspirates 87

§ 55. Spirants. 1. Sk. *y* = origl. *y* 88

2. Sk. *s* = origl. *s* 88

Sk. *š* = origl. *s* 88

Variation of origl. *s* to *š*, °, *r*, *ç*, acc. to sound-laws . . . 89

Change of *as* to *ō*; change of *š* to *k* before *s* 89

Change of *š* to *t*, *ḍ* 90

PAGE

3. Sk. v = origl. v 90

§ 56. Nasals. 1. Sk. n = origl. n 90

Loss of n before case-terminations 91

2. Sk. m = origl. m 91

Interchange of n, m, with $ṅ$, $ń$, $ṇ$, ˘, acc. to sound-laws . 91

§ 57. r- and l-sounds 91

Sk. r = origl. r 91

Sk. l = origl. r 92

§ 58. Sound-laws 92

§ 59. Medial. 1. Assimilation: before sonant consonants are
found sonants, before mute mutes 93

Dissimilation; s before s to t 94

2. Aspirates: sonant aspirates + t become sonant unaspirated consonants + dh; ht becomes gdh; ht, hth, hdh, also
become $ḍh$ with lengthening of preceding vowel . . . 94

Transposition of aspiration from termination to beginning
of roots 95

Law of reduplication 95

§ 60. Termination. 1. Only one consonant tolerated *in fine* (commonest exception ˘s) 96

2. None but mute consonants stand *in fine* 96

§ 61. GREEK. Consonants 97

§ 62. Origl. momentary mute unaspirated consonants:

1. k; κ, γ = origl. k 98

π, τ = origl. k 99

2. t; τ = origl. t 100

$\kappa\tau$ beside ks of other languages 100

3. p; π = origl. p 100

Note 2.—Unorigl. aspiration of mute momentary consonants 101

§ 63. Origl. momentary sonant unaspirated consonants.

1. g; γ = origl. g 101

β = origl. g 102

PAGE

2. d; δ = origl. d 102

3. b;. β = origl. b 102

    Note.—χ, θ, ϕ for γ, δ, β 103

§ 64. Origl. momentary sonant aspirated consonants.

1. χ = origl. gh 103

2. θ = origl. dh 104

    Note.—θ for χ 104

3. ϕ = origl. bh 104

    Note.—Roots beginning and ending with origl. aspirates 105

    Consonantal Prolonged-sounds 105

§ 65. Spirants: 1. y; Gk. ι (also transposed)=origl. y . . . 106

    ϵ, ζ = origl. y 106

    $'$ = origl. y; loss of origl. y 107

2. s; σ = origl. s, sometimes also *in initio*; $'$ = origl. s, sv . 108

    Transfer of $'$ from middle to beginning of a word . . . 109

    Note.—ἕος = *sevos 109

    $'$ as a later representative, esp. before υ 110

    Loss of origl. s 110

    Loss of origl. s before ν, ρ, μ and other consonants . . 111

3. v; υ (also transposed)=origl. v 112

    F = origl. v 112

    $'$ = origl. v 113

    Note.—β=v, $\sigma\phi$=sv 113

§ 66. Nasals: 1. ν=origl. n; the nasal dependent on following

    consonants 114

2. μ=origl. m; ν in terminations for origl. m 115

§ 67. r- and l-sounds; ρ=origl. r 116

    λ=origl. r 116

§ 68. **Sound-laws: Medial** 116

1. Assimilation. a. Complete assimilation of foregoing

    to following sound: ν, $\nu\tau$, $\nu\delta$, $\nu\theta$ before following s. 116

  PAGE

b. Complete assimilation of following to foregoing sounds:
    of F, y, σ; $\tau\tau=\tau y$, θy, κy, χy, $\delta\delta=\delta y$, γy . . . 117

c. Partial assimilation of foregoing to following sounds,
    before τ, σ, only mutes can stand, before δ only
    sonants, before θ only aspirates. Before ν labials pass
    over into their labial; ν before labials becomes μ;
    τ, δ, θ, before μ often become σ; κ, χ, before μ
    become γ; aspiration before nasals, ρ, λ; τ before
    ι becomes σ, sometimes also before ν 119

d. Partial assimilation of following to preceding sounds;
    $\delta y = \zeta$; aspiration of unaspirated consonants on acct.
    of preceding prolonged sounds. 121

e. Simultaneous assimilation, partial and complete, of
    sounds to one another; γy to ζ (ζ is not $=\beta y$); τy,
    θy, κy, χy to $\sigma\sigma$. 122
        $\sigma\sigma$ apparently $=\gamma y$ 123
        $\sigma\sigma$ not $=\pi y$. 123

f. Apparent sound-insertion between consonants coming
    together: $\nu\rho$, $\mu\rho$, $\mu\lambda$, become $\nu\delta\rho$, $\mu\beta\rho$, $\mu\beta\lambda$, for
    which $\beta\rho$, $\beta\lambda$ also occur ($\pi\tau$ *in initio* for π) . . 123

g. Elision of σ between consonants; loss of τ, ν, between
    vowels 124

2. Dissimilation; dentals before τ, θ, to σ; avoidance
    of two aspirates one after the other; avoidance of two
    similar or like consonants separated by vowels . . 124

3. Aspirates; retrogression of aspiration upon τ beginning
    a root. 125

4. Law of reduplication. 125

§ 69. Termination. Only σ, ν and ρ end a word; τ cast off or
    changed into σ; θ changed to σ 126
        τ falls off, sometimes also other consonants; m becomes
        ν; rejection of the last consonant from final groups of
        consonants; ν ἐφελκυστικόν, etc. 126

PAGE

§ 70. LATIN. **Consonants.** 128

§ 71. Origl. momentary mute unaspirated consonants:

    1. k; Lat. c, q, qv=origl. k 128

    Lat. g=origl. k 129

      Note.—Pronunciation of c before i; h=origl. k in pro-

      nominal stem hi-, ho-, and in $\sqrt{hab}$; Lat. p

      not = origl. k 129

    2. Lat. t=origl. t 130

    3. Lat. p=origl. p 131

§ 72. Momentary sonant unaspirated consonants:

    1. g; Lat. g, gv, v=origl. g 132

      Note.—*Flug* beside *flu*; b not=origl. g 132

    Mispronunciation of gn as $\dot{n}n$ 133

    2. d; Lat. d=origl. d; Lat. l=origl. d 133

    3. b; b of other languages 134

§ 73. Momentary sonant aspirated consonants:

    (f, *in medio* b represents all the aspirates; ch, th, ph are

    not Latin) 134

    1. gh; Lat. g, gv, v=origl. gh. 134

    h=origl. gh; loss of h (h wrongly written) 136

    f=origl. gh 136

    2. dh; Lat. d=origl. dh; r=origl. dh; $\dot{f}$=origl. dh . . . 137

    b=origl. dh 139

    2. bh; Lat. b=origl. bh 139

    Lat. f=origl. bh; Dat. h=origl. bh. *Note.* t, p, not=origl.

    dh, bh 139

§ 74 Spirants; 1. y; Lat. j=origl. y; i=origl. y 141

    Loss of y 141

    2. s; Lat. s (r)=origl. s 142

    3. v; Lat. v=origl. v; u=origl. v 142

    Note.—*suus, tuus, *sevos, *tevos* 143

    Loss of origl. v 143

PAGE

§ 75. Nasals; 1. *n*; before gutturals is found the nasal, before labials the labial guttural 144

　2. *m*=origl. *m* 144

§ 76. *r*- and *l*-sounds; Lat. *r*=origl. *r* 145

　Lat. *l*=origl. *r* 146

§ 77. Sound-laws. **Medial.**

　1. Assimilation. a. Complete assimilation of a foregoing to a following sound; doubling not characterized in the older spelling. 146

　　Loss of *d, t, n,* before *s* 147

　　Loss of *g* before *y*; of *g* before *v* 147

　　of *d* before *v* 148

　　Loss of *g, c, x,* before *n, m*; of *x* before *l*; of *t, d* before *c*; of *s* before sonants 148

　　Loss of *s* before *m*; of *s* before *l, d,* and *b* 149

　　Loss of *r* before *d*; of *r* before *s* 149

　　Loss of consonants before *sc*; *st* before and beside *xt, st,* for *rst*; loss of *c, g,* between *r, l,* and *t, s* . . . 150

　　br for *sbr, rbr*; *nt* for *nct* 150

　　b. Complete assimilation of a following to a preceding sound 151

　　ss for *st*; *rr, ll,* for *rt, lt*; *rr* for *rs,* etc.; *ll,* etc. perhaps for *ly*; *ns* for *nst*; *ss, s,* for *st,* from *dt, tt.* . . . 151

　　c. Partial assimilation of preceding to following sound; sonants before mutes become mutes; labials before *n* become *m*; in the earlier language *t* before nasals became *s*; *br* for origl. *tr* 152

　　d. Partial assimilation of following to preceding sound; *t* after nasals, liquids and *c* often becomes *s*. . . . 153

　　e. Change of *s* to *r* between vowels, or between vowels and sonant consonn. and after vowels in termination 153

　　f. Loss of consonants between vowels 154

　　g. Insertion of sounds (*mps, mpt*) 154

PAGE

2. Dissimilation; *t, d,* before *t* to *s* 154

Interchange of *-alis, -aris* 155

Avoidance of two perfectly or partially similar con-

sonants separated by vowels 155

§ 78. **Initial.** Consonant-loss *in initio* 155

m, n, for *sm, sn; r, l,* for *vr, vl* 155

f for *sf;* other sporadic cases 156

n for *gn; l* for *stl; v* for *dv* 156

y for *dy; v* for *qv; u* for *cu* 157

§ 79. **Final.** Consonant-groups *in fine;* no doubling, and no com-

bination of two momentary sounds in terminations . . 158

Later fixed system of termination in written language,

whereas in earlier times most final consonants were

sometimes written, sometimes omitted 158

Treatment of final *s* 159

Treatment of final *m, t* 159

Final *nt* 160

ERRATA.

PAG.	LINE.			
10, 11, 12	head	*for* Origl. language-vow ls	*read* Origl.-language.	Vowels.
17	9	*for* part. perf. pass.	*read* past part. pass.	
18	14	*for* pf. part.	*read* „ „ „	
25	3	*for* sub.	*read* post.	
34	13	*for* τονς	*read* τόνς.	
35	1	*for* κιρνημι	*read* κίρνημι.	
36	34	*for* μῆτερ-	*read* μητέρ-.	
39	22	*for* μῆτερ-	*read* μητέρ-.	
47	21	*for* σέομαι, σγομαι	*read* -σεομαι, -σγομαι.	
48	33	*for* ˘	*read* ῑ.	
54	7	*for* Old. Lat.	*read* Old Lat.	
ead.	28	*for* Indo-Germ.	*read* Indo-Eur.	
59	9	*for* uouos	*read* nouos.	
61	1	*for* dïco	*read* dīco.	
ead.	10	*for* and	*read* cf.	
64	17	*for* Sk.	*read* Gk.	
71	4	*for* φεροντς	*read* *φεροντς.	
72	last	*for* final ō . . . origl. ŏ	*read* final ŏ . . . origl. ō.	
78	16	*for* πυνζάνομαι	*read* πυνθάνομαι.	
100	3	*for* ab.	*read* Zend.	
104	last but one	*for* νεφελη	*read* νεφέλη.	
115	28	*for* μήτερ	*read* μητέρ-	
118	last but one	*for* ἥττων	*read* ἥττων.	
133	last but one	*for* δᾱήρ-	*read* δᾱήρ.	
148	19	*for* στίχω	*read* στίζω.	

INTRODUCTION.

I. Grammar forms one part of the science of language: this science is itself a part of the natural history of Man. Its method is in substance that of natural science generally; it consists in accurate investigation of our object and in conclusions founded upon that investigation. One of the chief problems of the science of language is the inquiry into, and description of the classes of languages or speech-stems, that is, of the languages which are derived from one and the same original tongue, and the arrangement of these classes according to a natural system. In proportion to the remainder but few speech-stems have hitherto been accurately investigated, so that the solution of this chief problem of the science must be looked for only in the future.

By grammar we mean the scientific comprehension and explanation of the sound, the form, the function of words and their parts, and the construction of sentences. Grammar therefore treats of the knowledge of sounds, or Phonology; of forms, or Morphology; of functions, or the science of meaning and relation, and syntax. The subject of grammar may be language in general, or one particular language or group of languages; grammar may be universal or special: it will in most cases be concerned in explaining the language as a product of growth, and will thus have to investigate and lay down the development of the language according to its laws. This is its exclusive province, and therefore its subject is the laying-down of the 'life of the language,' generally called historical grammar, or history of language, but more correctly 'science of the life of

1

a language' (of sound, form, function, and sentence), and this again may be likewise as well general as more or less special.

The grammar of the Indo-European languages is therefore a special grammar : because it treats of these languages as products of growth, and exhibits their earlier and earliest gradations, and would therefore be more accurately called a special historical grammar of Indo-European languages.

Note 1.—By comparative grammar is meant not that grammar which is merely descriptive, but that which throws light on speech-forms as far as possible, because as a rule it is not confined to the treatment of any one particular language.

Note 2.—The following work embraces only two parts, viz. scientific treatment of sounds and of forms. Indo-European function and sentence-formation we are not at present in a position to handle in the same way as in the case of the more external and intelligible branches—sounds and forms.

II. To assume one original universal language is impossible ; there are rather many original languages: this is a certain result obtained by the comparative treatment of the languages of the world which have lived till now. Since languages are continually dying out, whilst no new ones practically arise, there must have been originally many more languages than at present. The number of original languages was therefore certainly far larger than has been supposed from the still-existing languages. The easiest preliminary distribution of languages which we can make is suggested by their morphological constitution.

There are—

1. Languages which are simply composed of invariable disjointed meaning-sounds, M o n o s y l l a b i c, e.g. Chinese, Annamese, Siamese, Burmese. Such sounds we denote by *R* (radix). The Indo-European language would be in this stage of development when the word *ai-mi* (I go, εἶμι) was sounded not so, but as *i* or *i ma* (formula *R*, or *R+r*).

2. Languages which can link to these invariable sounds sounds of relation, either before, or after, or in the middle, or

in more than one place at once [denoted here as *s*. (suffix), *p*. (prefix), *i*. (infix)]. These are C o n f i x a t i v e languages, e.g. Finnish, Tatar, Dekhan, Basque, the languages of the aborigines of the New World, of South Africa.(Bântu), and most languages in fact. In this step of development the word *ai-mi* would be *i-ma* or *i-mi*.

3. Languages which for the purpose of expressing relation can regularly vary their roots as well as their confixes (which have sprung from independent original roots), and can at the same time preserve intact the means of compounding. These are I n f l e x i v e languages. Such a root as is regularly varied for the end of expressing relation is here denoted by R^x (R^1, R^2, etc.), a similar suffix by s^x.

Hitherto we have become acquainted with only two speech-stems of this class, the Semitic and the Indo-European. The latter has for all words only one formula, viz. $R^x s^x$ (s^x meaning one or more than one regularly variable suffix), and consequently a regularly variable root with a regularly variable expression of relation at the end of the suffix, e.g. *ai-mi*, εἶμι, √*i*.

The Indo-European is therefore a suffix-language, together with the neighbouring languages of the Finnish stem, including Tataric, (Turkish) Mongolian, Tungusian, Samoiedish, as also with the Dravidian (Dekhan)—all included in the formula *Rs*.

Note 1.—The Semitic, which is not akin to the Indo-European, has more word-forms, namely R^x and pR^x, forms quite strange to Indo-European, which has only one. Besides, its vowel-system is perfectly distinct from the Indo-European, not to mention other marked differences. Cf. Aug. Schleicher, 'Semitisch und Indogermanisch' in Beitr. ii. 236–244. An attempt to deduce the fundamental language of the Semitic speech-stem has been made by Justus Olshausen in his lehrbuche der hebräischen sprache, Brunswick, 1862.

Note 2.—The augment in Indo-European is no relation-affix, no prefix, but an adherent, though originally independent word, which may moreover be omitted.

III. The life of a language (generally called its 'history') falls under two heads—

1. *Development in prehistoric times.* As man has developed, so also has his language, *i.e.* the expression of his thoughts by sounds : even the simplest language is the product of a gradual growth : all higher forms of language have come out of simpler ones, the C o n f i x a t i v e out of the M o n o s y l l a b i c, the I n f l e x i v e out of the C o n f i x a t i v e.

2. *Decline in the historic period.* Language declines both in sound and in form, and in its decay changes of meaning take place alike in function and construction of sentences. The transition from the first to the second period is one of slower progress. To investigate the laws by which languages change during their life is a most important problem in the science of language, for unless we are acquainted with them we cannot possibly understand the languages in question, especially those which are still living.

Through different developments, at different points in the province of one and the same language, the self-same tongue branches out into the ramifications of the second period (whose beginning however is likewise earlier than the origin of historic tradition), and diverges into several languages (dialects) : this process of differentiation may repeat itself more than once.

All these changes took place gradually and at long intervals in the life of the language, since generally all changes in language unfold themselves gradually.

The languages which spring immediately from an original language we call f u n d a m e n t a l; almost every f u n d a m e n t a l-l a n g u a g e has split up into l a n g u a g e s; all these last-named l a n g u a g e s may further branch into d i a l e c t s; and these d i a l e c t s into s u b - d i a l e c t s.

All the languages which are derived from one original-language form together a c l a s s o f s p e e c h or s p e e c h - s t e m;

these again are sub-divided into f a m i l i e s or b r a n c h e s of s p e e c h.

IV. The name of Indo-European has been given to a distinct set of languages belonging to the Asiatico-European division of the earth, and of a constitution so consistent internally, and so different from all other languages, that it is clearly and un-doubtedly derived from one common original language.

Within this Indo-European class of speech however certain languages geographically allied point themselves out as more closely related to one another: thus the Indo-European speech-stem falls into three groups or divisions.

These are:

1. The Asiatic or Aryan division, comprising the Indian, Iranian (or more correctly Eranian), families of speech, very closely allied to one another. The oldest representative and fundamental-language of the Indo-European family, and gene-rally the oldest known Indo-European language, is the O l d - I n d i a n, the language of the oldest portion of the Vêdas; later on, after it had become fixed in a more simplified form, and subject to certain rules, as a correct written language, in opposition to the peoples' dialects, called S a n s k r i t. We are not acquainted with E r a n i a n in its original form: the oldest known languages of this stem are the O l d - B a k t r i a n or Z e n d (the Eastern), and the O l d - P e r s i a n, the lan-guage of the Achaimenid cuneiform inscriptions (the western). To this family besides is related the A r m e n i a n, which we know only from a later date, and which must have branched off even in early times from the E r a n i a n fundamental-language.

2. The south-west European division, composed of the G r e e k, next to which we must perhaps place the A l b a n i a n, pre-served to us only in a later form; I t a l i a n (the oldest known forms of this language are the L a t i n,—especially important for us is the O l d - L a t i n, as it was before the in-

troduction of the correct literary language formed under Greek
influence,—the U m b r i a n and the O s c a n), K e l t i c, of
which family the best known, though already highly decom-
posed, language is the O l d - I r i s h, Erse dating from
700 A.D.   Italian and Keltic have more in common with one
another than with the Greek.

3. The North-European division, composed of the S c l a v o n i c
family with its closely-allied L i t h u a n i a n,—the most important language for us of this group,—and the G e r m a n,
widely separated from both.   The oldest forms of this division
are the O l d - B u l g a r i a n (Old Church-Slavonic in MSS.
dating from 1100 A.D.) : the L i t h u a n i a n (and of course
the High-Lithuanian, South-Lithuanian, Prussian Lithuanian),
first known to us 300 years ago, but clearly of far greater
antiquity, and the G o t h i c from the fourth century.   Beside
the Gothic, however, are the oldest representatives of German
and Norse, O l d - H i g h - G e r m a n, and O l d - N o r s e, which
we may bring forward when they present earlier forms than
Gothic.

The greatest number of archaic particulars in point of sounds
and construction of language is found in the Asiatic division,
and within it, in the Old-Indian ; next in point of archaicisms
(*i.e.* preservation of similarity to the original language, by
having fewer strongly-developed and peculiar forms) comes
the S.W.-division, in which Greek is found to be most faithful ;
and lastly the N.-European group, which, if regarded as a
whole, may be shown to have the most characteristic development, and to be the least faithful to the original language.

By combining these facts with the above-named relationships
of the Indo-European languages, and drawing inferences as to
the process of separation of the Indo-European body of language in ancient times, we get the following result : The
Indo-European original language differentiates first, through
unequal development in different parts where it prevailed, into

two fundamental-languages, viz. the Sclavo-Teutonic, which afterwards divided itself into Teutonic and Sclavo-Lithuanian, and the Aryo-Graeco-Italo-Keltic, the remaining portion of the Indo-European language, which divided itself into Graeco-Italo-Keltic and Aryan; and the Graeco-Italo-Keltic soon split up into Greek and Italo-Keltic, while the first, the Aryan, remained undivided for some time. Later still the Sclavo-Lithuanian, the Aryan (Indo-Eranian) and Italo-Keltic, further divided themselves. It may be that at most or at all of the divisions there arose more languages than we now know of, since probably many Indo-European languages have died out through lapse of time. The further eastward an Indo-European people lives, the more archaicisms are found in its language: the further westward they have gone, the fewer archaicisms, and the more numerous new-formations are found in the language. From these and other indications we infer that the Sclavo-Teutonic race first began its wanderings westwards; next followed the Graeco-Italo-Keltic; and of the Aryans who remained behind, the Indians journeyed south-eastward, the Eranians south-westward. The home of the Indo-European original race must be sought in the highlands of Central Asia.

It is only of the Indians, who were the last to leave the parent stem, that it is quite certain that they expelled an aboriginal race from their later dwelling-place, a race of whose language much passed into their own: a similar process is highly probable in the case of many other Indo-European peoples.

The most ancient divisions of the Indo-European, up to the origin of the fundamental languages belonging to the families of speech formed from the speech-stem, may be seen in the following table (see next page). The length of the lines shows the duration of the periods, their distances from one another, the degrees of relationship.

Note.—In the present work an attempt is made to set forth the inferred Indo-European original language side by side with its really existent derived languages. Besides the advantages offered by such a plan, in setting immediately before the eyes of the student the final results of the investigation in a more concrete form, and thereby rendering easier his insight into the nature of particular Indo-European languages, there is, I think, another of no less importance gained by it, namely that it shows the baselessness of the assumption that the non-Indian Indo-European languages were derived from Old-Indian (Sanskrit), an assumption which has not yet entirely disappeared. This view has found supporters up to the present date, especially as regards Old-Baktrian (Zend). The term 'Sanskritist,' not seldom applied to Indo-European philologers (meaning that we concede to Sanskrit a position which it does not deserve, by deriving other languages from Sanskrit, or explaining them by it, instead of studying them fundamentally), is likewise shown to be quite inapplicable by the plan employed in the Compendium. The disadvantage of having in certain cases Indo-European original forms inferred which are more or less doubtful, does not weigh at all against the advantages which, according to our view, are attained by the arrangement of the subject used hereafter.

A form traced back to the sound-grade of the Indo-European original language, we call a fundamental-form [f.f.] (*e.g.* Lat. *generis,* f.f. *ganasas;* Gk. γένους, f.f. *ganasas*). Hence it is only when forms of different sound-grades are brought to one and the same sound-grade, that we can compare them with one another. When we bring forward these fundamental-forms, we do not assert that they really were once in existence.

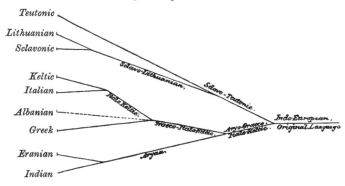

GRAMMAR.

PHONOLOGY.

A. VOWELS.

INDO-EUROPEAN ORIGINAL-LANGUAGE.   § 1.

Since in the citation of examples we make use not only of
vowels but also of consonants, before we treat of the vowels
we proceed to set forth a table of the speech-sounds collectively,
arranged according to the physiology of sound, followed by the
necessary remarks upon pronunciation, etc.

TABLE OF THE SOUNDS OF THE INDO-EUROPEAN ORIGINAL LANGUAGE,

i.e. those sounds from which arose the sounds of the different
Indo-European languages, according to the laws of sound-
change which come into play during the life of a language, and
to which accordingly, they may be traced as to a common source.

	CONSONANTS.							VOWELS.	
	MOMENTARY SOUNDS.			PROLONGED SOUNDS.					
	UNASPIRATED.		ASPIRATED.	SPIRANTS.		NASALS.	*r*-SOUND.		
	mute	sonant	sonant	mute	sonant	sonant	sonant		
Gutt.	*k*	*g*	*gh*					*a*	*aa, āa*
Pal.					*y*			*i*	*ȧi, āi*
Ling.							*r*		*au, āu*
Dent.	*t*	*d*	*dh*	*s*		*n*			
Lab.	*p*	*b*	*bh*		*v*	*m*		*u*	

§ 1.　*Note* 1.—The three aspirates and the vowel-diphthongs with *ā* (thus *āa*, *āi*, *āu*) probably were wanting at an earlier period in the life of the Indo-European original language; in the most archaic state of the language, while it was yet uninflected, all the vowel-diphthongs were absent.

Thus the Indo-European original language probably possessed six momentary sounds, viz. three mutes, and three sonants; six consonantal prolonged sounds, viz. three spirants, and three so-called liquids, *i.e.* the two nasals *n*, *m*, and *r* (*l* is a secondary offshoot of *r*), and six vowels. At a later period, shortly before the first separation, there were nine momentary, and nine vowel-sounds. We must not overlook the numerical proportion belonging to the number of sounds.

Note 2.—Sonants (or medials) are those consonants in whose production the glottis gives a simultaneous sound: this is the case with all nasals and *r*- and *l*-sounds, whilst the momentary consonants and spirants can be pronounced with or without the accompaniment of the vocal-sound. Sonants thus have something of the vowel in their composition. The aspirates are double sounds; both sounds of which they consist, the preceding momentary consonant and the subsequent aspiration, must be heard in pronunciation.

Note 3.—The momentary consonant which precedes the pronunciation of an initial vowel—the so-called spiritus lenis, the aleph or hamza of the Semitic,—which is formed by the sudden separation of the vocal chords, should properly be represented here and in the other languages in the tables, and expressed by a special character (perhaps ', after Gk. analogy). It is a consonant sound produced in the larynx alone, and must therefore be placed in a laryngal class of sounds (to which *h* also belongs, v. post. § 4). Nevertheless I have ventured to abide by the majority of Indo-European spelling-systems, and to leave this sound uncharacterized.

§ 2.　VOWELS OF THE INDO-EUROPEAN LANGUAGE.

Fundamental vowel.	1st Step.	2nd Step.
1.　*a*-scale　*a*	a+a=*aa*	a+aa=*āa*
2.　*i*-scale　*i*	a+i =*ai*	a+ai =*āi*
3.　*u*-scale　*u*	a+u=*au*	a+au=*āu*.

Note 1.—The second step occurs in the Asiatic, South-European, and North-European divisions of the Indo-European languages, and therefore in all probability traces its existence

from the original language, though the separate languages often § 2.
disagree in its use.

Note 2.—*aa* and *āa* were perhaps even in early times both
compressed into *ā*. But at the same time the two *ā*s which
thus arose are distinguished from one another, *e.g.* in Greek
and Gothic *ā* of the 1st is distinguished from *ā* of the 2nd step.
Notwithstanding that the earliest Indian and the Zend seem to
bear evidence against the contraction of both *a*s, we have placed
throughout hereafter an *ā* for *aa* and *āa* in original Indo-
European words, chiefly because it would be impossible to
distinguish always between a 1st and a 2nd step-form.

a, the commonest vowel, constitutes a class by itself; *i* and
u are by nature very similar, and are fundamentally different
from *a*. *i* and *u* have the consonants *y* and *v* as collateral re-
lations, and frequently as representatives, whilst *a* cannot pass
into any consonantal sound, and has therefore the vowel-nature
in a higher degree than the more consonantal sounds *i* and *u*.
a is by far the most frequent vowel in the Indo-European
language, occurring more often than *i* and *u* taken together.

Each vowel can move in its own scale only : this takes place
in the root itself for the purpose of expressing relation : the
vowels in stem-formative and word-formative suffixes likewise
are capable of step-formation, since these suffixes themselves
have arisen from roots originally independent. The fundamental-form of the root is always to be cited with the
fundamental vowel. Before two consonants the step-formation does not take place ; the fundamental vowel *a* (never *i* or
u) is found in all roots which end in two consonants.

The essence of inflexion depends upon the vowel-system.

Vowel-lengthening must not be conceded to the original
language as being of secondary origin.

Note.—Even where the correspondence between different
Indo-European languages seems to point to a greater antiquity
in the lengthening (*e.g.* in many nom. sing. as Sk. *pitā́r(s)*, Gk.
πατήρ, Old-Lat. *patēr*, Goth. *fadar*, i.e. **fathār ;* Sk. *dúrmanās*,
Gk. δυσμενής ; Sk. *áçmā*, Gk. ποιμήν, Lith. *akmŭ̀*, Lat. *homō*,

§ 2. Goth. *guma*, i.e. *gumā) we believe that we see an unoriginal phenomenon, which suitably to the nature of the case did not become developed in the different Indo-European languages till after their separation from the original language (not unfrequently the conformity is wanting even in this particular, cf. Sk. *bháran*, Gr. φέρων, Lat. *ferens*, Goth. *bairands*, Sclav. *bery*). In the original language we can cite here only the pure fundamental forms, *i.e.* the word preserved perfectly intact as regards all its parts (thus, e.g. *patars, dusmanass, akmans*).

EXAMPLES.

1. *a*-scale.

vak-mi (1 sg. pres.), √*vak* (speak), *va-vāk-ma* (1 sg. pf.), *vāk-s* (uox) ; *bhar-āmi, ba-bhar-mi* (I bear), *bhar-ta-s* (borne), √*bhar* (bear), *ba-bhār-ta* (3 sg. pf.), *bhār-a-s* (burden), *bhār-aya-ti* (3 sg. pres. caus. vb. ; φορεῖ) ; *da-ta-s, da-tā* (datus, data), √*da* (give), *da-dā-mi* (1 sg. pres.) ; *dha-ta-s, dha-tā* (past part. pass. n. sg. m. f.), √*dha* (set), *da-dhā-mi* (1 sg. pres.), etc.

2. *i*-scale.

i-masi (1 pl. pres.), √*i* (go), *ai-mi* (I go) ; *vid-masi* (1 pl. pres.), √*vid* (see, know), *vaid-mi* (I see), *vaid-aya-ti* (3 sg. pres. caus. vb.), *vi-vāid-ma* (pf.) ; √*div* (shine), *div-am* (acc. sg. word-st. *div*, light, bright sky, Ζεύς), *daiv-a-s* (shining, diuos, deus), etc.

3. *u*-scale.

bhug-na-s (past part. pass.), *a-bhug-am* (1 sg. aor.), √*bhug* (bend), *bhaug-āmi* (1 sg. pres.) *bu-bhāug-ma* (1 sg. pf.) ; *yug-a-m* (iugum), *yug-ta-s* (iunctus), √*yug* (iungere), *yu-yāug-ma* (1 sg. pf.), etc.

Note.—The agreement of Greek and Gothic proves the 2nd step in pf. ; πέφευγα gives no evidence against the 2nd step, but is a Graecism for *πέφουγα ; cf. forms like λέ-λοιπ-α, √λιπ, which therefore would lead us to expect ου here, because ει corresponds to εν ; v. sub Greek vowel-system.

§ 3.   VOWEL SOUND-LAWS

(*i.e.* influence of vowels and consonants on vowels) were not existent in the original Indo-European language.

A meeting of several vowels occurs but seldom, since hitherto no consonants have been elided, and prepositions, like separable §3. adverbs, stand before their verb.   Nevertheless, if two vowels do come into contact with one another in consequence of word-formation, hiatus perhaps occurred in the most original state of the language ; in early time, however, *a* may have become fused with following vowels: thus probably *i* (and *u*, but examples are wanting) after *a* becomes combined with it into a diphthong, in cases like *bharait* (3 sg. opt.), $\sqrt{bhar}$ (bear), pres. st. *bhara-*, *i* is the sign of the opt. ; the opt.-st. is thus *bharai-*, *t*=sf. of 3 sg. But the sequence of two vowels, of which the former is *i* or *u*, will not be considered as a hiatus, e.g. *i* and *u* (so also *ai, āi, au, āu*) remain unchanged before other vowels, as *i-anti* (3 pl. pres. $\sqrt{i}$, go), *ku-kru-anti* (3 pl. pf.) *krau-as* (neut. the hearing, $\sqrt{kru}$, hear).

Note.—The earliest Old-Indian points clearly to the non-avoidance of hiatus between *i, u* (and the diphthongs which have these vowels as their key-elements), and following vowels. We may nevertheless suppose that *iyanti, kukruvanti, krauvas* were pronounced, *i.e.* that *i* and *u* before vowels split up into *iy, uv*, as this pronunciation almost arises from them.

SANSKRIT.

TABULAR VIEW OF SANSKRIT SOUNDS.   §4.

	CONSONANTS.								VOWELS.	
	MOMENTARY.				PROLONGED.					
	UNASPIRATED.		ASPIRATED.		SPIRANTS.		NASALS.	*r-*&*l-*SOUND.		
	mute	sonant	mute	sonant	mute	sonant	sonant	sonant		
Gutt.	*k*	*g*	*kh*	*gh*	⸰	*h*	*ṅ*		$a\ \bar{a}$ ⎫	⎱
Pal.	*k̓*	*ǵ*	*k̓h*	*ǵh*	*ç*	*y(j)*	*ñ*		$i\ \bar{\imath}$ ⎬ $\breve{e}\ \bar{a}i$	
Ling.	*ṭ*	*ḍ*	*ṭh*	*ḍh*	*š̌*		*ṇ*	*r l*	$r\ \bar{r}\ l$	⎱ $\bar{o}\ \bar{a}u$
Dent.	*t*	*d*	*th*	*dh*	*s*		*n*			
Lab.	*p*	*b*	*ph*	*bh*		*v*	*m*		$u\ \bar{u}$	⎭

§ 4. The nasalised pronunciation of vowels (as **Fr.** *en, on*) is indicated by ˜ (*ã, ĩ,* etc.) : this pronunciation arises through the change of a following nasal consonant according to sound-laws.

The accented syllable is marked .

Note 1.—If we compare the above table with the table of Indo-European sounds in § 1, we shall find that the sounds collectively existed in the original language likewise (*ē*= original *ai, ō*=original *au*), but in addition to them we shall see a number of very similar unoriginal sounds, which have arisen from those original sounds according to the laws of language, and now stand side by side with them.

Note 2.—The doctrine of the Sanskrit alphabet belongs to Sanskrit special-grammar, as an appendix to the sound-rules.

Pronunciation. Known to us through the Hindu, which is on the whole a very good representative, and by means of the physiology of sounds, and the history of language.

The remarks on the pronunciation of the aspirates in § 1 hold good here also : they are distinct double sounds, and the *h* must be made audible after the momentary sounds.

We are accustomed to pronounce the momentary palatals *ḱ, ǵ, ḱh, ǵh*, like *tsch, dsch*, or, more accurately, like French *dj, tschh, djh*, a pronunciation which is correct only for a later state of the language; in the earlier period the correct pronunciation of *ḱ* and *ǵ* would be a close blending of *ky, gy*—almost like *k, g,* in German *kind, gieng* (in the case of the aspirates the aspiration is still naturally added). Our pronunciation of these sounds is nevertheless clumsy (especially before other sounds than *i, e*), and we therefore willingly abide by the somewhat incorrect traditional pronunciation, *i.e.* momentary dental + lingual spirant.

'Lingual,' for want of a better term, is used for that part of the mouth between the palate and the teeth. The momentary linguals are sounds like *t* and *d*, except that they are produced not by the teeth, but much further back towards the palate :

to effect this the tongue must be bent backwards : these sounds are called by the Hindus ' *head-sounds* ' (which has been mistranslated ' cerebral ') : in the conventional European pronunciation they are not distinguished from the dentals.

Of the spirants, the exact pronunciation of ḥ (a variation fr. *s* acc. to sound-laws) is not known ; it has no equivalent in sound : we pronounce it either as *h* or not at all.

h is always audible and equivalent to a sonant, and is therefore like our *h*, but must, however, be sounded emphatically. The *h* is a fricative noise formed in the upper part of the larnyx, and belongs (like ', § 1, Note 3) to the class of laryngal consonants. For convenience, here and in the other languages where it makes its appearance, we have placed it amongst ' Gutturals.' *h* can be produced either with or without vibration of the vocal chords, *i.e.* as a *sonant* or as a *mute.*

ç must be pronounced like *y*, but without its accompanying vocal-sound, and probably somewhat more sharply (with closer contraction of the organ), perhaps like *ch* in *sichel;* the conventional pronunciation as a sharp *sh* is wrong, and must be avoided ; ç has nothing in common with *s.*

š = Germ. *sch*, Fr. *ch.*

Nasals. ṅ is the guttural nasal, and must therefore be pronounced like Germ. *n* in *enkel*, or *ng* in *lange ;* ñ is the pal. nas., which must have been sounded as a close blending of *ny* (as Fr. *gn* in *campagne*) ; ṇ, the head-nasal, takes the place of formative *n*, where *ṭ* or *ḍ* follows : our pronunciation of it is unsuccessful, for we usually confuse it with *n.*

r and *l* as vowels are perhaps sounded as in Germ. *hadern, handeln,* pronounced with an inaudible *e* as *er, el ;* the existence of a strong vowel-sound in vowel *r* is expressly attested by Hindu grammarians (Benfey, Or. und Occ. iii. 25 *sqq.*). ṝ is = long *r*, and should therefore be distinguished from it by a more prolonged pronunciation. Also *r* before consonants was pronounced as a consonant, with a strongly perceptible vibration of the chords (as in other languages, especially in Zend), which even appears in spelling as a perfect vowel (*a, i*) after *r*. (Benfey, ib. p. 32.)

Note.—The Bohemian likewise has *r, l,* as vowels; the Slovack dialect has, moreover, the long form of each sound.

SANSKRIT VOWELS.

Of special importance are the change of *a* to *i, ī,* and *u, ū,* and its total loss (the latter rarely happens in the case of the other vowels). In the latter cases *r* and *l* after consonants form syllables, and count as vowels; *r* is then even capable of being lengthened to *ṝ* (as *i* and *u* to *ī* and *ū*).

Besides short *i* and *u,* Sanskrit has further their unoriginal lengthenings *ī, ū; ai* and *au* have been compressed into *ē* and *ō* (through approximation of *a* to *i* and *u,* whereby it became *e* and *o;* and through a further like assimilation of *i* and *u* to *a,* which thus passed into the same vowels *e* and *o;* from *ee, oo* arose *ē, ō*).

Here for the first time we are met by a very important law affecting the life of a language—the law of assimilation (partial and total), and by the no less frequent 'vowel-weakening,' a favourite change, especially in the case of *a.* The vowel-scales of the Sanskrit are now therefore as follows:—

			Weakening.	Fund.-vowel.	1st Step.	2nd Step.
1.	*a*-scale	loss;	*i, u; ī, ū;*	*a*	*ā*	*ā*
2.	*i*-scale			*i*	*ē*	*āi*
3.	*u*-scale			*u*	*ō*	*āu*

Note.—The *a*-scale is thus enriched by one member: a negative step-formation (*i.e.* the weakening) has thereby placed itself in a parallel line with the positive.

EXAMPLES.

1. *a*-scale.

The weakening occurs principally through the influence of the accent; a similar influence is likewise exercised by assimi-

lation to *i*, *u* of the following syllable, or the preceding con- § 6.
sonant has an effect equivalent to this assimilation.

Loss of *a* occurs most frequently before *r*, also after *r*, in
which cases *ar* and *ra* followed by a consonant become vowel *r;*
in parallel cases *al* becomes vowel *l*, *va*=*u*, *ya*=*i* ; loss of *a* is
however by no means confined to these instances.

Examples of complete loss of *a* are :

r=*ar*; √*bhar* (bear, pres. *bhár-āmi*, φέρω, fero), *bhr-tá-s* (n. sg.
masc. part. perf. pass.); √*kar* (make, 3 sg. pres. *kar-ọti*), *krt-á-s*
(made), *ḱa-kr-má* (1 pl. pf.); √*mar* (mori), *mrt-á-s* (mortuos,
βροτός=*μρο-το-ς) ; st. *mā-tár-* (μητέρ-, mater), *mā-tr-bhyas*
(matribus), *mā-tr-šu* (μητράσι), etc.

This *r* is subsequently treated acc. to analogy of the other
vowels, and thus is also lengthened; e.g. acc. pl. *mā-tṝ-s*
(matres, μη-τέρ-ας), *dā-tṝ-n* (datores, δο-τῆρ-ας), st. *dā-tár-* (dator,
δοτήρ).

l=*al* occurs only in √*kalp* (3 pres. med. *kálp-a-tē*, keep oneself right, succeed), which stands for original *karp* (v. ‘Consonants’), *klp-tá-s* (n. sg. masc. past part. pass.).

r=*ra* ; *prḱh-áti* (3 sg. pres.), √*praḱh* (pray, cf. Goth. *frah*,
Lat. *prec*, e.g. in *prak-šyáti*, 3 sg. fut.) ; *prth-ú-s* (broad), √*prath*
(cf. πλατ-ύ-ς, Lith. *plat-ù-s*), etc.

Note.—The Hindu grammarians treat *r*, *l*, as fundamental
vowels, *ar*, *al*, as their first step-formations. As a vowel of the
first step it is generally=*a* (for it often stands parallel to *ē*, *ō*,
also), in the second it is perfectly=*ā*. The first step is called
by the Hindu grammarians *guṇá-s* (masc. ‘quality’), the second
step *vṛddhi-s* (fem. ‘increase,’ √*vardh*, to increase, fmd. with sf.
ti), expressions which have often been introduced into European
works on language.

Loss of *a*, without admitting vocalisation of consonants, occurs
not only before other consonants, but also before *r*, which is
capable of being vocalised, in those cases where a vowel follows *r*
(from *ar*) ; in which case, as in all others where *a* is lost before
a consonant, the latter alone remains. Examples : *ḱa-kré*

§ 6. (1. 3. sg. pf. med.), √*kar* (make), for **k̑a-kar-ē*, and this fr. 1. *ka-kar-mē, 3. **ka-kar-tē; k̑a-kr-ús* (3. pl. pf. act.), fr. *ka-kar-anti.

Loss of *a* before other consonants, e.g. *g̑a-ghn-ús* (3. pl. pf.), √*han*, *ghan* (kill), for *g̑a-ghan-ús* (sg. *g̑a-ghắn-a*); *g̑a-gm-ús* (3. pl. pf.), √*gam* (go), for **g̑a-gam-us* (sg. *g̑a-gắm-a*); *s-ánti* (3. pl. pres.), √*as* (esse), for *as-anti (as *s-unt* for *es-unt); *s-yáti* (e.g. in *vy-ava-syáti*, he determines), for *as-yati, √*as*, *sa*, so too *ç-yáti* for *aç-yati, f.f. *ak-yati, √*aç*, *ça* (acuere); *á-pa-pt-at* (3. sg. aor.) for *a-pa-pat-at, √*pat* (fall, fly, πτ-έσθαι), etc.

u=va (*a* is lost and *v* becomes *u*); *uk-tá-s* (n. sg. masc. past part. pass.), √*vak* (speak, 3. sg. pres. *vák-ti*), *u-vák̑-a* (3. sg. pf.) for **va-vák̑-a*, *ūk̑ús* (3 pl. pf.) for **va-vak̑-ús*, f.f. *va-vak-anti, *ávōk̑am* for **a-va-uk̑-am* (1. sg. aor.), f.f. *a-va-vak-am (Gk. εἶπον fr. **ė́-Fϵ-Fϵπ-ον*); *sup-tá-s* (pf. part.), √*svap* (sleep; *sváp-iti* 3. sg. pres., *á-svap-am*, 1. sg. aor.); *urú-s* (wide, εὐρύς) for *varú-s (comp. st. *váriyās-*, superl. *váriṣtha-*), etc.

i=ya (*a* is lost and *y* becomes *i*); *iš-tá-s* (past part. pass.) for *yag-ta-s, √*yag̑* (offer, worship; 3 sg. pres. *yág̑-ati*), *i-yắg̑-a* (3 sg. pf.). for **ya-yắg̑-a*, *īg̑ús* (3 pl. pf.) for **ya-yag̑-ús*, f.f. *ya-yag-anti; *vidh-yati* (3 sg. pres.), √*vyadh* (wound, slay), *vi-vidh-ús* (3 pl. pf., 3 sg.=*vi-vyắdh-a*), etc.

§ 7. Weakening of *a*—1. to *i* and *u* occurs before *r*, sometimes with assimilation to vowel of following syllable; weakening of *a* to *i* often occurs without influence of following sounds. *u* in certain cases corresponds to original *an*, *am* (the nasal is lost, after dulling the preceding *a* into *u*).

Examples. *gir-i-s* (mountain), √*gar* (be heavy), Zend *gairis*, both from *gar-i-s (cf. Scl. *gor-a*, with another st.-termn.); *gur-ú-s* (heavy), cf. Gk. βαρ-ύ-ς, f.f. of both *gar-ú-s, the original √fm. *gar* comes to light only in the Sk. step-forms of this word, e.g. *gár-iṣtha-s* (superl. of *gurú-s*); *kur-ú* (2 imper. act.), *kur-u-té* (3 sg. pres. med.), and other like forms of √*kar* (make),—these stand for *kar-u, *kar-utē, etc., whilst the latter again stand for *kar-nu, *kar-nutē, etc. (v. post. 'Rules of Conjugation'), *kur-más* next for **kur-umas*, fr. **kar-nu-mas*, where, § 7. as in the similar forms, the *u* which caused the assimilation is lost; *pur-ú-s* (many), f.f. and Old-Persian *par-u-s*, cf. πολ-ύ-ς, √*par* (fill), *pur-á-m*, *pur-í* (state), from same √*par*, with *a* changed to *u* before *r*, without assimilating influence (cf. πόλ-ι-ς, f.f. *par-i-s*).

Weakening of *a* to *i* is frequent, e.g. *kir-áti* (3 sg. pres.), √*kar*, pf. *ka-kǎr-a* (pour out); *gir-áti* (3 sg. pres.), √*gar*, pf. *ǵa-gǎr-a* (throw); *çiš-más* acc. to sound-laws for **çis-mas* (1 pl.), beside *çǎs-mi* (1 sg.), pres. st. and √*çās* (pure √fm. *ças*, bid). This weakening occurs especially in the case of roots in *a* (which by-the-bye we find wrongly classified with √termns. *ā, ē, āi, ō*, acc. to the system of the Hindu grammarians), e.g. *sthi-tá-s* (*sta-tu-s*, στα-τό-ς), √*stha* (stand); *hi-tá-s* for earlier (Vêd.) *dhi-tá-s* (θε-τό-ς), √*dha* (set); *mi-tá-s* (like the preceding, past part. pass.), √*ma* (measure); st. *pi-tar-* for **pa-tar-*, cf. πα-τέρ-, *pa-ter-*, √*pa* (protect); further in pres. redupln. e.g. *bi-bhár-mi*, √*bhar* (bear), *ti-šthā-mi* = ἵστημι, f.f. of both is **sti-stā-mi*, earlier **sta-stā-mi*, √*stha* (stand; cf. Sk. *dá-dhā-mi*, *dá-dā-mi*, and Gk. τί-θη-μι, δί-δω-μι, where the Sk. does not yet show that weakening which has occurred in Gk.).

u = an, *am*, e.g. in termn. of 3 pl. *-us*, fr. *-anti, -ant*, e.g. *bhárēy-us* = φέροιεν = **bharay-ant* (3 pl. opt. pres. act.), *babhrús* = **babharanti* (3 pl. pf. act.), *ubhǎ*, *ubhǎu* = ἄμφω, *ambō*; thus later languages show the more original form, etc.

2. *a* becomes weakened to *ĭ, ŭ*, likewise in the combination *ar*, so that *ĭr, ŭr*, the latter after labial consonants, are considered as of the same force as vowel *r*; the weakening to *ĭ*, however, occurs not only before *r*, but also not seldom in other cases.

ŭr = r (vowel) = *ar* after labial initial √sounds, e.g. *pūr-ná-s* (plenus) for **pr-na-s*, Zend *pere-na-s* (Zend *ere* = Sk. vowel *r*), f.f. **par-na-s*, √*par* (fill), etc., yet also *kań-kūr-*, intensive pres. st. √*kar* (go), and the like.

ĭr = r (vowel) = *ar* after all except labial initial sounds, e.g.

§ 7. *stīr-ṇá-s* (past part. pass.) for *str-ṇá-s*, f.f. *star-na-s*, √*star* (strew); *dīrghá-s* for *drgha-s (long), Zend *daregha-s*, Gk. δολιχό-ς, etc., f.f. *dargha-s, cf. compar. and superl. formed in Sk. with step-fmn. of √vowel *a*, compar. st. *drágh-īyās-*, superl. st. *drágh-iṣṭha-*.

i as a weakening of *a* often occurs, especially in cases of roots in *a* (like its weakening to *i*), nevertheless it also often occurs in the case of a non-radical *a* belonging to formative affixes, e.g. *hī-ná-s* for *ha-na-s (past part. pass.), √*ha* (leave, 3 sg. pres. *já-kā-ti*); *pī-ta-s* (past part. pass.), √*pa* (drink, 3 sg. pres. *píba-ti* for *pi-pa-ti, fr. *pa-pa-ti); *yu-nī-más* for *yu-na-mas (1 pl. pres.), cf. *yu-ná-ti* (3 sg. pres.), pres. st. *yu-na-*, √*yu* (iungere), etc.

Note 1.—Through this weakening are developed also roots with *i*, which originally were in *a*, e.g. Sk. *kri* (buy), e.g. pres. *krī-ṇá-ti*, fut. *krē-ṣyáti*, pf. *kikráy-a*, etc., thus with pure *i*, seems nevertheless to have come from original *kra*=*kar*, cf. Gk. πέρ-νημι, Lith. *perkù* (buy), where the √ with *k* is a further formation. The weakenings of original *a* are altogether not rarely formed by steps like original *i* and *u*; e.g. fr. *pi-tā-mahá-s* (masc. grandfather; on *pi-tar-*, √*pa*, v. supr.) is formed a st. *pāi-tā-maha-* (adj. grandfatherly); fr. st. *dhĭr-a-* (adj. firm, stable), √*dhar* (hold), weakened to *dhĭr*, sf. *-a-*, *dhāir-ya-m* (neut. stability); fr. *pur-ṇá-māsa-s* (masc. full-moon; on *pūr-ṇá-*, √*par*, v. supr.), *pāur-ṇa-māsá-* (adj. of a full-moon), etc. A change of *a*-scale to *i*- and *u*-scales is accordingly seen, especially in later formations, having arisen after the language-instinct had lost the root-forms.

Note 2.—Cf. the cases where *ī* apparently stands for *a*, though it really is a contraction of *ya*, *yā*, or an auxiliary vowel, § 15, c, f.

§ 8.   The fundamental vowel *a* appears in Sk. as the commonest vowel in roots and relation-sounds, e.g. *ád-mi* (1 sg. pres.), √*ad* (edere); *ás-ti* (3 sg. pres.), √*as* (esse); *bhár-asi* (2 sg. pres.), *á-bhar-at* (3 sg. impf.), *bhár-antas* (φέροντες, n. pl. masc. pres. part. act.), √*bhar* (bear); *áp-as* (opus), *áp-as-as* (operis); *mán-as* (μέν-ος), *mán-as-as* (*μεν-εσ-ος, μένους); *áç-va-s*, f.f. *akvas* (equos, ἵππος for *ikϜos); *sa* (ὁ), *ta-m*, (τό-ν, *is-tu-m*); *çata-tamá-s* (centesimus), etc.

The step-formation of *a* to *ā* cannot further be analysed § 9. into first and second steps (as in Gk., Lat., Goth.), and, moreover, can scarcely—only by means of the analogy of completely corresponding words in *i* and *u*—be distinguished from lengthening. Therefore we hesitate to make the distinction between lengthening and step-formation in the case of f. vowel *a*, and accordingly probably admit many forms as steps, which would be more accurately denoted as lengthenings. The step-formation of *a* to *ā* occurs in roots and in relation-sounds.

Examples of step-formed roots with √ vowel *a* are *ba-bhắr-a* (3 sg. pf.) bes. *bhár-āmi* (1 sg. pres.), √ *bhar* (bear) ; *u-vắk-a* (3 sg. pf.) bes. *vák-ti* (3 sg. pres.), √ *vak* (speak) ; *vắs-as* (uestis) bes. *vas-tế* (3 sg. pres. med.), √ *vas* (clothe) ; *kār-áyati* (3 sg. pres. causat. vb.) bes. *kar-ố-ti* (3 sg. pres.), √ *kar* (make), etc.

Note.—The roots which end in *a* occur mostly in step-raised forms [whence arose the grammatic rule that roots in *a* appear only in pronominal functions, as *ta* (n. sg. masc. *sa*, acc. *ta-m* dem.), *ya* (n. sg. masc. ntr. *ya-s*, *ya-t* rel.), *ka* (n. acc. sg. masc. *ka-s*, *ka-m*), etc., whilst all verbal roots end in *ā*—acc. to Hindu grammarians in *ā*, *ē*, *āi*, *ō*]. Also the un-raised forms, indeed the shortened forms of these roots are not rare, e.g. *ǵi-gā-ti*, *ǵá-gā-ti* (3 sg. pres.), but *ga-tá-s* (past part. pass.), *ga-hi* (2 sg. imper.), *gá-kkhati*, f.f. *ga-skati* (3 sg. pres.), cf. βέβᾰμεν, βᾱτήs, √ *ga* (go) ; *dá-dā-mi* (1 sg. pres. δί-δω-μι), but *da-d-más* for *da-da-mas* (1 pl. pres.), cf. δί-δο-μεν, δό-σιs, δο-τήρ, *dămus*, √ *da* (give) ; *dá-dhā-mi* (1 sg. pres.), but *da-dh-más*, fr. *da-dha-mas*, cf. τί-θε-μεν, θέ-σιs, θε-τόs, √ *dha* (set) ; *á-pā-t* (3 sg. aor.), *pā-syá-ti* (3 sg. fut.), but *pi-ba-ti* for *pi-pa-ti*, fr. *pa-pa-ti* (3 sg. pres.), cf. πέ-πο-μαι, πό-σιs, √ *pa* (drink) ; *pĭ-ti* (3 sg. pres.), but *pá-ti-s*, cf. πό-σιs, Goth. *fa-th-s*, i.e. *fa-di-s*, Lith. *pà-t-s*, for *pa-ti-s* (lord), with weakening of *a* to *i* in *pi-tar-* (n. *pitắ*), cf. πα-τήρ, f.f. *pa-tar-*, √ *pa* (protect) ; *ti-šthā-mi*, ἵ-στη-μι (1 sg. pres.), but *ti-štha-ti* for *sti-sta-ti*, fr. *sta-sta-ti* (3 sg. pres.), with weakening of *a* to *i* in *sthi-tá-s*, f.f. *sta-tá-s*, cf. στᾰ-τό-s, *stă-tu-s*, √ *stha*, original *sta* (stare), etc. Here accordingly, as in many other like cases, the root-forms are evidently *ga, dha, da, pa, pa, stha ;* so too *a* is everywhere to be assumed to be the root-sound, even where it happens that the raised forms only are seen in

§ 9. the existing language. Cf. my treatise on '*a*-roots in Indo-germanic,' Beitr. ii. 92–99.

a as a sound expressing relation is found raised in termin. *a* of pres. st. *bhárā-mi* (1 sg. pres.), *bhárā-masi* (1 pl. pres.) bes. *bhára-si* (2 sg. pres.), *bhára-ti* (3 sg. pres.), etc., *bhára-* is pres. st. of √ *bhar* (bear); in almost all cases of the fem. of *a*- st., e.g. *náv-ā náv-ām* (n. acc. sg. fem. nou-a, *νέϜα*) bes. *nava-s nava-m* (n. acc. sg. masc.), st. *nava-* (nouos); *áç-vā* (equa) bes. *áç-va-s* (equos), st. *áç-va-* (*ak-va-*), and generally before certain case-sff., e.g. *dēvá-s*, earlier *dē-vá̄-sas* (n. pl.) bes. *dēvá-s* (n. sg.), st. *dēvá-* (deus); further in final syllables of sundry consonantal noun-stems before certain case-sff., e.g. *dā-tár-am* (acc. sg.), *dā-tár-as* (n. pl.), fr. st. *dā-tár-* (da-tor), which appears pure in e.g. *dā-tár-i* (loc. sg.), in *dā-tŕ-bhis* (instr. pl.), *dā-tr-é́* (d. sg.), and others it is weakened to *dā-tr*.

§ 10.   2. *i*-scale.

Fundamental vowel *i*; *i-más*, cf. *ἴ-μεν* (1 pl. pres.), √ *i* (i-re); *vid-más* (1 pl. pres.), cf. *Ϝίσ-μεν*, Hom. *Ϝίδ-μεν*, √ *vid* (uid-ere, scire); *viç-áti* (3 sg. pres.), *viç-as* (n. pl. people, husbandmen), √ *viç* (go in, dwell); *div-am div-ás* (acc. g. sg. of n. *dyāu-s*, sky), √ *div* (shine; cf. *ΔιϜ-ós*, similarly fr. *Ζεύς* = *Δγευς*); *pák-ti-s* (fem. coctio), cf. *πέπ-σι-ς* for *πεπ-τι-ς*, √ *pak*, *πεπ*, origl. *kak*, cf. Lat. *cŏc*, Lith. *kep* (coquere), formed through sf. *-ti-*, f.f. therefore *kak-ti-s*.

ī is not seldom a lengthening of genuine *i*, just as we have already found it to be a lengthening of *i* = *a*. The laws under which this lengthening takes place are not discovered in every instance. The lengthened *i* is often interchanged with the un-lengthened *i*, and is subject to step-formation and change (to *iy, y*), like the latter.

In cases like *pátī-n* (acc. pl. msc.), f.f. *pati-ms*, st. *páti-* (lord); *páktī-s* (acc. pl. fem.), f.f. *pakti-ms*, st. *pákti-* (coctio), we clearly see a compensatory lengthening, v. post. (§ 15, d), where also the lengthening bef. *y* is yet to be mentioned (§ 15, a), as e.g. *i-yát* bes. *i-yãt* (3 sg. opt.) √*i* (ire). Bef. final *r* in noun- § 10. stt., as bef. *r* folld. by a sf. which begins with a conson., lengthening occurs in the case of *i* and *u*, e.g. st. *gir-* (speech ; acc. sg. *gir-am*), n. sg. *gīr* for **gir-s*, loc. pl. *gīr-šú*, instr. pl. *gīr-bhis* for **gir-su*, **gir-bhis*.

So also in roots *ī* appears bes. *i*, and is grammatically arbitrary, since in these cases the √fm. is usually characterized by the long vowel, as e.g. √*bhī*, not *bhī* (frighten), cf. *bi-bhi-más* and *bi-bhī-mas* (1 pl. pres. ; 3 sg. *bi-bhé-ti*) ; in other roots it happens that only the lengthened vowel appears, e.g. *nī-tá-s* (past part. pass.), √*ni* (*nī* acc. to Grammarians and Dictt. ; ' lead ') ; *prī-tá-s*, √*pri* (*prī*, delight), etc.

Note 1.—Root-fms. with final vowels are particularly often mentioned in the lengthened fm. in gramm. and dictt., because the lengthening was particularly popular in these cases. On the unoriginality of *ī* and *ū* in Indo-Eur., cf. my remarks in Beitr. i. 328–333.

Note 2.—On *tr-tíya-s* (*ter-tiu-s*), in wh. *tr* can be taken as a weakening fr. *tri* (st. of numeral 3), v. sub. ' Numerals.'

The 1st step of *i* is in Sk. *ē*, e.g. *é-mi* (*eἶ-μι*), f.f. *ai-mi*, § 11. √*i* (ire) ; *véd-a* (*Foῖδa*), *véd-a-s* (n. sg. ; sacred writings of the Hindus, Vēda), √*vid* (see, know) ; *vi-véç-a* (3 sg. pf.), *véc-a-s* (n. sg. house, cf. *Foῖκ-o-ς*, *uἶc-u-s*), f.f. *vaik-a-s*, √*viç* (go in) ; *dēv-á-s* (deus), f.f. *daiv-a-s*, √*div* (shine) ; *pák-tē-s* (g. sg.), *pák-ti-s* (coctio), *pát-ē-s* (g. sg.), *pát-i-s* (lord) ; *bi-bhé-ti* (3 sg. pres. redupl.), √*bhi* (frighten) ; *né-tra-m* (eye, lit. ' the guiding one '), *náy-ati* (3 sg. pres.), *nay=nē* (v. post. § 14, d), √*ni* (lead) ; *cé-tē* (*κεῖ-ται* 3 sg. pres. med.), √*çi* (rest, lie), etc.

The 2nd step of *i* is in Sk. *āi*, e.g. *vãiç-ya-s* (man of third caste), √*viç* (go in ; cf. *viç-as* and *véç-a-s*) ; *vãid-ya-s* (vēdic, learned), √*vid* (see, know ; cf. *Véd-a-s*) ; *dãiv-a-s* (godly), whence *dãiv-a-m* (destiny), st. *dēv-á-* (deus), √*div* (shine) ; *çãiv-a-s* (belonging to the god Çiva, Çiva-worshipper), fr. *Çivá-s* (the god Çiva) ; *vāišnavá-s* (belonging to Vishnu, Vishnu-worshipper

§ 11. fr. *Víšṇu-s* (the god Vishnu); bef. vowels not *ai* but *ay* is found (§ 14), e.g. *nǎy-aka-s* (masc. leader), *nāy-áya-ti* (3 sg. pres. causat. st.), √*ni* (lead), etc.

§ 12. **3. *u*-scale.**

This scale, in all its parts, runs parallel to the *i*-scale, also the lengthening of *u* to *ū* occurs here, like *i* to *ī* above.

Fund. vowel *u*, e.g. *buddhá-s* for *budh-ta-s (past part. pass.), *bu-budh-é* (1, 3 sg. pf. med.), √*budh* (learn, know); *tud-áti* (3 sg. pres.), √*tud* (thump); *yug-á-m* (iugum, ζυγόν), *yuk-tá-s* (past part. pass.) for *yug-ta-s (iunctus), *á-yuǵ-at* (3 sg. aor.), √*yuǵ*, *yug* (iungere); *su-tá-s* (past part. pass.), √*su* (produce, sow); *çru-tá-s*, κλυ-τό-ς (past part. pass.), *çru-dhí* (vēd. 2 sg. imper. aor. κλῦ-θι), √*çru* (hear), etc. In pres. st. *çr-ṇu-*, e.g. *çr-ṇó-mi* (1 sg. pres.), √*çru* (hear), *ru* is exceptionally weakened to *r*, by complete loss of *u*.

The lengthening of *u* to *ū* occurs here, just as in the *i*-scale *i* becomes *ī*, e.g. *á-bhū-t* (ἔ-φυ(τ), 3 sg. aor.), *bhū-tá-s*, *bhū-tá-m* (masc. ntr. past part. pass.), √*bhu* (*bhū*, be), cf. φŭ-τό-ν, *fŭ-turu-s*; *sū-nú-s* (son), cf. Lith. *sūnùs*, Goth. *sunus*, √*su* (bear, sow, sts. also given as *sū*); *sū-nú-n* fr. *su-nu-ns (acc. pl.), Goth. *sununs*, st. *sūnú-* (n. sg. *sū-nú-s*, cf. § 15, d). Like *i*, so *u* bef. *r*, and bef. *r*+conson. in noun-stt. is lengthened (§ 10), e.g. st. *dhur-* (fore-part of a coach-pole, e.g. acc. sg. *dhúr-am*), n. *dhūr* for *dhur-s, instr. pl. *dhūr-bhis* for *dhur-bis, etc.

§ 13. **1. step ō**, e.g. *bódh-ati* (3 sg. pres.), √*budh* (learn, know); *pra-tōd-a-s* (masc. goad), √*tud* (push); *yu-yóǵ-a* (1, 3 sg. pf.), *yóg-a-s* (joining, speculation), √*yuǵ* (iungere); *bháv-ati* (3 sg. pres.), *á-bhav-at* (3 sg. pf.), *bhav*=*bhō* (v. § 14, d), √*bhu* (be); *sóš-yáti* (3 sg. fut.), √*su* (bring forth); *cró-tra-m* (ntr. ear), √*çru* (hear), *sū-nó-s* (g. sg.), st. *sūnú-* (n. sg. *sū-nú-s*, son), cf. Lith. *sūnaús*, Goth. *sunaus*, etc.

2. step āu, e.g. *bāuddhá-s* (masc. Buddhist) fr. *buddhá-s* (past part. pass. n. propr. *Buddha*), √*budh* (know); *á-tāut-sam* for *a-tāud-sam (1 sg. aor.), √*tud* (push); *yáug-ika-s* (adj. fr. *yóga-s*

supr.), st. *yóga-*, √*yug* (iungere) ; *bhắv-a-s* (being, nature), § 13.
bhāv=*bhāu* (v. § 14, d), √*bhu* (be) ; *sắu-ti* (3 sg. pres.), *su-šắv-a*
(1, 3 sg. pf.) for **su-sắv-a* (v. sub. consonn.), *sāv*=*sāu* (v. § 14, d),
√*su* (bring forth) ; *á-çrāu-šam* (1 sg. aor. compos.), √*çru*
(hear), etc.

Note.—" *ī* and *ū* are subject to step-formation only when they
are at the end of roots," is the rule of Sk. grammar, *i.e.* they are
in these cases lengthenings of real *i, u ;* as medial root-sounds
however, they are felt by the language-instinct to be unorigl.,
and are therefore not treated like genuine *i, u.* Real *i* and *u*
appear besides only before root-termns. which consist of one
consonant.

VOWEL SOUND-LAWS. § 14.

Note.—Only the most important Sk. sound-laws are here
mentioned—those which operate within the word : the changes
undergone by the termn. of a word in consequence of its place
in a sentence belong to the department of Sk. special-grammar,
not to the Indo-Eur. (the so-called ' Comparative ') Grammar.

1. L a w s   o f   t h e   c o n c u r r e n c e   o f   v o w e l s.

Fundamental law : Sk. permits hiatus in its earliest remains
of language alone (in the Vēdic hymns), where we find even
two like vowels in juxtaposition. In classical Sk. hiatus is
avoided, a. by contraction, b. by loss of the former vowel, c.
by separation, d. by change of vowel to corresponding spirant.

Contraction occurs when *a* happens to stand before another
vowel, except in those cases where *a* is lost bef. the following
vowel. Change to the consonn. takes place when *i, u* (including
their furthest formations *ē*[=*ai*], *ō*[=*au*], *āi*, *āu*). This contrast
between *a* and *i, u*, arises from the fact that *a* has no corresponding spirant, whereas *i, u,* have by their side *y, v*, which
are only different from them through a slight distinction in
pronunciation ; the change from *i, u*, to *y, v*, is through intermediate *iy, uv.*

a. E x x.   o f   c o n t r a c t i o n : pres. st. *bhára-*+*i* of opt. mood=
bhárē-, e.g. *bhárē-t* fr. **bhara-i-t* (3 sg. opt. pres., √*bhar*, bear) ;

§ 14. noun st. *áçva-+i* of loc. case=*áçvē* (loc. sg. of n. sg. *áçva-s*, equos), etc.

Note.—v. older peculiar contractions post. (§ 15, c).

b. Loss of *a* occurs e.g. in cases like *dhanín-* (rich, n. sg. masc. *dhanî*), fr. st. *dhána-* (neutr. n. sg. *dhána-m*, wealth)+sf. *in ;* only bef. sf. *ya* is *a* regularly lost, e.g. st. *dhán-ya-* (adj. rich, n. sg. masc. *dhán-ya-s*), from same st. *dhána-*. Roots in *a* do permit this loss of *a* not unfrequently, e.g. *da-d-más, da-dh-más* (1 pl. pres. act.), fr. pres. stt. *da-da-, da-dha-* (1 sg. *dá-dā-mi, dá-dhā-mi*), √*da* (give), √*dha* (set); so also in pf. they lose their termn., and subsequently even assume an auxil. vowel *i*, as if they ended in a conson., *da-d-i-má, da-dh-i-má* (1 pl. pf.), like *tu-tud-i-má,* √*tud* (push), so that it becomes probable that *a* was lost bef. *i,* and not *ma,* but *ima,* etc., was considered to be the termn.

c. The splitting-up of *i* and *u* (and of their lengthenings *ī, ū,*—perh. it is more correct to suppose no lengthening to take place before vowels) to *iy, uv,* is retained where these vowels are radical in monosyll. words, more rarely also in ordinary Sk. otherwise, *i.e.* when two consonn. stand before the vowel.

Exx.: *bhiy-i* (loc. sg.), cf. n. sg. *bhī-s* (fear), st. thus *bhī- ; iy-áy-a* (3 sg. pf.), √*i* (go), fr. **i-ái-a ; āi* is √*i* in 2nd step, *i* in fund. fm.

çu-çruv-ús (3 pl. pf.), √*çru* (hear), f.f. *ku-kru-anti ; āp-nuv-ánti* (3 pl. pres. fmd. by *nu* fr. √*āp*, work); *bhruv-i* (loc. sg.), n. sg. *bhrū-s* (ὀ-φρύς), st. therefore *bhrū-.*

Note.—*y-anti* (3 pl. ind. pres.), √*i,* contrary to rule where we should have expected *iy-anti ; i* is here exceptionally treated according to the plan laid down below.

d. The change into corresponding semi-vowel is regular in ordinary Sk., that is, occurs exclusively in the case of *i* and *u* as 2nd part of diphthongs *e* (=*ai*), *āi, ō* (=*au*), *āu,* e.g. *pákty-ā* (instr. sg. of n. sg. *pákti-s*, coctio) for **pakti-ā, ni-ny-é* (1, 3 sg. pf. med.), √*ni* (*nī,* lead) for **ni-ni-ē.*

náy-ati (3 sg. pres.), √*ni* (lead), here raised to 1st step *nē*, § 14. i.e. *nai*.

ni-nā́y-a (1, 3 sg. pf. act.), √*ni*, *nāi*=2nd step of *ni*.

çr-ṇv-ánti (3 pl. pres. act.), √*çru* (hear), pres. st. √*çr-ṇu-* (cf. § 12) for **çr-ṇu-anti*, f.f. *kru-nu-anti;* cf. supr. *āpnuv-ánti*, with splitting of *nu* into *nuv*, whereas here two consonn. stand before *u*.

çráv-ana-m (the hearing, ear; n. sg. ntr.), √*çru* (hear), raised to *çro=çrau* + sf. *ana; çráv-as* (ntr. the hearing, ear =κλέƑος, Scl. *sloves-*), likewise fr. same root + sf. *as*.

çu-çrā́v-a (1, 3 sg. pf.),√*çru* (hear), here raised to 2nd step *çrāu*.

Note 1.—The earlier lang. shows the splitting-up only in the case of *i, u*. The scale of variation is as follows: 1. *i, u*+ vowel, e.g. *pákti-ā;* but there arises very easily, 2. *iy, uv* + vowel, e.g. *páktiy-ā;* and finally the vowel element is lost entirely, 3. *y, v* + vowel, e.g. *pákty-ā*.

Note 2.—The fms. explained in § 6, such as *ūḱ-us*, *íǵ-us*, form no exception to the laws above laid down, and are prob. not contracted fr. **uuḱús, iiǵús*, but rather arise fr. resolution of *v, y*, into *u, i; *va-vaḱ-us, *uvaḱus, *uvḱus, ūḱús; *ya-yaǵ-us, *iyaǵus, *iyǵus, íǵús*, are the gradations of change here to be understood.

2. Vowel-change caused by the neighbouring § 15. consonn.

Note.—A single instance had to be mentioned as early as § 7, as *pūrnás* with *ū* on acct. of *p;* generally the weakenings of *a* bef. *r* are intrinsically caused by this conson.

a. *y* often lengthens preceding *u, i, a* (for splitting-up of *y* to *iy, īy*, v. supr. § 14, 1, c.), e.g. *crū-yá-tē* (3 sg. pres. pass.), √*çru* (hear); *ǵī-yá-tē* (3 sg. pres. pass.), √*ǵi* (conquer, e.g. in *ǵi-tá-s*, past part. pass., *ǵáyati* 3 sg. pres.); *ǵā-ya-tē* (is born, 3 sg. med.), √*ǵa* (generally *ǵan*, and thus means bring forth, bear; cf. Zend *za-yē-itē*, f.f. therefore *ga-ya-tai*), etc.

Note.—Bef. *y=i*, *ī* also may be explained as splitting-up of *i* to *iy*. Perh. fr. this source arise also the lengthenings of *u* to *ū*, and *a* to *ā*, bef. *y*. Cf. sq.

§ 15.   b. *iy* sometimes occurs instead of *y*, and also *īy* with the favourite vowel-lengthening bef. *y*.

After *a* in certain cases *iy* (with *a* or *ā* therefore *ēy*) instead of *y* (with *a* or *ā* therefore *ay, āy*), e.g. pres. st. in *a* + opt. element *ya* forms not *-a-ya*, but *-a-iya*, i.e. *-ēya*, e.g. *bódhēyam* for **bōdha-ya-m* (1 sg. opt. pres.), pres. st. *bodha-*, √*budh* (learn, know); *dé-ya-s* (part. necessitatis, n. sg. masc.) for **dā-ya-s*, st. *dā-ya*, consisting of step-formed √*da* (give), and sf. *ya* ; *gāṅgēya-s* (found in or on the Ganges), fr. *gáṅgā* (nom. pr. Ganges), step-fmd. *gāṅgā* + sf. *ya*, for **gāṅgā-ya-s*.

Also after consonn. occurs *īy* for *y*, thus in compar. st. fmd. with origl. sf. *yans*, e.g. st. *lághīyās-* (n. sf. masc. *lághīyān*), fr. *laghú-s* (light)=ἐ-λαχύ-ς, for **lagh-yās-*, cf. ἐ-λάσσων for **λαχ-ψων*, and superl. *lágh-iš-tha-s*, ἐ-λάχ-ισ-το-ς, where *is-* is a relic of *-yas-, -yās-*. So moreover the sf. *ya* has also a fm. *īya*, e.g. st. *karaṇ-īya-* (faciendus) for **karan-ya-*, st. *kára-ṇa*, which loses its termn. bef. *ya* (§ 14, 1, b), etc.

Note.—*īy*=*y* is not developed in Indian until after the division of Aryan into Ind. and Eran.; the Zend, which stands so close to Old-Ind., still has *y*=Sk. *īy*.

c. *yā* was sometimes compressed into *ī*. So esp. in fem. stt. in *ī*, which prob. can only be=*yā*, e.g. *bháranti* (the bearing one, f.) = **bharant-yā* = φέρουσα = **φεροντ-yā* ; *ganitrí* = **ganitr-yā* fr. **gan-i-tar-ya* (genetrix)=γενέτειρα, i.e. **γενετερ-ya*, etc., *ya-* stt. fr. usual masc. stt., Sk. *bhárant-*, *gani-tár-*, Gk. φέροντ-, γενε-τήρ- ; *dēvī*́=**daivyā* (dea), cf. Lith. *deivė̃*, i.e. **deivyā̃*, f.f. *daiv-yā* (once 'goddess,' now='ghost'), later fmn. fr. st. *dēvá-*, Lith. *dė̃va*, f.f. *daiva-* (deus); Vēd. *ávī* (instr. sg. for Sk. *ávy-ā*, both fr. *áviā* (*ávi-s*, ouis, *ā* sf. of instr. sg.), etc. : *ī* is clearly a weaker vowel-fm. for *yā* in opt., *e.g.* 3 sg. act. *bibhr-yá̄-t*, but 3 sg. med. *bíbhr-ī-ta*, √*bhar* (bear, pres. st. *bibhar-*), etc.

Sometimes *ī* is a product of a similar earlier contraction of *i-a* or *ya* after loss of conson. betw. *i* and *a*, as in *sīd-áti* (3 sg. pres.), fr. **si-adati* for **si-sad-ati*, √*sad* ·(sit, pf. *sa-sā́d-a*, aor.

á-sad-at), like *ἵζω* fr. **ἵἑζω=*si-sed-yō*, f.f. *si-sad-yami*, Lat. *sĭd-o* § 15. fr. **sisdo* for *si-sed-o*, f.f. **si-sad-ami* (with not unfreq. pres. redupln.), also the *īr* now used as a root, e.g. *īr-té* (3 pres. med., rises, causat. *īr-áyati*, he arouses), is recognized as a product of pres. redupln. ; *īr=*i-ar*, **iyar*, √*ar* (go), etc.

d. **Compensatory lengthening**   Esp. in declens.-fms. (n. sg., acc. pl.) is found lengthening of the foregoing vowel after loss of conson. Exx. :

N. sg. *rā́jā* for **rājan-s*, st. *rājan-* (masc. rex) +nom. sf. *s*, cf. *ποιμήν* for **ποιμεν-ς* ; *dhaní* for **dhanin-s*, st. *dhanin-* (rich) ; *mātā́* for **mātar-s*, st. *mātar-* (mater), cf. *μήτηρ* for **μητερ-ς* ; *dúr-manās* for **dur-manas-s* (masc. fem. evil-minded, compounded of *dus*, evil, *mánas* ntr. mens), cf. *δυσμενής* for **δυσ-μενεσ-ς* ; *agnimā́n* for **agnimant-s* (fiery, st. *agni-*, ignis+sf. *-mant*). Notice *bháran* without compens. lengthening for **bharant-s* (n. sg. part. pres. act., whilst the corresponding Gk. *φέρων* for **φεροντς* has the lengthening).

Acc. pl. *áçvān* for **açvan-s*, n. sg. *áçva-s* (equos) ; *pátīn* for **patin-s*, n. sg. *patis* (lord) ; *sūnū́n* for **sūnun-s*, n. sg. *sūnú-s* (son) ; *mátīs* for **mati-ns*, n. sg. *máti-s* (fem. thought) : *dhēnū́s* for **dhēnun-s*, n. sg. *dhēnú-s* (milch cow).

Bef. sonant consonn. we ought prob. to consider *ō* to be a compens. lengthening=*as*, with dulling of the vowel, e.g. *mánōbhis*, instr. pl. for **manas-bhis*, fr. *mánas-* (neutr. mens, *μένος*) and *bhis* (sf. of instr. pl. consisting of *bhi*+pl. sf. *s*), etc. This change of *as* to *ō* often takes place in case of final *as*.

Note.—In the case of compens. lengthening in Sk. and in the other languages, we might make a more accurate distinction as follows: 1. ˘+conson.=¯ (cf. O.-Bulg. instr. sg. *-mĭ*=origl. *bhi*, bes. instr. pl. *-mi*, i.e. *-mī*=origl. *-bhis*), in terminations; medially this case is not found: 2. ˘+conson. 1+conson. 2=¯ (e.g. *mātā* for **mātars*) in termn.: 3. ˘+conson. 1+ conson. 2=¯+conson. 2, final and medial (e.g. *matīs* for **matin-s* ; Gk. *εἰμί* for **ἐσμι* ; a subdivn. forms here ˘+cons. 1+cons. 2+cons. 3=¯+cons. 3 (e.g. *ἱστάς* for **ἱσταντς*): 4. ˘+

§ 15. conson. 1 + cons. 2 = ˉ + cons. 1 (e.g. μήτηρ for *μητερς), or
ˇ + cons. 1 + cons. 2 + cons. 3 = ˉ + cons. 1 (e.g. φέρων for
*φεροντς, finally and medially, the latter, e.g. Gk. ἔφηνα for
*ἔφανσα). The physiological explan. of this sound-process is
difficult, esp. in case No. 4.

e. Dulling of *ā* to *ē* and *āu* bef. lost conson. and *in fine.*
For *ā* there occurs a dulled fm. in *ē*, in certain cases in the middle
of a word, when *ā* has been produced through compens.
lengthening (§ 15, d), in the case of unusual and late consonantal loss: in termn. it occurs, but is likewise confined to
certain cases; also we find *ē* for *ā*, like *āu* for *ā*, the latter of
which is retained in the old lang. Exx.:

ē for *ā* when consonn. have been lost; thus in imperat. pres.
ēdhi for **ā-dhi*, **as-dhi* (√ and pres. st. *as-*, esse, *dhi* termn. of
2 sg. imper.); *dhēhi* for **dhāhi*, with asp. (v. § 59) for Vēdic
daddhi for **dadh-dhi* (pres. st. *dadh*, √*dha*, set); *dēhi* for **dāhi*,
fr. **dadhi* for *daddhi* (pres. st. *dad*, √*da*, dare); in pf. fm. as
Sk. *pēt-i-má* for **pāt-i-ma*, Vēd. *papt-i-má* fr. **pa-pat-ma* (1 pl.
act.; pf. st. *papat-*, √*pat*, fly, fall); *tēn-i-ré* for **tān-i-rē* fr.
older *ta-tn-i-rē* (3 pl. med.; pf. st. *tatan-*, √*tan*, stretch), etc.;
finally in voc. of fem. *a-* st., e.g. *áçvē* (but earlier still *áçva*),
voc. of *açvā* (equa). *āu* for earlier *ā* (cf. *ō* for *as* in termn. bef.
sonants, § 15, d) occurs in n. acc. dual, e.g. *áçvāu*, earlier *áçvā*
(n. *áçvas*, equos); further in 1, 3 sg. pf. act. of roots in *a*, e.g.
dadắu, archaic *dadá̄*, √*da* (dare).

f. An auxil. vowel *i, ī*, occurs betw. stem-termns. and
termns. which begin with a conson. in word-fmn., esp. in conjugation fms., in which origly. and partly still in the earlier lang., the
termn. was added immediately to the stem-termn., e.g. pres. fm. of
single vbs., as *sváp-i-mi, sváp-i-ši, sváp-i-ti, svap-i-más* (1, 2, 3 sg.,
1 pl. pres.), etc., for **svap-mi*, etc., √*svap* (sleep); in pf. this
occurs regularly in case of certain persons, e.g. 1 pl. *tutud-i-má*,
√*tud* (tundere), etc. Here we often see even now the older
fms. without inserted *i*, partly even in ordinary Sk., as e.g.
kakár-tha (2 sg. pf.); √*kar* (faćere), partly in the earlier lang.

of the Vēdas, in which a fm. *tutudmá*, etc., may be found. In § 15.
fut. e.g. *gam-i-ṣyắmi* (1 sg. fut.), √*gam* (ire); in part. pres.
pass., e.g. *vid-i-tá-s*, √*vid* (see, know), and many similar fmns.,
this insertion of *i* occurs in certain roots.

ī occurs as auxil. vowel in aor.-fms., e.g. 2 sg. *á-nāi-ṣ-ī-s*, √*n*
(*nī*, lead), bes. 1 pl. *ánāi-ṣ-ma* ; in pres. fms. as 1 sg. *bráv-ī-mi*,
3 sg. *bráv-ī-ti*, bes. 1 pl. *brū-más*, √*bru* (*brū*, speak), and in
impf. fms., as *á-brav-ī-s*, *á-brav-ī-t* (2, 3 sg.) (id.); *ắs-ī-s*, *ắs-ī-t*
(2, 3 sg.), √*as* (esse), etc. ; *ghr-ī-tá-s* past part. pass., √*grah*
(grasp), has likewise this *ī*, which is therefore used just like *i*,
only not so often.

The Vēd. *ās* for *ās-t (acc. to a sound-law of Old-Ind., which
must be discussed under ' Consonants'), instead of later *ás-ī-t*,
favours the view that *ī* is an auxil. vowel inserted at a later time.

Note.—Since beside *sváp-i-mi* for *svapmi, etc., we see *svápāmi*,
etc., we must simply suppose that here, as often elsewhere, beside
the pres. st. *svap-*, there was a pres. st. in *a*, *svapa-*.

GREEK.

§ 16.

SUMMARY OF SOUNDS.

	CONSONANTS.						VOWELS.
	MOMENTARY SOUNDS.			PROLONGED SOUNDS.			
	UNASPIRATED.	ASPIRATED.	SPIRANTS.	NASALS.	*r-* & *l-*SOUNDS.		
	mute sonant[1]	mute	mute sonant[1]	sonant[1]	sonant[1]		
Gutt.	κ γ	χ	ʽ	γ·			*a ā* ⎫
Pal.							*ι ῑ* ⎭ > *ε η* ⎫
Ling.				ρ λ			⎫ > *o ω*
Dent.	τ δ	θ	σ	ν			*υ ῡ* ⎬
Lab.	π β	φ	(*F*)	μ			(*ου*) ⎭ ⎭

[1] Or medial.

§ 16.   In this table only the indivisible sounds are mentioned.

ζ is a consonantal diphthong, namely *d* with the sonant dental spirant (e.g. Sclavonian *z*). ψ, ξ, are only characters for two sounds πς, κς. The vowel-diphthongs are *αι, ει, οι*; *αυ, ευ, ου* (older pronunciation); *υι*; also *ᾳ, ῃ, ῳ* (older pronunciation, by which the *ι* was still heard); *ᾱυ* (perhaps in the word γρᾱῦς [γρηῦς], perhaps pronounced distinctly from *αυ* with short *a*), *ηυ, ωυ.*

Note 1.—*υ* at an earlier period of the language was equivalent to *u*, but became pronounced like *y, ü*, as early as classical times; *ου* in the earlier language was the genuine diphthong *ou*, but even in the classical period it had become equivalent to *ū*, as indeed it did in other languages, *e.g.* French, the older *ou* became *ū*, whilst the spelling retains the earlier sound-grade.

To pronounce Old-Greek after the fashion of modern Greek is a mistake, which arises from utter ignorance of the laws of development and phonology of a language.

We should be careful to distinguish *αι* from *ει* in pronunciation, because they are distinct sounds : they are pronounced as they are written, i.e. *αι* like German *ai* or *ei*, but *ει* like *e + i* tacked on, a diphthong, which is found dialectically in German, and characterized in other languages by *ey (ej)* (cf. Curt. Erl. § 8 sqq.).

Note 2.—Like most other written languages, the Greek does not characterize its long vowels throughout; in earlier Greek, however, they were not indicated at all : *a* serves as *a* and *ā, ι* for *i* and *ī, υ* for *ü* and *ū̄*, in the earlier writing ε for *e* and *ē* (η) ; *o* for *o* and *ō* (ω). These incomplete indications of sounds have nothing to do with the language itself, τες, e.g., must be read τῆς, τει=τηι, i.e. τῇ, τοι=τωι, i.e. τῷ, etc.; in all cases the long vowels are derived from the original language. Cf. ' Declensions.'

The system of Greek writing belongs to Greek special-grammar, as an appendix to the phonology.

§ 17.   THE GREEK VOWEL-SYSTEM.

The most important deviation from the original language lies in the colouring of *a* into *e* and *o*, which takes place alike in the case of *a* and *ā* by the side of the original vowel preserved : the archaic dialects (Dôric) have remained most faithful § 17. to the older order of sounds : *o* has a double duty; it is not only 1. the representative of the original *a*, but also 2. (opposed to *ε*=*a*) the representative of the original *ā*.

Through the differentiation of *ā* into *o*, *ā*, *η*, *ω*, it became possible to separate *ω* as the second step from the first *o*, *a*, *η*.

The weakening of *a* into *ι* and *υ*, as well as loss of *a*, occurs comparatively seldom.

This same colouring of the *a*-sound into *e* and *o* occurs when it is combined with *i* and *u* in a diphthong ; here too *ε* (=*a*) is the first, *o* (=*ā*) the second step, which however is replaced in the *u*-scale almost always by the first step (*ει*, *ευ*=original *ai*, *au* ; *οι*, *ου*=original *āi*, *āu*). It is only wherever the language has lost the living variability of the vowels according to their scales, *αι* and *αυ* appear as steps raised from *ι* and *υ*.

A large number of vowel-sounds, especially diphthongs and long vowels, arise in Greek through the elision, permutation, and change of position of the original spirants *y*, *v*, *s*, which were entirely, or in certain combinations, unbearable to Greek pronunciation. The vowel-sounds so formed are consequently entirely unoriginal, being products of the peculiar sound-laws of the Greek language, and foreign to the original state of the language.

The Greek vowel-system, in many parts differing from the original one, reminds us in several respects of the Zend ; whilst we find on the other hand the greatest conformity with that of the Latin language.

The vowel-scales of the Greek language are then as follows :

		Weakening.	Fundamental-vowel.	1st Step.	2nd Step.
a-scale	loss	*ι*, *υ*	*ε*, *o*, *a*	*o*, *ā*, *η*	*ω*
i-scale			*ι*	*ει* (*αι*)	*οι*
u-scale			*υ*	*ευ* (*αυ*)	*ου* (*āυ*)

Note.—More than one sound accordingly occurs here in different functions, as is the case with *i* and *u* in Sanskrit, and

3

§ 17. partly also in Zend.   In the Greek, however, we meet with the
ambiguity of the sounds for the first time to a greater extent ;
we may here therefore speak of it briefly.   Besides the permu-
tations shown above, ι=original *i* and *a*; υ=original *u* and *a*;
ο=original *a* and *ā* : that is, the diphthongs are ambiguous
because they stand, sometimes for scale-sounds, sometimes for
results of contraction, sometimes for protracted vowels.   e.g. ει
in εἶμι (εο, ibo), fundamental-form *ai-mi*, originally distinct from
εἰμί (sum), from *ἐσμι, fund.-form *as-mi*; εἰ in εἶπον (dixi), fr.
*ἔεπον, *ϝεϝεπον, √ϝεπ; εἰ in εἴην (opt. pres.) for *ἐσγην, f.f.
as-yā-m; κτείνω (kill) for *κτενγω; ου in σπουδή (haste ; raised
to ευ in σπεύδω, √ σπυδ) is altogether different, as ου in πούς
(foot) for *ποδ-ς, f.f. *pad-s* ; ου in τούς for τονς (acc. pl. of το-),
f.f. *tams*; ου in νέου, fr. *νέοο, for νέοιο, *νεϝοσγο, f.f. *navasya*
(gen. sing. masc. and n. fr. νεο-, young) ; ου in γουνός for
*γονϝος (gen. sing. fr. γόνυ, knee):—similarly in the case of οι,
λοιπ-ός (remaining), √λιπ, but μοῖρα (lot, fate) for *μορ-ya,
√μερ (divide) ; οἷς, fr. ὄις (older form ὄϝις, Lat. ouis) ; αι in αἴθω
(burn), √ιθ, but μέλαινα (nom. sing. fem. st. μελαν-, black) for
μέλανya, etc.

§ 18.   EXAMPLES.
1. *a*-scale.
Weakening. Loss. e.g. γί-γνο-μαι (become) for *γι-γέν-ομαι,
√γεν, original *gan*; πί-πτ-ω for *πι-πετ-ω, √πετ, original *pat*
(fall) ; ἔ-σχ-ον (1 sing. aor.), fund.-form *a-sagh-am*, √σεχ,
original √*sagh*; ἐ-σπ-όμην (1 sing. aor. ἕπ-ομαι), √σεπ (follow), original √*sak*, etc.

There takes place not unfrequently a complete loss of an
original *a* in the elements of stem-formation, e.g. πα-τρ-ός,
πα-τρ-ί, from stem πατέρ- (father), original *pa-tar-*, thus stand
for πατέρ-ος, πατέρ-ι (Homêric), f.f. *patar-as, patar-i*, etc.

Note.—Loss of initial *a* in Greek is not common, cf. ἐσ-μέν
(we are), f.f. *as-masi*, Sansk. *s-más*, and Lat. *s-umus*; εἴην=
*ἐσγην, f.f. *as-yām*, Sansk. *s-yām*, Lat. *s-iēm*; εὖ (εύ) for *ἐσύ,
f.f. *asu*, Sansk. *su* (well).

The weakening of original *a* to ι (cf. Curt. Gk. Et.,
p. 641 sqq.) is not frequent or regular in roots, and occurs most
often before two consonn., e.g. ἴσ-θι, f.f. *as-dhi* (2 sing. imper.),

√ἐς, origl. and Sansk. *as* (to be); πίτ-νημι beside πετ-άννυμι § 18. (spread out), cf. *pateo;* πιτ-νέω (fall), √πετ, Sk. *pat;* κιρ-νημι beside κερ-άω, κερ-άννυμι (mix); τίκ-τω (bring forth), √τακ, origl. √*tak,* cf. ἔ-τεκ-ον, τέ-τοκ-α; ἵππος for *ἵκ-Fος, Sk. *áç-vas,* Lat. *eq-uos,* f.f. *ak-vas,* √*ak* (run). The passing of original *a* into *i* is through intervening *e,* to which fact the examples cited bear witness.

This weakening of the fundamental *a* into ι occurs regularly in the reduplicated form of the present, e.g. τί-θη-μι, Sk. and origl. *dá-dhā-mi,* √θε, Sk. and origl. √*dha* (place); δί-δω-μι, Sk. and origl. *dá-dā-mi,* √δο, Sk. and origl. *da* (give); γί-γν-ομαι, √γεν, origl. *gan* (bring forth); πί-πτ-ω, √πετ, origl. *pat* (fall). This *i* (weakened from *a*) occurs lengthened to ῑ, e.g. in πί-νω (drink), √πο (πό-σις, πο-τήριον, πέ-πω-κα), origl. *pa;* παρθεν-οπ-ίπ-ης (looker-at-maidens), cf. ὀπ-ωπ-ή (sight), √ὀπ, origl. *ak* (see); ὑσ-μίνη, ὑσ-μῖνι (loc. sing. moil), f.f. *yudh-manā, yudh-mani,* the latter to the st. *yudh-man-,* √*yudh* (join battle), suff. *man.*

Dialectically (in Dôric, Aiolic) this weakening of origl. *a* to *i* is more common; e.g. Dôr. ἰσ-τία, Iôn. ἰσ-τίη, for ἑσ-τία (hearth), origl. √*vas;* ἰν Arkad. and Kuprian for ἐν (in), related to the pronoml. stem *an;* Boiôtian ἰών=Iôn. ἐών for *ἐσ-ων (n. sing. masc. part. pres. act.), √ἐσ- (be), etc. Through the dulling of *a* to *o,* and further of *o* to *u,* a change of origl. *a* to *u* takes place. ·

This weakening of *a* to υ (cf. G. Curt., p. 644 sqq.) occurs merely unconnectedly, in most cases through the influence of a nasal or *r, l;* and herein we must not forget that υ represents an older *u,* so that in Greek we have the same weakening from *a* to *u* as in Lat. and German, etc., e.g. νυκτ-ός (gen. sing.), stem νυκτ- (night), (Sk. adv. *nákt-am=noctu*), Lat. stem. *noct-:* the root-vowel thus is *a,* and the root clearly √*nak* (necare, nocere); in ὄνυξ (stem ὀνυχ-, nail), root νυχ, cf. Goth. *nag-ls,* Sk. *nakh-ás,* etc., the origl. vowel is no doubt *a;* γυνή (woman),

§ 18. √γαν (bring forth), cf. Sk. *ǵán-a-s* (mensch), *ǵánī* (wife), Gothic *kven-s* (wife, spouse); κύκλος (ring), cf. Sk. *kakrá-m*; μύλ-ος, μύλ-η (mola), √*mal* fr. *mar*, cf. *mola, molere*, Lith. *malù*, Gothic *malan*; ἀν-ώνυμος (nameless) beside ὄνομα (name), f.f. *gnāman*, etc.

Dialectically this change is more frequently observed, esp. in Aiolic, e.g. ὄνυμα=ὄνομα; ὕμοιος=ὅμοιος, f.f. *samaias*, from stem *sam*=Gk. ὁμο (ὁμός, like), the origin of which is found in the pronoml. origl. √*sa*=Gk. ὁ; Aiolic locative ἄλλυι, τυῖδε, for ἄλλοι (ἀλλο-, other), τοῖδε (το- demonstr. pronoml. st.); Boiôtian τύ for *τυι=τοι (n. pl. masc. same st.), τῦς ἄλλυς= *τυις *ἀλλυις=τοῖς ἄλλοις (dat. loc. pl.), by contraction of υι to υ.

Note.—I hold it inadmissible to separate from the rest those cases in which original *ka, ga*, become κυ, γυ, and to explain them collectively from *kva, gva*, with loss of *a*; neither will a fm. *κϝακλος seem to me to be Gk., and yet we must suppose some such form. No one, so far as I know, has had recourse to a fm. *νϝαξ, *ὀνϝαξ, *μϝαλη, in order to explain the υ in these words. Here υ must have arisen from *a* without passing through *va*, and the same process must have taken place after gutturals.

§ 19. Root-vowel *a* in the original language.

As a rule, ε is the representative of origl. *a* in roots; whilst ο generally takes its place in the stem-formative and word-formative particles, *a* is found in roots; in word-formative additions it is mostly dependent on a nasal now lost, but once in existence.

ε=*a*. ἔδ-ω, Sk. *ád-mi* (eat), √ἐδ, origl. *ad* (edo); √ἐδ in ἔζ-ομαι=*σεδ-yομαι (sed-eo), ἔδ-ος (sed-es), origl. *sad* (sit); √γεν in γέν-ος (gen-us), origl. *gan* (gi-gu-ere) of *gan-as*; ἐσ-τί, Sk. and origl. *ás-ti* (√ἐσ, origl. *as*, esse); φέρω, Sk. and origl. *bhár-āmi*, ἔφερ-ον, Sk. and origl. *á-bhar-am*, √φερ, origl. *bhar* (ferre), etc. So also ε is common in elements of relation, e.g. st. πα-τέρ- (n. sing. πατήρ, father), origl. *pa-tar-*; st. μῆ-τερ- (n. sing. μήτηρ, mater), origl. *mātar-*; st. μέν-εσ- (n. sing.

μένος, might), Sk. and origl. *mán-as* ; φέρ-ετε, Sk. *bhár-atha* ; § 19.
origl. evidently *bhar-a-tasi* (2 pl. pres. act.), etc.

o=a. ποδ-ός, Sk. and origl. *pad-ás* (g. sing.), st. and √*pad*
(foot, go), where of course, in accordance with the sensibility
of the Greek, the *o* may also be considered as a raised step
from ε in πεδ; ὁ, τό, origl. and Sk. *sa, ta-t*, root and st. *sa, ta*
(pron. dem.) ; πό-σι-ς (lord)=origl. and Sk. *pá-ti-s* (lord) ;
μέν-ος (n. acc.), μέν-ους (gen. sing.) for *μένεσ-ος, Sk. and
origl. *mán-as, mán-as-as* ; similarly in *a*-stems, *a* changes to *o*,
as νέϜο-ς (n. sing. masc.), νέϜο-ν (acc. sing.)=Lat. *nouo-s, nouo-m*,
Sk. and origl. *náva-s, náva-m*, etc.

Dialectically *o* takes the place of *a*. Aiolic βροχέως for
βραχέως (adv.), from st. βραχύ- (breuis=*breguis*, short) ; Ar-
kadian ἑκοτόν for ἑκατόν (100), f.f. of -κατον is *kata-m* or
kanta-m, cf. Sk. *çatá-m* ; Kuprian κόρζα=καρδία (heart), cf.
Lat. *cord-*, f.f. of this stem is *kard-* ; st. τεκταν- in τέκταινα, i.e.
*τεκτανγα (fem.), τεκταίν-ομαι (build), *i.e.* *τεκτανγομαι stands
by the form τέκτον- (n. sing. τέκτων, builder), f.f. *taktan-* ; the
older *a* is preserved in the Dôric Ϝίκατι for the newer Attic εἴκοσι
(twenty), f.f. of the second part of the word is (*da*)*kati* ; in
δια-κάτιοι for διακόσιοι (200), -κατιοι is derived from an origl.
stem *kata-* or *kanta-* (100).

a=a. ἀκ-ωκ-ή (point), st. ἄκ-οντ- (n. ἄκων, dart), origl. √ἀκ
(Lat. *ac-, ac-utus*) ; ἄγ-ω (lead)=Lat. *ago*, Sk. *áǵ-āmi*, origl.
√*ag* ; ἄχος (grief), ἄχ-νυμαι (am grieved), origl. √*agh* ;
ἐ-λαχ-ύς (little), Sk. *lagh-ús* (old *ragh-ú-s*) (light) ; πλατύ-ς
(broad, wide), Sk. *prthú-s*, origl. *pratu-s* ; λα-μ-β-άνω (take),
ἔ-λαβ-ον, Sk. *á-labh-am*, √λαβ, Sk. *labh-* (get) ; δάκ-νω (bite),
ἔ-δακ-ον, cf. Sk. *dáç-āmi*, f.f. √*dak* ; ἔ-λακ-ον (I spoke), cf. Lat.
loq-uor, Sk. *láp-āmi* (cry out), √λακ, origl. *rak* ; st. πα-τέρ-
(father)=Lat. *pa-ter-*, origl. *pa-tar-*, √*pa* (protect).

a stands beside ε, e.g. ἔ-ταμ-ον beside ἔ-τεμ-ον (τέμ-νω, cut), in
ἔ-τραφ-ον, ἔ-τραπ-ον, ἔ-κταν-ον beside τρέφ-ω (cherish), τρέπ-ω
(turn), κτείν-ω (kill) (=*κτεν-γω). We cannot trace herein a

§ 19. step from ε to *a*, but only a vowel-colouring, originally merely dialectic, which indeed was used in Greek for the purpose of expressing the relation of the aorist. As ἐ-ταμ-ον is to ἐ-τεμ-ον, so are the present forms τέμνω, τρέφω, τρέπω to the Dôric τάμνω, τράφω, τράπω, which we have to consider as the presents corresponding to the aorists ἔταμον, ἔτραφον, ἔτραπον; κρείσσων (better) (i.e. *κρετ-γων) beside κράτ-ιστος (best). Cf. Dôric ᾱ=Iôn. Attic η.

a=*a*+nasal. πόδα (acc. sing.), Sk. and origl. *pád-am* (pedem), πόδ-ας, Sk. *pád-as*, origl. *padam-s*; φέρον-τα, Sk. and origl. *bháran-tam* (feren-tem), φέροντ-ας, Sk. *bhárant-as*, origl. *bharant-ams* (acc. pl. ferent-es); ἑπτά, Sk. and origl. *saptán* (septem); δέκα, Sk. *dáçan*, origl. *dakan* (decem); -σα (1 sing. aor. in comp.) =Sk. and origl. *-sa-m*, cf. ἔ-δειξα (=ἐ-δεικ-σα) and Sk. *á-dik-ša-m*, √*diç*, origl. *dik* (show).

§ 20. **Step-formation in the *a*-scale.** Rule for the **first step** is: radical ε is raised to *o*, *a* to *ā* (i.e. η). There are, however, exceptions to this rule.

1. ε : *o*. φόρ-ο-ς (tax), φορέω (bear (durative), wear)=Sk. and f.f. *bhár-a-s* (burden), *bhār-áyāmi* (causat.) beside φέρ-ω, Sk. and f.f. *bhár-āmi* (fero); Fόχ-ο-ς (waggon), Sk. *vah-a-s*, f.f. *vāgh-a-s* (waggon), √Fεχ, Sk. *vah*, origl. *vagh* (vehere), which, however, as a verb becomes intermixed with √σεχ, Sk. *sah* (have, hold); μέ-μον-α (strive), f.f. *ma-mān-a*, beside μέν-ος (might), Sk. and f.f. *mán-as*, √μεν, origl. √*man* (think); γον-ή (birth), γόν-ο-ς (thing born, bairn), γέ-γον-α, f.f. *ga-gān-a*, Sk. *ǧaǧā́na*, beside ἐ-γεν-όμην, γέν-ος (genus), Sk. *ǧán-as*, f.f. *gan-as*, √γεν, origl. √*gan* (gi-gn-ere); τόκος (thing born, bairn), τοκ-εύ-ς (parens), beside τεκ-έσθαι, τίκ-τω, √τεκ (produce); τέ-τροφ-α beside τρέφ-ω, ἐ-τράφ-ην, √τρεφ (nourish); ἔ-κτον-α beside κτείν-ω (i.e. *κτεν-γω), ἔ-κταν-ον, √κτεν (kill); εἴ-λοχ-α, λόγ-ος, beside λέγω, √λεγ (legere); ἔ-φθορ-α, φθορ-ά, beside φθείρω, i.e. *φθερ-γω, √φθερ (destroy); ὄψ (voice), i.e. Fόπ-ς, origl. *vāk-s*, Sk. *vāk* for *vāk-s* (cry), beside Fέπ-ος (word),

origl. *vāk-as*, Sk. *vak̄-as*, origl. √ *vak* (cry) ; γόν-υ, gen. γόνατος, § 20. older (Iôn.) γούνατος=*γονϜατος, γουνός=*γονϜος, cf. Sk. *g̑ā́nu* (genu) ; ὄ-νο-μα, older (Hom.) οὔ-νο-μα (name), from ὄ-γνο-μα, cf. Lat. *gno-men*, (Sk. *nãm-an*, also, with root-vowel raised).

In Greek, on account of the prosodic quantity of *o*, this step is possible only before two consonants, e.g. δέδορκα=Sk. *da-dárç-a*, origl. *da-dark-a*, beside δέρκ-ομαι, ἔ-δρακ-ον, √ δερκ, origl. *dark* (see).

Note.—The same kind of step-formation of *e=a* to *o=ā* occurs in Latin, also in Sclavonic, e.g. O.-Bulg. *vez-ą*=original *vagh-āmi*, Lat. *ueho*, bes. *voz-ŭ*=original *vāgh-a-s*, Gk. Fόχ-o-ς, v. infr.

2. *a* : *ā*, η. two equivalent sounds. e.g. λέ-ληκ-α, λέ-λᾱκ-α, beside ἔ-λακ-ον, √ λακ (cry out), cf. Sk. *lap*, origl. *rak* ; κέ-κληγ-α beside ἔ-κλαγ-ον, κλάζω=*κλαγ-yω, √ κλαγ (sound) ; λέ-ληθ-α, Dôr. λέ-λαθ-α, λήθη (forgetfulness), beside ἔ-λαθ-ον, λα-ν-θ-άνω, √ λαθ (escape notice) ; εἴ-ληχ-α beside ἔ-λαχ-ον, λα-γ-χ-άνω, √ λαχ (get by lot) ; δέ-δηχ-α beside δάκ-νω, ἔ-δακ-ον, √ δακ (bite); εἴ-ληφ-α, λῆψ-ις (i.e. ληπ-σις=ληβ-τις), beside ἔ-λαβ-ον, λα-μ-β-άνω, √ λαβ (take) ; κέ-κρᾱγ-α beside κράζω, *κραγ-yω, √ κραγ (cry aloud); ἔ-ᾱγα, Iôn. ἔ-ηγ-α, i.e. Ϝε-Ϝᾱγ-α, f.f. *va-vāg-a*, beside ἄγ-νυμι, √ Ϝαγ (break) ; st. μῆ-τερ-, origl. and Sk. *mā-tar-*, etc.

In elements belonging to the formation of words, *o* will be found raised to η, *ā* : this rule is observed regularly in the stem-termination *o=a* in such stems as are raised in the feminine termination, e.g. νέο-ς (n. sing. masc.), νέο-ν (n. sing. neut.), origl. and Sk. *náva-s*, *náva-m* (nouo-s, nouo-m), but fem. νέ-α, Iôn. νέη=origl. and Sk. *návā* (noua). In ἡ, ʽ*ā*, origl. and Sk. *sā*, beside ὁ, origl. and Sk. *sa* (pron. demonstr.), and other pronominal stems, is found radical *o* raised to η, *ā*, the root being equivalent to the stem as often.

Note 1.—μέ-μηλ-α beside μέλ-ει, √ μελ (be a care to), shows also the raising of ε to η.

§ 20.   *Note* 2.—Sometimes $\bar{a}$ is shortened to $\breve{a}$, e.g. Ƒάστυ (city), Sk. *vắs-tu* (house), Sk. and original √*vas* (inhabit) ; similar shortenings often occur in the *a*-termn. of feminine stems.

Note 3.—The laying-down of the laws for the use of $\bar{a}$, η, belongs to the special-grammar of Greek: the Dôric predilection for the more ancient $\bar{a}$ and that of Iônia for η are well known. In Attic likewise $\bar{a}$ changes to η, yet *a* repeatedly occurs, owing to the surrounding sounds, especially in the case of ρ, ε, η, ι, *y* (i.e. ζ, σσ, λλ, etc.), preceding, and ε, η, following, when its change to η is stopped.

For the s e c o n d   s t e p we have ω in examples such as ἔρ-ρωγ-α, ῥώξ, ῥωγ-ός (cleft), beside ῥήγ-νυμι, √Ƒραγ (break), cf. Goth. *brak*, Lat. *frag* ; πτώξ, i.e. πτώκ-ς, gen. πτωκ-ός (cowering), πτώσσω, i.e. *πτώκ-yω (cower), beside πτήσσω = *πτήκ-yω, ἔ-πτακ-ον, √πτακ (cower), clearly a further formation from √πτα, cf. πε-πτη-κώς ; ἀρωγ-ός (helper) beside ἀρήγ-ω (I help). From these examples we gather an equation η : ω :: ε : ο.

Also where there is no parallel first step to ω, we must hold it to be in the position of a second step, e.g. τρώγ-ω beside ἔ-τραγ-ον, √τραγ (gnaw, chew) ; ὄδ-ωδ-α beside ὄζω = *ὄδ-yω, ὀδ-μή, ὀσ-μή, √ὀδ (smell) ; ὠκ-ύς=Sk. *āç-ús*, origl. *āk-us* (sharp), ἀκ-ωκ-ή (point), √ἀκ, cf. ἵππος (equos), origl. *ak-vas* ; ὠ-όν, better ᾠόν (Sappho, ὤιον acc. to Ahrens, ὤβεον Hêsuch.), origl. *āvya-m* (ouom, *lit.* bird-, of a bird), from origl. *avi-s*, Sk. *vi-s* (auis) ; ἀγ-ωγ-ή (leading), ἀγ-ωγ-ός (leader), beside ἀγ-αγ-εῖν, ἄγ-ειν (lead) ; δί-δω-μι beside δί-δο-μεν, √δο (dare) ; ἐδ-ωδ-ή (food), √ἐδ, Lat. *ed*, origl. and Sk. *ad* (eat) ; γνω-τός (known), γι-γνώ-σκω (learn, come to know), cf. Lat. *(g) nō-tus, (g) nō-sco*, √*gna*, from *gan*.

Note.—Dialectically ου occurs for ω, i.e. $\bar{u}$, in isolated instances (a weakening which occurs also in Lat.). ω : ου ($\bar{u}$) :: ο : υ (*u*), e.g. Thessal. γνούμα=γνώμη (insight, opinion), √γνο, original *gna=gan* (learn) ; -ουν=-ων, fund. -*ām* in gen. pl., cf. Lat. -*um*, etc.

§ 21.   2. *i*-s c a l e.

R o o t - v o w e l ι. ἴ-μεν, ἴ-θι, Sk. *i-más-i, i-hí*, origl. *i-masi, i-dhi*, √*i* (ire) ; ἔ-λιπ-ον, √λιπ, Lat. *lic*, Sk. *rik̂*, origl. *rik* (leave) ; Ƒίδ-μεν

=Sk. and origl. *vid-mási*, st. *Fίσ-τορ-* [n. sing. *ἴσ-τωρ* and *ἴσ-τωρ* § 21. (knower, witness)], for **Fιδ-τορ-*, f.f. *vid-tar*, √*vid* (know); *ἔ-πιθ-ον, ἐ-πιθ-όμην, πίσ-τις* (faith), for **πίθ-τι-ς*, √*πιθ* (persuade), and element of stem-formation *τι*; *σχίδ-η* (splinter), *σχίζω* (split) =**σχίδ-yω*, √*σχιδ*=Sk. *k̆hid*, Lat. *scid*, origl. *skid* (scindere); *ὀ-μιχ-εῖν*, √*μιχ*=Sk. *mih*, origl. *migh* (mingere); *λίχ-νος* (daintiness), *λιχ-μάω*, √*λιχ*, Sk. *lih, rih*, Lat. *lig*, origl. *righ*; *στίχ-ος* (rank), *ἔ-στιχ-ον*, √*στιχ* (march, tread), Goth. *stig*, Sk. and origl. *stigh*; *τί-ς*, fund. *ki-s*, Lat. *qui-s*, Goth. **hi-s*, pronl. root, origl. *ki* (dem. and interrog.), etc.

Lengthened *ī* is a parallel form to *i* (often depending on fixed proportion of sound), e.g. Hom. *ἴ-ομεν* and *ἴ-ομεν* beside *ἴ-ωμεν* (1 pl. pres. conj.), origl. *i-a-mas*, √*i* (ire); *ἰδ-ος* (ntr. sweat), *ἰδ-ίω* (I sweat), √*ἰδ*, origl. *svid*, cf. Sk. *svid-yāmi*; *πῖ-νω* (*πῖνε*), *πῖθι*, beside *ἔ-πῖ-ον*, √*πι* (drink), cf. Sk. *pī* beside *pa*.

i raised by steps. § 22.

1. *i* raised to *ει*; e.g. *εἶ-μι* (go), Sk. *é-mi*, origl. *ai-mi*, √*i*; *πείθ-ω* (1 sing. pres.), √*πιθ*, so *λείπ-ω*, √*λιπ*; *λείχ-ω*, origl. *raigh-āmi* (1 sing. pres.), √*λιχ*, origl. √*righ*; *στείχ-ω*, origl. *staigh-āmi*, √*στιχ*; *Fείδ-εται, εἴσομαι* (for **Fειδ-σομαι*), *Fεῖδος* (ntr. outward-form), √*Fιδ*; *εἰκ-ών* (likeness) beside *ἔ-ικ-τον, ἐ-ίκτην*, √*Fικ*, clearly (=resemble); *κεῖ-ται* (3 sing. pres. med.)=Sk. *çé-tē*, √*ki* (lie), etc.

αι occurs in the main perhaps only as a lifeless step-formation where the language has lost all sense of the derivation, and hence for the most part no *ι, ει*, or *οι*, is parallel to *αι*, e.g. *αἴθ-ω* (I kindle), *αἴθ-εσθαι* (burn), *αἰθ-ήρ, αἰθ-έρος*, (aether), *αἴθ-ουσα* (porch), cf. Lat. *aed-es, aid-ilis*, √*ιθ*=Sk. *idh, indh* (burn), Germ. *it*, in O.H.G. *eit* (fire); *αἰ-Fών*, origl. *ai-vān-s* (time, long time), cf. Lat. *ae-uo-m*, origl. *ai-va-m*, Sk. *é-va-s*, origl. *ai-va-s* (a going), Goth. *aiv-s*, f.f. *āi-va-s* (time, long time), with other step-forms, √*i* (go), with sf. *van, va* (here the language no longer felt the connexion with *ἴ-μεν, εἶ-μι, οἶ-μος*); *και-ρό-ς* (point of time), cf. Goth. *hvei-la* (hour, time, Engl. '*while*'), origl. *kai-rā*, origl. √*ki*.

§ 22. *Note.*—In medial termns., e.g. φέρο-μαι, *φερε-σαι, φέρε-ται, φέρον-ται, αι is not a step-form, but the product of a contraction from f.f. *bharā-mami, bhara-sasi, bhara-tati, bhara-ntanti,* v. sub. ' Conjugation.'

2. *i* raised to οι, e.g. οἶ-μος, οἴ-μη (road, a going), cf. αἰ-Fών, εἶ-μι, ἴ-μεν, √ι (go) ; πέ-ποιθ-α beside πείθ-ω, √πιθ (ἐ-πέ-πιθ-μεν) ; λέ-λοιπ-α, λοιπ-ό-ς (left, remaining), beside λείπ-ω, ἔ-λιπ-ον, √λιπ ; *Foîδ-a* (know)=Sk. *véd-a,* with the 1st, Goth. *vait* with 2nd step, beside *Feîδ-ος,* √Fιδ (Fίδ-μεν) ; ἔ-οικ-α (seem) beside εἰκ-ών, for *FéFοικα,* √Fικ, (ἔ-ικ-τον, ἐ-ίκ-την) ; *Foîκ-ο-ς* (house), cf. Sk. *véç-a-s,* Lat. *uîc-u-s,* i.e. **ueic-o-s,* with 1st step, √Fικ=Sk. *viç,* origl. *vik* (settle) ; *Foîν-ο-ς* (wine), cf. Lat. *uin-um,* Germ. *wein* with 1st step ; λοιβ-ή (lib-atio) beside λείβ-ω (pour), and λίβ-ο-ς (drop), λιβ-άς, -άδ-ος (moisture), √λιβ ; στοῖχ-ος (rank) beside στείχ-ω, ἔ-στιχ-ον, √στιχ ; αἱματο-λοιχ-ό-ς (blood-licking) beside λείχ-ω, λίχ-νος ; κοίτ-η (bed), κοι-μᾶσθαι (sleep), beside κεῖ-ται, √ki, etc.

Note.—In opt. φέρ-οις (etc.)=fund. *bhar-ai-s,* also in nom. pl. e.g. οἱ, original *sai* (*tai*), οι is the result of a contraction, not a step of a vowel-scale ; v. ' Conjugation and Declension.'

§ 23.   3. *u*-scale.

Radical υ, e.g. ἔ-φυγ-ον, φυγ-ή (fug-a), √φυγ, Sk. *bhug̓* (*bhug-ná-s,* bent), Goth. *bug* (bend), Lat. *fug* (only here and in the Greek with a narrower sense) ; ζυγ-όν (yoke)=Lat. *iug-um,* Sk. and origl. *yug-ám,* √yug (join, iungere) ; ἐ-ρυθ-ρό-ς (red) =Sk. *rudh-irá-s,* f.f. *rudh-ra-s,* √ρυθ, origl. and Sk. √*rudh,* Goth. *rud* (be red), etc. ; σύ, τύ (thou, du), cf. Sk. *tv-am,* Lat. *tu,* Lith. *tu,* Sclav. *ty ;* κλύ-ω (hear), √κλυ, Sk. *çru,* Goth. *hlu* (Eng. *loud, lud*=voice), origl. *kru ;* ρυ-τό-ς (flowing), √ρυ, Sk. and origl. *sru* (flow), so ἐρρύ-ην=*ἐ-σρυ-ην, Germ. *stru* (in *strōm,* stream, with inserted *t*) ; φύ-ω (am), φύτ-ον (being), √φυ, Sk. *bhu,* Lat. *fu,* origl. *bhu* (be) ; κέ-χυ-μαι (perf.), √χυ, Goth. √*gu-t* (pour) (with a *t* for further formation) ; ἔσ-συ-μαι, (pf.), σύ-το (aor.), √συ (rush) ; ὠκ-ύ-ς=Sk. *āç-ú-s,* origl. *āk-u-s*

(sharp) ; πλατ-ύ-ς, Sk. *prthús*, origl. *prat-u-s* (broad), sf. *u ;* § 23.
ἄσ-τυ (city)=Sk. *vãs-tu* (house) ; βοη-τύ-ς (shout), μάρ-τυς
(witness), etc., with sf. -τυ, Sk., Lat., origl. *tu.* The lengthening of υ to ῡ is not uncommon, e.g. ῞ῠδωρ, cf. Sk. *ud-a-m,*
ud-aká-m, Lat. *unda,* with inserted nasal, Sk. √*ud* (be wet);
κλῠ-θι (imper. aor.)=Sk. *çru-dhí,* origl. *kru-dhi,* cf. κέ-κλῠ-θι,
κλῠ-τός, √κλυ, origl. *kru* (hear) ; πέ-πνῡ-μαι, πε-πνῡ-μένος
(prudent), √πνυ (blow) ; ξΰ-ω, √ξυ (shave) ; ῦς and σῦς (swine),
cf. Lat. *sūs,* Sk. *sū-kara-,* O.H.G. *su,* √*su ;* δρῦ-ς (tree),· Goth.
triu (arbor). We cannot decide with any certainty where origl.
au stands as a lengthening for a root-vowel, and where it stands
for a step of a vowel-scale. In the last-mentioned examples
perhaps originally a step-form was in existence.

Note 1.—The older sound *u* has been kept in Boiôt. (τού=σύ,
κούνες=κύνες, etc.), and in diphth. *av.* The later υ=ü occurs
proportionately early, however. The same transition of sound
occurs also in other languages. Lat. *una* became Fr. *une,* pronounced *ün.*

Note 2.—In Greek as well as in Umbr., *ι* occurs as a weaker
representative form of *υ.* In mod. Gk. it is well known that υ
has universally become *ι.* So φῑ-τυ-ς (father, begetter), φῑ-τύ-ω
(beget)=Lat. *fu-tu-o,* √φυ, original *bhu ;* δρί-ον, also δρί-ος
(forest), and δρῦ-ς (tree), cf. Sk. *dru-,* masc. n. wood, m. tree),
Goth. *triu* (tree); σί-αλο-ς (hog) and σῦς. Curt. Gk. Et.²
p. 647 sqq.

Step-formation of *u.*   § 24.

1. step ευ, e.g. φεύγ-ω (flee), πέ-φευγ-α, √φυγ ; ἐλεύ[θ]-σομαι
(shall come), √ἐλυθ in ἤλυθον=*ἐ-ελυθ-ον ; κλέϜ-ος=Sk. çráv-as
(fame), origl. *krav-as,* √κλυ ; πλέϜ-ω (sail)=Sk. and origl.
plàv-ãmi, √πλυ ; ῥεῦ-μα (stream), ῥεύ-σομαι, ῥέϜ-ω (flow)=Sk.
and origl. *sráv-ãmi,* √ῥυ, origl. and Sk. √*sru* (flow) ; πνεῦ-μα
(breath), πνεύ-σω, πνέϜ-ω (blow), √πνυ ; σεύ-ω (rush), √συ ;
χέϜ-ω (pour), √χυ ; ξέϜ-ω (I scrape), √ξυ ; Ζεύ-ς (nom.
propr. God), for *δγευ-ς, in Sk. with 2nd step *dyāu-s* (heaven),
in the other cases from √*div,* √διϜ=*dyu,* *δγυ, ζυ, etc.

av is here too a lifeless step-formation, e.g. αὔ-ω for *αὐσ-ω

§ 24. (kindle), ἔν-αυσ-μα (tinder), cf. εὔ-ω, Lat. *uro*=*ous-o, *eus-o
(see Lat. 'Vowels'), Sk. *ṓś-āmi*, origl. *aus-āmi*, √*uš*, origl. *us*;
αὐγ-ή (glance), √ὐγ, cf. Sk. *ṓgas* (force); αὔξ-άν-ω, i.e. *αὐγ-σανω
(make to grow), cf. Lat. *aug-eo*, √*ug* (which occurs pure in
Lith.).

2. Second step *ov* occurs seldom, espec. when *u* is medial
(no *πε-φουγ-a=Goth. *baug,*=*bu-bāuga, like λέλοιπα), while we
find it compensated for by the first step, yet cf. εἰλήλουθα
(Hom.) from √ἐλυθ, cf. ἤλυθον and ἐλεύ(θ)σομαι [origl. √ἐλ=
ἐρ, origl. *ar* (go), in ἔρ-χομαι (come, go), f.f. *er-skomai*, further
formed in Greek by sf. *υ* (προς-ήλυ-τος ἔπ-ηλυς, newly come),
to which is added the frequent accompaniment of a verb-stem θ
(v. sub. 'Formation of Present-stem'); the secondary √ἐλυθ so
formed sts. was treated as if the √vowel was really *υ* (exx. in
text), sts. is merely equivalent to an auxiliary vowel (§ 29), which
moreover may disappear, ἤλθον]; ἀ-κόλουθος (follower), and
κέλευθ-ος (way); ῥούσ-ιος (reddish), for *ῥουθιος (or perhaps
*ῥουθ-τιος, *ῥουθ-σιος ?), beside ἐ-ρεύθ-ω (blush), and ἐ-ρυθ-ρός
(red); σπουδ-ή (haste) beside σπεύδ-ω (hasten); λοῦσσον=
*λουκ-γον (white pith of deal), cf. λευκ-ός (white), ἀμφι-λύκ-η
(twilight), λύχ-νος. More often beside final *u*, e.g. πνοϝ-ή
(blast) beside πνέϝ-ω, √πνυ; ῥοϝ-ή, ῥόϝ-ος (stream), beside
ῥεῦ-μα, √ῥυ; χοϝ-ή (outpouring) beside χέϝ-ω, √χυ; πλόϝ-ος
(voyage) beside πλέϝ-ω, √πλυ; θόϝ-ος (swift) beside θέϝ-ω,
√θυ, Sk. and origl. *dhu*; ξοϝ-ίς (chisel), ξόϝ-ανον (carved-work),
beside ξέϝ-ω, √ξυ; σόϝ-ος (quick motion), σοῦ-μαι=*σοϝ-ομαι
(Trag. haste), beside σεύ-ω, √συ.

In separate instances also *av* (*āv*) is a second step fr. *u*, e.g.
ναῦς (nauis) (i.e. νᾱῦς on acct. of νηῦς)=Sk. *nāu-s*, Iôn. νηϝ-ός,
Dôr. νᾱϝ-ός, Sk. *nāv-ás*, point to √*nu*.

ωυ is only Iôn.=*av*, e.g. θωῦ-μα (wonder)=θαῦ-μα, θέϝa,
θεϝά-ομαι (show, gaze), point to √θυ.

ω also occurs sts. as second step from *υ*, e.g. ζω-μός (broth),
cf. ζῦ-μη (yeast), Sk. *yū-ša-m*, Lat. *iū-s*, similarly belonging to

√/yu, Gk. ζυ (with which ζέ-ω (cook) for *ζεσ-ω, cf. ἔ-ζεσ-μαι, § 24. ζεσ-τό-ς, has no connexion, cf. O.H.G. √/jas, cook); ζώ-ννυμι (gird), √ζυ, origl. yu (join) ; χώ-ννυμι, √χυ, χέω (pour). If we compare πλώ-ω for πλώϜω, Iôn. parallel-form to πλέϜ-ω, Dôr. βῶς=βοῦς=Sk. gāus, and Iôn. ων=αυ, hence we infer in Greek a step-formn. ōu, ον=origl. āu, āv, where the 2nd element has become assimilated to the first, so that only ō, ω (=ωο, ου) remains.

Note 1.—Cases such as οὐρανό-ς (heaven) beside Sk. *váruna-s* (name of a deity) ; οὐλ-ή (scar) beside Lat. *uolnus*, Sk. *vranam* and *vranas* (wound) ; εὐρύ-ς (wide) beside Sk. *urú-s* for *varú-s*, show ον, ευ, in place of the expected Ϝο, Ϝε. The explanation of this is difficult ; perhaps it is to be considered less as a transposition of Ϝο, Ϝε, to ον, ευ, than a shortening fr. original *va* to *u* and a step-formation from the latter.

Note 2.—There are three roots θυ in Gk. : 1. θύω, hasten ; 2. θύω, offer ; 3. in θαῦμα, θεάομαι, gaze.

Note 3.—All vowel-sounds which do not appear in the vowel-scales are therefore unoriginal products of the sound-laws (especially of contraction after the elision of consonants).

SOUND-LAWS OF VOWELS. § 25.

The laws laid down in ordinary Greek grammars, i.e. the laws of contraction, etc., may be passed over as already understood.

At first sight we are struck by the frequently occurring hiatus which arises from elision of spirants *y*, *s*, *v*, and their vocalisation, and which is not by any means invariably obviated by contraction ; thus arise forms such as Homêric δηϊόφεν, five vowels (together), 3 pl. opt. from δηϊόω (slay), fr. δήϊος (hostile) ; δήϊος evidently=*δήσιος=Sk. *dāsya-s* (hostile), adjectival form in *ya*, fr. *dā́sa-s* (demon, slave, originally 'foe'), whence *dāsya--yā-mi* (=*δησιο-yω-μι, whence δηϊόω), of which 3 pl. f.f. *dās-ya-yai-nt*, in Gk. with superfluous unoriginal ε before personal termination, *dāsya-yai-ant* as f.f.=δηιο-οι-εν, and in that case with φ=αι, in consequence of an unoriginal lengthening of οι to ω, comes δηιόφεν. (Acc. to Aufrecht in Kuhn's Zeitschrift, vii. 312,

§ 25. sqq., δήιος proved to be Aiolic in δάϝιος belongs to √δυ; f.f. accordingly of δήιος, δηιόφεν=*dāvya-s, *dāvya-yai-ant.) Diphth. ᾳ, ῃ, ῳ, are only secondary products of contraction.

Whilst the termination (except a few instances, e.g. partial shortening of ā to ă in fem. and the like, cf. § 20) does not yet exercise a destructive influence on the vowels,—and also the vowels of syllables which follow medially upon one another (excepting the working of the ι of σι on the vowel of the preceding syllable) have no essential influence upon one another,—we perceive a variation of the older vowel-system, caused by consonantal influence,—a variation of considerable importance and characteristic of the language.

Important above all are the changes in consequence of the Greek distaste for the original and frequent Indo-European spirants y, v, s; y and v become ι and υ, y also becomes ε; v and y as ι and υ change position from a following to a preceding syllable; y, v, and s, further fall out from between two vowels. After the disappearance and softening of consonants, frequent vowel-lengthening takes place. A consonantal sound in the beginning of a word is not unfrequently accompanied by an introductory vowel-sound, and besides occurs the so-called vowel-insertion between two consonants.

§26a.   Introduction of i into a preceding syllable in case of termn. -σι. e.g. (1.) loc. dat. pl. ταῖσι, Iôn. τῇσι, thence ταῖς, fr. *tāsi (pronoml. st. ta raised to tā, and loc. termn. pl. si), and also τοῖσι, τοῖς, fr. *to-si, *tā-si (although another explanation offers itself here, v. sub. 'Declension'). (2.) 2 sing. ind. and conj. act., e.g. φέρεις (indic.), fr. *φερεισι, *φερε-σι, f.f. bhara-si; φέρῃς (conj.), fr. *φερησι, *φερηισι, *φερησι, f.f. bharā-si.

§26b.   Vocalisation and transposition of y and v.

1. y changes to ι and u to υ, e.g. original stem-formative particle ya=Gr. ιο; πάτρ-ιο-ς (paternal), cf. patr-ius, st. πατέρ-, cf. Sk. pitr-ya-s, origl. patar-ya-s; ἅγ-ιο-ς (holy), cf. Sk. yaǵ-ya-s (to revere); compar. suff. -ιον, origl. -yans, e.g. ἡδ-ίων, st.

ἡδ-ίον- (ἡδ-ύ-ς, sweet), f.f. svād-yāns, st. svād-yans-, cf. ἐλάσσων §26b. for *ἐλαχγων, f.f. lagh-yāns (ἐλαχ-ύ-ς, small, f.f. lagh-u-s), in the latter of which instt. y as such has disappeared; pres.-st.-suff. origl. ya, e.g. ἰδ-ί-ω (sweat), f.f. ´svid-yāmi, δα-ίω (kindle), fr. da-yāmi, cf. κράζω (howl), for *κραγ-yω, with same suff. which here has retained y; in Dôr. fut. form. -σίω for *σyω, origl. syāmi; in gen. sing. masc. neut. of a-stem, origl. -asya (Gr. with loss of σ, οιο), e.g. ἵππο-ιο fr. *ἰκFοσ-yo=Sk. áçvasya, origl. akva-sya; optat. particle ιη, origl. and Sk. ya, e.g. εἴην for *ἐσ-yη-μ= origl. as-ya-m, with s lost between two vowels; perf. part. act. fem. υια fr. origl. -vant-yā, -vans-yā, from the latter form with elision of an came *-vsyā, hence -usyā=Gk. *υσια=υια; δύο, δύω =*δFω, cf. δώδεκα fr. *δFωδεκα, Sk. and origl. dva.

Note.—Esp. in Lesbo-Aiolic v between two vowels is pre-ferred to be=v, e.g. χε-ύ-ω=χέFω (pour), √χυ; so πνεύ-ω= *πνέFω (breathe), √πνυ; θεύω=θέFω (haste), √θυ, etc.

2. Further, ε occurs sts. undeniably for y (not however for v, F) especially after consonants; in the cases from y there remains only the accompanying vowel-sound itself, as a short and in-determinate vowel which is nearly=ε, e.g. ε=y in fut. forms, πλευσοῦμαι, φευξοῦμαι=σέομαι, *σyομαι, fund. f. -syāmai; further in κενέος (empty), Aiol. κέννος, both fr. *κενyος, f.f. kvanyas, Sk. çūnyás; ἐτεός (true) = Sk. satyás; στερεός (firm, solid) beside στερρός, f.f. *στεργyος, staryas, fem. στεῖρα, staryā; Epic ἠνορ-έη =ἀνδρ-ία (manliness), f.f. of suff. is yā (st. ἀνέρ-, ἀνδρ-), n. sing. ἀνήρ (man).

Note 1.—In cases of declens., e.g. πόλεως, ε is not=y, but there was a step-raising of ι to ει, and the representative y was lost; e.g. πόλεως=πόλεος, fr. *πολεy-ος, st. πολι (city), f.f. parai-as, st. pari.

Note 2.—Original v also does not change to ι. In poetry perhaps the metrical forms such as πλείειν for πλεύειν (sail), √πλυ, raised to πλευ, πλεF, may be traced to a present st. in ya, which the Gk. has strangely liked, thus πλείω=*πλεF-yω, while πλέω = πλέFω; νεῖος beside νέFος (new), νεώς beside νεFός

§26 b. (fallow), brings us to a f.f. *navyas*, which clearly occurs in Lith. *nau-yas*, Goth. *niuyis*, st. *niuya-* (new). From such cases ει may have become a more widespread representative of ε by analogy. In πνοιή for πνοή, we find *ya*-stems, whilst πνοϜή (√πνυ) has suff. *a*, πνοιή=*πνοϜιή=*πνοϜγη, suff. *ya*.

Note 3.—ἑός=ἑϜ-ός, Lat. *sou-os, suus*, f.f. of both *sev-os ; τεός=τεϜός, Lat. *touos, tuus*, f.f. *tevos (yet σός, fr. σϜος=*τϜος, not raised from √τυ); through the Latin the Italograec f.-forms are made clear.   In forms like ἡδεῖα, fem. of ἡδύς (sweet), there is a clear step-raising, thus f.f. is ἡδεϜ-ια=*svā-dav-yā*, diverging from the unraised Sk. *svādvī́*, fr. *svādvyā.

Note 4.—G. Curt. Gr. Et.[2] p. 500 sqq., treats of ο, ω, as representatives of original *v*. This occurs on the whole but seldom, and mostly in words of uncertain etymology, e.g. δοάν (Alkman), for *δϜαν, *δϜην, δήν (long while), and these must stand for *διϜα-ν, *διϜη-ν, acc. of a st. *διϜα-=Lat. *diue-, in *die-s*= *dive-s* (day, for meaning cf. Lat. *diu*, long).

3. When *y* and *v* stand after ν, ρ, they regularly occur as ι and υ before the consonants : in Aiolic dialects, however, assimilation takes place to the preceding consonant : this assimilation occurs in the case of λ in the other dialects, transposition in the case of λ is merely the exception. The origin of the transposition we must hold to be this, that at first, whilst *y* and *v* were yet in existence, an *i* and *u* arose by assimilation in the foregoing syllable (as in Zend), and that long afterwards the *y, v*, disappeared.

y; e.g. κτείνω (kill), Aiolic κτέννω, for *κτεινγω, fr. *κτενγω ; μέλαινα (fem. fr. stem μέλαν- black), fr. *μελανγα ; χείρων (worse), Aiol. χέρρων, for *χειρ-γων, fr. *χεργων ; φθείρω (destroy), Aiol. φθέρρω, for *φθεργω ; κλίνω (lay), Aiol. κλίννω, for *κλινγω ; κρίνω (sift), Aiol. κρίννω, for *κρινγω ; πλΰνω (wash), for *πλυινω, *πλυινγω, *πλυνγω, contrn. of υι and υι to ˉ and ῡ.

In the case of λy the assimln. occurs outside the Aiolic dial., ἀφείλω, however, for *ὀφελγω, Hom. ὀφέλλω (ought).

Note 1.—After ν, ρ, λ, original *y* very often=ι, e.g. χρόν-ιο-ς, ἐλευθέριο-ς, μακάριο-ς, παράλλιο-ς, collectively constructed with § 26b. original suff. *ya*.

Note 2.—For epenthesis of *y* beside other consonants, we have good instances in μείζων (greater) for *μειγ-γων, fr. *μεγ-γων, μεγ- with compar. suff. original -*yans*; ζ=γy, consequently this is a clear case of genuine epenthesis; κρείσσων (stronger, better) for *κρειτ-γων, fr. *κρετ-γων (κρέσσων preserved in diall.); σσ=τy (v. post.) formed just like μείζων; πείκω (beside πέκω, comb) for *πεκγω, which by the laws of sound (κy=σσ) must coincide with πέσσω (cook) in form; st. γυναικ- (γυναικός, gen. fr. γυνή, woman) for *γυνακι, cf. φυλακίς (female-guard); st. αἰγ- (n. sing. αἴξ for αἰγ-ς, goat) for *ἀγι-, cf. Sk. *agá-s* (stag), *agá* (goat) (Curt. Gr. Et.² p. 608). It cannot be denied that πείκω for *πεκ-γω is very doubtful phonetically.

v; e.g. γουνός, γοῦνα (Aiol. γόννος, γόννα), γούνατος, for γονϜός, γόνϜα, γόνϜατος, st. γόνυ (knee); οὖλος, Ion.=ὅλος (all), fr. ὅλϜος, cf. Sk. *sárva-s* (every, all), Lat. *saluo-s*, *sollus* (Fest. totus), fr. *soluo-s; παῦρο-ς (small, few) fr. *παρϜο-ς, cf. Lat. *paruo-s*; νεῦρο-ν (sinew) fr. *νερϜο-ν, cf. Lat. *neruo-s*.

In consequence of the evanescence of *y, v, s*, vowel- § 27. accumulation and contraction occur frequently.

Thus *s* disappears, e.g. in φέρῃ fr. *φέρεσαι (2 sing. pres. med. fr. φέρω, bear), Sk. *bhárase*; μένους (gen. sing. fr. μένος, might) fr. *μενεσος, Sk. *mánas-as*; εἴην (1 sing. pres. opt. of ἐσ-, esse) fr. *ἐσ-γην, f.f. *as-yā-m*; εἰπόμην fr. *ἐ-σεπ-ομην, √ἐπ (follow), i.e. σεπ, Sk. *sak*, Lat. *seq*, in ἔπομαι; εἷρπον fr. *ἐ-σερπ-ον, √σερπ (crawl), Sk. *sarp*, Lat. *serp-o*; πεποιθυῖα (fem. part. pf. act.) fr. -υσια, and the latter fr. *v(an)tyā*, etc.

Ϝ disappears in εἰργασάμην (Ϝεργάζομαι, work) fr. *ἐ-Ϝεργ-ασαμην; εἶπον, εἰπεῖν, older ἔ-ειπον, fr. *ἐ-Ϝε-Ϝεπ-ον=f.f. *a-va-vak-am*, redupl. aor. of √Ϝεπ (speak), Sk. *vak*, Lat. *uoc*, f.f. *vak*, etc.

Loss of *y* is common above all in the stems whence arise the contr. vbs. in έω, άω, όω, fr. *εγω, *αγω, *ογώ=Sk. and origl. -*ayāmi*, e.g. φορῶ, φορέω (bear)=Sk. *bhāráyāmi*, etc.

Note.—The sound-laws by which concurring vowels are regulated in different dialects do not belong in this place;

§ 27. because they extend to explain the Greek forms alone. The fundamental-forms, however, in the commonest and most important cases, conform to the rules laid down in the construction of stems and words.

The forms peculiar to the Greek, e.g. ὁρόω, ὁράᾳς, by assimilation for ὁράω, ὁράεις; δρώωσι beside δράουσι, δρῶσι, etc., frequently offer difficulties in their explanation.

§ 28. After the evanescence and medial and final loss of consonants, there often occurs a compensatory lengthening.

1. *n* lost before *s*, followed by lengthening of preceding

o to *ου*—e.g. φέρουσι (they bear)=*φερονσι fr. φέροντι= *bháranti*, φέρουσα=*φερονσα fr. *φεροντya, etc. ; λύκους (acc. pl. st. λυκο-, wolf)=*λυκο-νς, cf. Goth. *vulfa-ns*; Krêtan τό-νς=τούς (acc. pl. st. το- demonstr.), f.f. *ta-ns, ta-ms*.

ε to *ει*—e.g. τιθείς (n. sing. m. part. pres. act. fr. τίθη-μι, place, √θε)=Krêtan τιθένς fr. *τιθεντ-ς; χαρίεις (n. sing. masc. conn. c. χάρις, grace)=*χαρι-Fεντ-ς (but fem. χαρίεσσα= *χαρι-Fεтya, without *ν*, cf. Sk. sf. *-vant*, fem. *-vatī=vatyā*, likewise with loss of *n*), etc.

a to *ā*—e.g. ἱστάς (n. sing. m. part. pres. act. ἵστη-μι, place, √στα)=*ἱστανς fr. *ἱσταντ-ς, etc.

υ to *ῡ*—e.g. δεικνύς (δείκνυ-μι, show)=*δεικνυνς fr. *δεικνυν-τς, etc. Similarly εἰμί (am) for *ἐσ-μι, by compensatory lengthening (cf. Aiol. ἐμμί by assimiln.), Sk. and f.f. *ás-mi;* ὀρεινός (mountainous) for *ὄρεσ-νος, Aiol. ὀρεν-νός (fr. ὄρος, mountain, Iôn. οὖρος, therefore older *ὀρ-Fος, √ὀρ, or-iri, exsurgere), st. ὀρες-, with sf. -νο-, etc.

2. Moreover medial compensation is found in the formn. of l aor. after the loss of σ, preceded by λ, μ, ν, e.g. ἔνειμα (νέμω, distribute) for *ἐνεμ-σα, cf. Aiol. ἐ-νέμμ-ατο, by assimiln. ; ἔφηνα (φαίνω for *φανyω, point out) for *ἐφαν-σα, ἔστειλα (στέλλω for *στελyω, send) for *ἐστελ-σα, Aiol. representation of compensation, ἔστελλα, etc.

3. Compensation by lengthening is frequently found in nom. sing. masc. of consonantal stems to compensate for lost

final ς or τς, e.g. ποιμήν (shepherd) for *ποιμεν-ς, cf. Sk. rā́ǵā § 28.
for *rāǵan-s, Lat. homo for *homon-s, Goth. guma (man), i.e. *gumā
for *guman-s; μήτηρ (mater) for *μητερ-ς, cf. Sk. mātā́ for *mātar-s;
πατήρ (father) for *πατερ-ς, cf. Sk. pitā́ for *pitar-s, Old Lat. patēr
for *pater-s, Goth. fadar, i.e. *fadār, for *fadar-s; εὐμενής (well-
meaning) for *-μενεσ-ς, cf. Sk. sumanā́s for *-manas-s; φέρων
(bearing) for *φεροντ-ς; πεποιθώς (perf. pt. act. πέποιθα, trust)
for *πεποιθ-Fο-τς.

Vowel insertion and addition. § 29.

1. Vowel insertion occurs in Gk. in the same way as in
Oscan and O.H.G., only less regularly. Acc. to G. Curtius, Gr.
Et.² 656, sqq., this change takes place only in the neighbourhood
of r, l, and nasals, so that it clearly arises from the vowel-sounds
contained in these consonants. a and ε occur most frequently,
o and ι are rarer, υ rarest, as vowels attached to these consonantal
sounds: e.g. ὀ-ρέγ-ω (reach, stretch), √ὀρεγ fr. ὀργ, cf. Sk. arǵ
(reach), beside ὀριγ-νάομαι (stretch) and ὀρό-γ-υια beside ὀργ-υιά
(fathom), where clearly ὀρεγ, ὀριγ, ὀρογ=ὀργ, origl. arg; ταράσσω
=*ταραχ-yω (make uneven, disturb), beside τέ-τρηχ-α (perf.)
and τραχ-ύς (rough, uneven), √τραχ, therefore; ἀλεγ-εινός (pain-
ful) beside ἄλγ-ος (pain); δολιχ-ός (long)=Sk. dīrgh-ás, √dargh,
beside ἐν-δελεχ-ής (unbroken, uninterrupted), fr. same root;
ἤλυθ-ον beside ἦλθ-ον (v. supr. § 24); χάλαζα (hail), i.e. *χαλαδya,
cf. Skl. grad-ŭ, Lat. grand-o, Sk. hrād-unī (storm); κολεκ-άνος,
κολοκ-άνος (lank), κολοσσός (colossus) for *κολοκ-yος, cf. Sk.
krç-á-s (lank), √karç (make lean), Lat. crac-entes (graciles),
origl. √krak, kark; κονίς, pl. κονίδ-ες (dust, nits), cf. O.H.G.
hniȝ, Bohem. hnid-a. Even long vowels clearly arise in this
way, e.g. ἐρωδ-ιός (heron), Lat. ard-ea.

Note.—But ε is no auxiliary vowel in such forms as ἡδεῖα, i.e.
*ἡδεF-ια (v. supr. § 26 b. 2, n. 2): and also in ἐπέεσσι fr. *ἐπεσε-σσι,
*ἐπεσε-σFι, κύνε-σσι, loc. pl. st. ἐπες- (ἔπος, word), κυν- (κύων,
dog, g. κυν-ός), and other loc. pls. in consonantal stems. These
are probably constructed on the analogies of the ι- and υ- stems,
cf. πόλε-σι, st. πόλι- (state), γλυκέ-σι, st. γλυκύ- (sweet), as

§ 29. doubtless in other languages consonantal stems have often become allied to vowel stems, especially to the *i*-stem (e.g. Lat.
pedi-bus, st. *ped-*). [Curt. has suggested doubts which I do not
understand, especially on account of the Hêrakl. πρασσόντ-ασσι;
he maintains a helping-vowel in these cases.] Less still do futs.
of verb-stems in λ, μ, ν, ρ, belong here, e.g. τενῶ fr. *τενεσω,
*τενεω; βαλῶ fr. *βαλεσω, *βαλεω. In these cases we come upon
the verb-stem -εσω, original *asyāmi*, fut. of √*as* (esse) (v. sub.
' Conjugation ').

2. Vowel addition (prefix).

This phenomenon of sound also is to be referred to the slight
development of the vocal-sound before the following consonants.
Acc. to G. Curtius (Gr. Et.[2] p. 649, etc.) prefixed-vowels are very
rare before simple momentary sounds ; they never occur before
τ, π, φ, but on the contrary, most frequently before more than
one consonant, before liquids, and before nasals. Exx. a) before
two consonants, ἀ-στήρ (star), cf. Latin *stella* for **sterula*, Goth.
stairnō, Sk. st. *star-* ; ὀ-φρύ-ς (brow), Sk. *bhrŭ-s*, O.H.G. *brāwa*,
Skl. *brŭvĭ*; Lesb. Aiol. ἄ-σφε, ἄ-σφι=σφέ, σφί, origl. st. *sva* ;
ἐ-χθές beside χθές (yesterday), Sk. *hyas*, etc.

b) before λ, μ, ν, ρ ; ἐ-λαχύς (small), Sk. *laghŭs*, Lat. *leui-s*,
fr. **legu-is*; ἐ-μέ, ἐ-μοί, beside μέ, μοί, origl. st. *ma* (pron. 1
pers.) ; ὀ-μιχέω (mingo), ὀ-μίχ-λη (mist), origl. √*migh*, cf. Sk.
mih (mingere), Lat. *mig*, *mi-n-go*, etc. ; ἀ-νήρ (man), Sk. st.
nar-, Umbr. *ner* (prince) ; √ἐ-νεκ- (bear), in ἠνέχ-θην, ἤνεγκ-ον ;
δι-ηνεκ-ής (thorough), for νεκ, cf. O. Bulg. *nes-ti*, Lith. *nèsz-ti*
(bear) ; ἐν-νέϝα (nine), with redupld. ν, cf. Lat. *nouem*, Sk.
návan, etc. ; ὄ-νυξ (nail), st. ὀνυχ-, Sk. *nakha-s*, *nakha-m*,
O.H.G. *nagel;* ὄ-νομα, name, cf. Lat. *(g)nōmen*, Sk. *nāman-*,
Goth. *naman-*, where in the Gk. the o did not arise until the
origl. initial *g* had disappeared, ἐ-ρυθρός (red)=Sk. *rudhirás*,
Lat. *ruber*, fund.-fm. *rudh-ra-s*, √*rudh;* ἔ-ρεβος (n. lower-world,
gloom), Sk. *rağas* (gloom), Goth. *rikvis* (dimness) ; ἐ-ρεύγ-εσθαι
(belch), cf. Lat. *ructare* for *rug-tare*, etc.

c) before origl. *v;* ἐ-ϝέργ-ειν beside ϝέργ-ειν (keep in), cf. Sk.
varğ (keep off) ; ἐ-ϝέρση (Il. xxiii. 598), Krêt. ἄ-ϝερσα beside

Ϝέρση, ἔρση (ros, dew), cf. Sk. √varš (rain); ἐ-Ϝείκοσιν (Il. vi. § 29. 217) beside εἴκοσι (twenty), Boiôt. Ϝίκατι, Sk. viçáti, Lat. *uiginti;* the initial was origly. *dv* (*dvi*=two), the ε was not prefixed until the *d* had disappeared (cf. ὄ-νομα); and more frequently in the case of Ϝ.

d) before other consonants; ὀ-δούς (tooth), st. ὀ-δοντ-, cf. Lat. st. *dent-*, Sk. st. *dant-* and *danta-*, Goth. *tunthu;* in this word the *o* arises clearly, I think, from the vowel-sound of δ, and my view is confirmed by the consonance of the *o* with the *o* of the second syllable, as well as by the agreement of all the other languages in initial *d.* [ἔδ-οντες in Aiolic should, I think, be separated fr. ὀδόντες, and be regarded as a ´ poetical expression; it is a part. of ἔδω (eat), 'the eating ones,' i.e. 'teeth'; the origl. *dant-* (tooth) may arise from √*ad, da* (eat), but in my opinion *da-nt-* more probably belongs to √*da, ad,* 'separate, cut'; cf. Zend st. *dā-ta-*, 'tooth.'] ἀ-δαγ-μός (itch), ὀ-δάξω, ἀ-δαξέω (bite, itch), fr. √δακ in δάκ-νω (bite), Sk. *daç.* For other inst. of prefixed-vowel before other mom. consonn., more or less probable, see Curt. Gr. Et.[2] p. 653.

LATIN. § 30.

TABLE OF SOUNDS IN THE LATIN LANGUAGE.

	CONSONANTS.					VOWELS.	
	MOMENTARY SOUNDS.				PROLONGED SOUNDS.		
	UNASPIRATED. mute sonant		ASPIRATED. mute sonant		NASAL. sonant	r- & l-SOUND. sonant	
Gutt.	c, q	g	h		n		a, ā
Pal.				j			i, ī
Ling.						r, l	o ō
Dent.	t	d	s		n		
Lab.	p	b	f	v	m		u, ū

e, ē, ae · oe

§ 30.   *Note* 1.—I have placed *h* amongst the mute spirants, because it is nowhere pronounced with a vowel-sound except in Sk.

   Note 2.—Guttural *n* has no peculiar character; *n* is gutt. before gutt. consonn. *c, q, g* (*n* adulterinum), but not after *g*, where, contrary to the German usage, it must be pron. like ordinary dental *n*.

   Diphthongs, almost exclusively peculiar to Old. Lat., are *ai* (*ae*), *au, ei, eu, oi* (*oe*), *ou, ui*.

§ 31.   LATIN VOWEL-SYSTEM.

   The Lat. vowel-system has suffered frequent changes in the course of time.   Classical Lat., like Umbrian, shows a distaste for diphthongs, and these have changed to more compact sounds : the old diphthongs are vouched for by Old Lat., and esp. by Oscan.   In the above cases the Lat. is insensible to vowel-development.   A movement of root-vowels in their scales (confined, however, generally to two steps only) is not still shown except in a few roots.

   The influence of final sounds, and further of sounds generally on one another (of consonant upon vowel, vowel upon vowel), has reached a high pitch in Lat.   Unoriginal shortenings and lengthenings also occur frequently, so that the vowel-system of the Latin has diverged very widely from the original sounds. Besides, Old-Lat. and Osc. (both Italic languages with more origl. vowel-systems) have reached us only in a very frag-mentary condition, while Classical Lat. has the characteristics of a written language which became stereotyped under foreign influence, and Umbr. is in the highest degree unoriginal in its vowels.   Accordingly, of all Indo-Germ. languages, Lat. offers the greatest difficulties to a scientific investigator.

   a is frequently weakened to *u* and *i*, and passes in a great measure into *e* and *o* (later generally to *u*), as in Gk.; similarly *ā* into *ē* and *ō*, only in Lat. the influence of neighbouring sounds is clearly the reason for vowel-colouring.   In conse-quence of the full and thorough conformity of the Lat. with the Greek vowel-scales, we are probably entitled to treat *ō* in § 31. Latin also as a vowel of the second step.

The *i*- and *u*- scales were in the oldest form of the language exactly like the Greek, especially in the distinction of *ai* and *au* from *ei* and *eu*. In the *u*-scale the second step takes throughout the place of the first, whilst *e* before *u* (*v*) passes into *o*, according to Lat. sound-laws (vid. § 34) [as in Gk. the converse takes place]. The later language, however, has preserved only *au* of the old diphthongs; yet even this diphthong shows a marked tendency to become a simple sound in certain cases.

Latin vowel-scales (Old Lat. sounds distinguished by upright characters):

	Weakening.	Fund.-vowel.	1st Step.	2nd Step.
1. *a*-scale loss.	*i, u*	*e, o, a*	*o, ē, ā*	*ō*
2. *i*-scale		*i*	**ei** *ī ē*, **ai** *ae*	**oi** *oe ū*
3. *u*-scale		*u*	**eu** *au ō*	**ou** *ū*

In Class. Lat. *eu* no longer exists as a vowel-step, but has become *ou* (i.e. *ū*).

The change from diphth. to monophth. is capable of simple physiological explanation (assimilation of both sounds, each to the other, e.g. *ei* to *ē*, *ai* to *ae*, *oi* to *oe*, *au* to *ō*, or of one to the other, as *ei* to *ī*, *ou* to *ū*), the change from *oi*, *oe* to *ū*, is caused by the common passing of *o* into *u* (change-scale *oi*, *ui*, *ū ;* possibly also *oe*, *ue*, *ū*).

EXAMPLES. § 32.

1. *a*-scale.

Weakening. 1. **L o s s** of radical *a*, e.g. *sum, sumus, sunt, siēm,* etc., for *es-um fund.-fm. *as-mi,* *es-umus f.f. *as-masi,* *es-unt f.f. *as-anti,* *es-iēm f.f. *as-yām* (√*es*, to be, cf. Gk.); *gigno* (produce, cf. γί-γνο-μαι), fr. *gi-gen-o, √*gen* (cf. *gen-ui, gen-us*), origl. *gan ;* especially in the second member of compounds is this loss frequent, as in *malo* fr. **maulo,* and this again fr. *mage-uol-o

§ 32. (*magis uolo*), and in like cases (v. 'Sound-laws,' § 42) : sf. *-br-um* (in part at least fr. **ber-um*), √*ber*, origl. *bhar* (ferre), so that here we have a compound, not a stem-formative sf.; the same remark applies to *-gnus* fr. **-genus* (√*gen, gi-gn-ere*), e.g. *mali-gn-us* (ill-disposed, malus, evil), and others, and *-gium* in *iur-gium* (lawsuit) for **iur-igium*, cf. *rem-ig-ium* (rowing), √*ag* (agere), etc.

In stem-formative suffixes, loss of origl. *a* occurs, as in the kindred languages, e.g. *patr-is*, older **patr-us, *patr-os*, for *pater--os*, st. *pater*, f.f. *patar-as* (gen. sing.), and in many other cases.

2. W eakening of *a* to *i* is very frequent, esp. in the second member of a compound, e.g. *ac-cipio* (receive) beside *capio* (take); *per-ficio* (complete) beside *facio* (make); *as-sid-eo* (sit by), √*sad*, Lat. *sed*; *me-min-i* (bring to mind), √*man*; *co-gni-tus* (known), √*gna*, fr. *gan*; *in-si-tus* (implanted), √*sa*, etc.; moreover in stem- and word-formative particles, e.g. *ueh-is*, *ueh-it* (2, 3, sing. pres., √*ueh*, carry), for **ueh-isi, *ueh-iti*, origl. *vagh-asi, vagh-ati*; *nō-min-is* (gen. sing. *nōmen*, name), origl. *gnā-man-as*, etc.

It occurs even in the accentuated syllable of the word (as in Germ.), e.g. *in-ter* (between), Umbr. *an-ter*, compar. of pronoml. st. *an*, cf. Sk. *an-tár, án-tara-s* (inter, interior), Gk. ἔν-τερα; *in-* (neg.), Umbr. *an-*, Sk. *an-*, Gk. ἀν-; *igni-s* (fire), Sk. *agni-s*; *quin-que* (five), f.f. *kankan*, Sk. *páṅkan*.

In the reduplication-syll. of pres. stems fr. roots in root-vowel *a*, this weakening takes place regularly, e.g. *gi-gno* (beget) fr. **gi-gen-o*, f.f. *ga-gan-āmi*, cf. Gk. γί-γν-ομαι, √*gan*; *ser-o* (sow) =**siso* (*i* changed to *e* on acct. of the *r*), f.f. *sa-sā-mi*, √*sa*; *si-st-o* (set), f.f. *sta-stā-mi*, √*sta*; *sīdo* (set myself) fr. **si-sdo*, **si-sed-o*, f.f. *sa-sad-āmi*, √*sad*.

Note.—The lengthening of *e* weakened from origl. *a* into *ī* (*ei*) is hardly susceptible of proof: *scrībo* (write) beside γράφω, since both words are generally akin, we must perhaps assume to be a case of *a*-scale passing into *i*-scale, as often in Sclavo-

Teutonic: in cases such as *uirī-tim* (man by man) fr. st. *uiro-* § 32.
(*uir*, man), the analogy of other forms (verbal stems) is followed (cf. *tribu-tim*, etc.).

3. **Weakening** of *a* to *u* is common, esp. in stem- and word-formative elements, but also in roots, through the influence of certain consonants. *i* is clearly the furthest weakening from *a*, for *u* through intermediate *ü* ("medius quidam inter *i* et *u* sonus—pinguius quam *i*, exilius quam *u*—sonum *y* Graecae uidetur habere" Gramm.; imp. Claudius Caesar ordered the character ⊢ to be used for this sound) often changes to *i*, whilst older forms in *u* exist beside later ones in *i*; *u* is also an unimportant representative of weakening from *a* through *o*, the older lang. very often retaining *o* where later *u* occurs. The vowel-scale of change from *a* to *i* is therefore evidently: *a, o, u, ü, i*. Thus, e.g. a f.f. *ap-tama-s* becomes **op-tomo-s, op-tumu-s, op-tümu-s, op-timu-s* (best), Ital. *ottimo*; *dakama-s*, **decomo-s, decumu-s, decimu-s* (tenth), Ital. *decimo*; beside *cap-io* (take), *man-cup-ium* (property; Plaut.), *oc-cup-are* (seize), *in-cip-ere* (begin), *man-cip-ium*; *con-cut-io* (shake violently) beside *quat-io* (shake), *in-sul-sus* (unsalted) beside *salsus* (salted), etc. *u* is frequent as a merely later change fr. older *o* (cf. Gk., where *o* remains), especially in word-formative elements, e.g. nom. acc. sing. masc. neut. of origl. *a*-stem *-u-s* fr. Old-Lat. *-o-s*, Gk. *o-ς*, origl. *-a-s*; *-u-m*, Old-Lat. *-o-m*, Gk. *-o-ν*, origl. *-a-m*, e.g. *da-tu-s* (given) fr. *da-to-s*, Gk. δο-τό-ς, origl. *da-ta-s*; acc. *da-tu-m* fr. *da-to-m*, Gk. δο-τό-ν, origl. *da-ta-m*. Lat. *os, us*, generally represents origl. final *as*, e.g. *gen-us* (race), earlier *gen-os*=γέν-ος, Sk. *ǵán-as*, origl. *gan-as*; *op-us* (work), Old-Lat. *op-os*, Sk. and origl. *áp-as*; *-bus* (sf. dat. abl. pl.), earlier *-bos* for *-byos*, Sk. *bhyas*; *ferunt* (they bear), Old-Lat. *fer-ont, fer-onti*, Gk. φέρ-οντι (φέρ-ουσι), Sk. and origl. *bhár-anti*; also in pres. part. *o* clearly is the form of the earlier lang., cf. *e-unt-em* (him who goes), i.e. *e-ont-em*, where beside *e*, *o* has become *u*, whilst *e* regularly occurs; *uol-unt-arius* (willing)

§ 32. points to a once-existing *uolont-, *uolunt-, beside usual uolent- (willing), etc.

After consonantal *u*, *o* remains, e.g. *uolt* (later *uult*, he will), Sk. and origl. √*var*; *loquontur* (*loquuntur*, they speak); *quom* (*quum*, conj. 'when,' 'since,' cf. *quon-iam*), f.f. *kam*; *quo-d* (which), f.f. *ka-t* (but *is-tu-d*, f.f. *ta-t*); *nouo-s*, new (*nouus*), Sk. and f.f. *náva-s*, etc.

Note.—Through the older *o*-forms, Latin approaches near to Greek.

§ 33. The root-vowel of the *a*-scale, origl. *a* is represented by—

1. *a* preserved in a very few cases, appearing by preference before *g*, *c*, e.g. *ac-us* (needle), *ac-ies* (point), *ac-erbus* (sour), √*ac*, Sk. *aç*, origl. √*ak*; *ag-o* (drive), ἄγ-ω, Sk. *áǵ-āmi*, √*ag*; *mag-is* (more), *mag-nus* (great), μέγ-ας, Sk. st. *mah-ánt-* (n. sing. masc. *mah-ā́n*), Goth. *mik-ils*, √*mag*, Sk. *mah* fr. *magh*; *frag-ilis* (breakable), *frag-or* (crash), *fra-n-go* (break), Goth. √*brak* (pres. *brik-a*, pf. *brak*); *ang-uis* (snake), Sk. *áh-is*, Gk. ἔχ-ις, Germ. *unk*; *ans-er* (goose) for *hans-er, Germ. *gans*, Sk. *hās-ás*, f.f. *ghans-*; *al-ius* (other), ἄλλος=*ἀλ-yος, Goth. *al-is*; *ap-iscor* (get), *ap-tus*, cf. Sk. *āp-nó-mi* (1 sing. pres. ind. adipiscor) √*ap*; *sta-tus* (placed), Gk. στα-τός, f.f. *sta-tas*, √*sta*; *sa-tus* (sown), √*sa*; *da-tus* (given), *da-tor* (giver), Gk. δο-τός, δο-τήρ, √*da*, etc.

2. Origl. *a* appears as *o*, especially in roots before and after *v*, and further in stem- and word-formative elements.

After *v*, as *uom-o* (spue), Gk. Ϝεμ-έω, Sk. *vám-āmi*; *uol-o* (will), *uol-t*, *uol-im*, later *uult*, *uel-im*, cf. Sk. *vár-āmi* (*vr-ṇómi*, *vr-ṇā́mi*), √*var*; *uoc-are* (call), Sk. √*vak̂*, Gk. Ϝεπ, origl. *vak*; *uort-o* (turn), later *uert-o*, cf. Sk. *várt-atē* (3 sg. pres. med. uertitur, est), √*vart*; *uo-s* (you), *uoster* (your), later *uester*, cf. Sk. *vas* (uos, uobis); *uolu-ere* (twirl), Goth. *valv-yan* (uoluere); cf. *quatuor* (four) for *quatuors, *quatuores, beside τέσσαρες=*τετϜαρες, f.f. prob. *katvāras*; even *uocuus* (empty) in inscrr. for *uacuus*.

Origl. *sva* is regularly *so* in Lat., prob. fr. *suo* for *sue*, origl.

sva, by the above rules; *u* falls out, as in *te* (thee), *se* (himself), § 33. etc., for *tue, *sue, e.g. *socer* (father-in-law) fr. *suocer, *suecer, Gk. ἐκυρός for *σϜεκυρος, Sk. *sváçuras* (written *çváçuras*), Goth. *svaíhra*, cf. *socrus* (mother-in-law), Sk. *sváçrūs* (written *çváçrūs*); *sorōrem* (sister, acc.), Sk. *svásāram*, f.f. *svastāram*; *sop-or*, *somnus* (sleep), for *sop-nus (cf. ὔπ-νος), Sk. and f.f. *sváp-nas*, *sváp-i-mi* (I sleep); *son-us* (sound), Sk. *svǎn-as*.

Before *v*, e.g. *ou-is* (sheep), Gk. ὄϜις, Sk. *áv-is*, Lith. *av-ìs*; *uou-os*, later *nou-us* (new), Gk. νέϜ-ος, Sk. *náv-as*; *nou-em* (nine), Gk. ἐν-νέϜα, Sk. *náv-an*.

In other combinations, e.g. *mor-ior* (die), origl. and Sk. √*mar* (mori); *dom-are* (tame), Gk. √δαμ (ἔ-δαμ-ον), Sk. *dam*, Goth. *tam*, H.G. *zam*; *op-us* (work), Old-Lat. *op-os*, Sk. *áp-as*; *loq-uor* (speak), cf. Gk. ἔ-λακ-ον, Sk. √*lap*; *po-tis* (powerful), *po-tens* (mighty), *po-tiri* (become master of), cf. Gk. πό-σις (lord), Sk. and origl. *pá-tis* (master) [perh. in these instances the lab. *m*, *p*, and the lab. vowel which in Lat. accompanies *l*, are the causes of *o* representing *a*]; *coq-uere* (cook), Gk. √πεπ, Sk. *pak̓*, Lith. *kep*, etc., origl. *kak*.

In terminal particles (stem- and word-formative) *o* is remarkably regular before *s* and *m* (as in Gk.); for later weakening of *o* to *u*, v. sup. §§ 32, 3); e.g. suff. -*to* in n. sing. m. and acc. masc. and neut. -*to-s*, -*to-m*, Gk. -το-ς, -το-ν, Sk. -*ta-s*, -*ta-m*, e.g. *in-clu-to-s* (famed), acc. *clu-to-m*, cf. Gk. κλυ-τό-ς, κλυ-τό-ν, Sk. *çru-tá-s*, *çru-tá-m*, origl. *kru-ta-s*, *kru-ta-m*; neut. termn. -*os*, later *us*, e.g. *gen-os* (*gen-us*, race), Gk. γέν-ος, Sk. *ǵán-as*, origl. *gan-as*, so also *Ven-os* (prop. n. fem., -*os* authenticated); Lat. pl. -*bos* (-*bus*), Sk. -*bhyas*, etc.

3. *a* passes into *e* very frequently, without assignable reason, in neighbouring sounds: e.g. *fer-o* (bear), √*fer*, Gk. φέρ-ω, Sk. and origl. *bhár-āmi*, √*bhar*; *es-t* (he is), √*es*, Gk. ἐσ-τί, Sk. and f.f. *ás-ti*, √*as*; *sed-eo* (sit), √*sed*, Sk. and origl. *sad*; *gen-us* (race), Old-Lat. *gen-os*, √*gen*, √Gk. γέν-ος, Sk. *ǵán-as*, origl. *gan-as*, √*gan*; *ueh-it* (he carries), √*uch*, Sk. *váh-ati*, f.f.

§ 33. *vagh-ati*, √*vagh; pecu-* (cattle), Sk. st. *paçú-* (n. sing. masc. *paçú-s*), f.f. stem *paku-* ; *eq-uos* (horse), √*ec*, Gk. ἵππος=*ἰκ-Ϝος, Sk. *áç-vas*, √*aç*, f.f. *ak-vas*, √*ak* ; *dec-em* (ten), Gk. δέκα, Sk. *dáçan-*, f.f. *dakan-* ; *septem*, Gk. ἑπτά (seven), Sk. and f.f. *saptán-* ; *dent-em* (tooth, acc.), ὀ-δόντ-α, Sk. *dánt-am ; men-te-m* (mind, acc.), f.f. *man-ti-m*, √*man* ; *fer-ent-em* (bearing, acc.), φέρ-οντ-α, Sk. and f.f. *bhár-ant-am ;* the origl. sound-combn. *ant* also becomes *ont, unt*, in Lat., e.g. *fer-unt* (they bear) fr. **fer-onti*, Sk. and origl. *bhár-ant-i, e-unt-em* (going, acc.; cf. § 32), beside *fer-ent-em ;* st. *pa-ter-* (father), *mā-ter-* (mother), origl. *pa--tar-, mā-tar-* ; *(g)nō-men* (name), Sk. *nắ-man-*, f.f. *gnā-man*, etc.

e is often an evident weakening from *a*, e.g. *per-fec-tus* (made thoroughly) beside *fac-tus* (made), etc.

e has proceeded from *o* in cases such as *uert-o, uester*, etc., fr. older *uorto, uoster*, f.f. *vart-ā-mi*, Sk. and origl. √*vart*, Goth. *varth ; uos-ter*, cf. Sk. *vas* (uos, uobis) (cf. § 33). Accordingly *e* comes after *a* and *o* as a lighter vowel.

§ 34.   Step-formation of *a*.

1. Corresponding to *e* we find *o* as the equivalent heavier vowel, and *o* sometimes occurs as a step-formn. fr. *e*=*a* (cf. Gk. and Sclav.) ; thus in these cases *o*=*ā* ; *e* : *o*=*a* : *ā*, e.g. *mon-eo* (warn), i.e. *mān-āyami*, caus. vb. fr. origl. √*man* (think, thus simply=make to think), beside *mens* (mind) for **ments*, **men-ti-s*, f.f. *man-ti-s* (sf. *ti*), fr. √*man*, cf. *me-min-i* (I remember), later with weakening of *e* to *i* ; *noc-eo* (hurt), f.f. *nāk-ayāmi*, caus. vb. fr. origl. √*nak*, Sk. √*naç* (die) (so simply 'make to die'), *nex, nec-is* (death), *per-nic-ies* (ruin), *nec-are* (kill), cf. νέκ-υς, νεκ-ρός (corpse) ; *tog-a* (wrapper) beside *teg-o* (cover), √*tag* (H.G. *tak*), prob. for *stag*, cf. στέγ-ω, Sk. *sthág-āmi* (cover), in Lith. *steg-iù* (cover) stands beside *stóg-as* (tectum) ; *socius* (comrade) beside *seq-uì* (go with), *ad-sec-la* (escort) ; *doc-eo* (teach), caus. f.f. *dāk-ayāmi*, beside *di-dic-i, disco* (learn) for **dic-sco*, prob. for **di-dac-sco*, cf. δι-δά(κ)-σκω (teach) beside διδάξω, i.e. διδάκ-σω, διδαχ-ή (teaching), √*dak* (not *dic*, as in

dĭc-o, δείκ-νυμι, which must be kept distinct) ; *proc-us* (wooer) § 34. beside *prec-ari* (beg) ; *for-s* (chance), *for-dus* (pregnant), beside *fero* (bear), √*fer*, origl. √*bhar*.

When *o* is short, the step-formations can take place also before two consonants, e.g. *pond-us* (n. weight) beside *peñd-ĕre* (weigh) ; *ex-torr-is* (exile), *torr-eo* (roast)=*tors-eo*, cf. *tos-tus* (p. part. pass. torreo) for *tors-tus*, beside *terra* for *ters-a* (the 'dry land' in contrast to the 'water'), √*tars*, Goth. *thars* (in *thaírsan*, roast, *thaúrsyan*, thirst, vb.), Sk. *tarš* (thirst). Beside *a*, *o* occurs in *scob-s* (sawdust), *scob-ina* (rasp), and *scăb-o* (scratch) ; *port-io* (share) beside *part-em* (*pars*, part), *im-pert-io* (give, share).

2. *ē* is not common, e.g. *tēg-ula* (tile) beside *tĕg-o* and *tŏg-a ;* *rēg-em* (*rex*, king), cf. Sk. *rāǵ-am*, *rā́ǵ-ānam* beside *rĕg-o* (rule) ; *lēg-em* (*lex*, law), *col-lēg-a* (comrade in office) beside *lĕg-o* (pick out, read), *sēd-es* (seat) beside *sĕd-eo* (sit), √*sad ;* *sē-men* (seed) beside *să-tus*, so chiefly as a step-formn. of *e ; ē* corresponds to origl. *ā* in *plē-nus* (full), f.f. *prā-nas*, √*pra*, par (fill) ; *ēd-i*, cf. Sk. *ā́da*, i.e. *aāda* (perf.), fr. *ĕd-o* (eat), Sk. *ád-mi; sēmi-* (half), Gk. ἡμι-, Sk. *sāmi-*, O.H.G. *sāmi- ;* *siēm, siēt* (1, 3, opt. fr. *es*, be), cf. εἴην, εἴη, Sk. *syām, syāt*, origl. *as-yā-m, as-yā-t*, in which cases perh. *i* has had an assimilating influence.

3. As *ē* is to *ĕ*, so is *ā* to *a* in the sound-scale, which, therefore, occurs most often before guttural consonants, ẹ.g. *ăc-er, ăc-ris* (sharp), beside *ăc-ies* (point) ; *plāc-are* (appease) beside *plăc-ēre* (please) ; *pāc-em* (*pax*, peace), thence *pāc-ạre* (to pacify), beside *păc-isci* (bargain) ; *māc-ero* (soften) beside *măc-er* (thin) : *amb-āg-es* (roundabout-way), cf. *amb-ĭg-ere* (be in doubt), fr. √*ag* in *ăg-o* (drive, lead), Gk. ἄγ-ω, Sk. *áǵ-āmi*, origl. *ag-āmi ;* st. *con-tāg-io-* (*con-tāg-iu-m*, contact), and further formed from it the commoner *con-tāg-iōn-* (n. sing. *con-tāg-io*), fr. √*tag* in *tango* (touch), *tac-tu-s* (past part. pass.) for *tag-tus*, cf. *con-tingo* (touch, hit) ; st. *suf-frāg-io* (*suffrāg-ium*, origly. 'sherd' ; vote) beside *frăg-or* (crash), √*frag*, cf. *fra-n-go* (break), *in-fri-n-g-o*

§ 34. (break into); *sāg-ire* (perceive), *sāg-us* (sooth-sayer), *sāg-a* (witch) beside *săg-ax* (knowing); *pāg-ina* (page, leaf), *com-pāg-i-* (compages, union), *com-pāg-in-* (compago), fr. √*pag* in *pa-n-g-o* (fix), cf. *com-ping-o* (fix together); *uăd-o* (go) beside *uăd-o-* (uadum, ford); *lāb-i* (glide) beside *lăb-are* (totter); *dā*, *dā-s*, beside *dă-tus*, √*da* (give); *fā-ri* (speak), *fā-ma* (fame), *fā-cundus* (eloquent), beside *fă-teri* (own to), origl. √*bha* ; *mā-ter* (mother), Sk. *mā-tar-*, √*ma* ; *frā-ter* (brother), Sk. *bhrā-tar-*, √*bhra*, transposed fr. *bhar*.

The fem. of the *a*-st. had origly. in the Lat. also long *a*, e.g. *nou-ā*, *coc-tā*, origl. *nav-ā*, *kak-tā*, cf. Sk. *náv-ā*, *pak-tā (this form does not happen to occur, but is replaced by an entirely different form *pak-vắ*), Gk. *νέϜ-ā*, *πεπ-τή*, fr. *nou-o-s*, *coc-to-s*, *nou-u-s*, *coctus*, origl. *nav-a-s*, *kak-ta-s*, Gk. *νέϜ-o-ς*, *πεπ-τό-ς*. Remains of this *ā* have been preserved in Latin.

4. Not unfrequently *ō* is a step-formation from *a*, especially beside *o*=*a*, and where *a* is a root-termn., further in stem-formative elements, e.g. *per-sōn-a* (mask) beside *sŏn-us* (sound), *sŏn-are* (sound), Sk. and origl. √*svan* ; *sōp-io* (put to sleep), i.e. Sk. and origl. *svāp-áyāmi*, causat. verb, beside *sŏp-or* (sleep), Lat. √*sop*, Sk. and origl. *svap* ; *uōc-em* (uox, voice)=Sk. *vắk-am*, Gk. *Ϝόπ-a*, origl. *vāk-am* beside *uŏc-o* (call), origl. √*vak* (speak) ; *ōc-ior* (swifter), comp. fr. lost adj. corresponding to Gk. *ὠκ-ύ-ς*, Sk. *āç-ú-s* (swift) (perh. sounded *oquis), origl. √*ak* ; *dō-num* (gift), Sk. and f.f. *dắ-na-m*, *dō-te-m*, n. *dōs* (dowry,=*dō-ti-s*), f.f. *dā-ti-m* beside *dă-tus*, √*da* ; *gnō-sco* (*nō-sco*, learn), *gnō-tus* (known, cf. *γι-γνώ-σκω*, *γνω-τός*), *gnō-men* (name) beside *(g)nŏta* (mark), *co-gni-tus* (known), √*gna*, fr. *gan* (as later forms show) ; *pōd-ex* beside *pēd-o* and *pēd-ico*, Sk. and origl. √*pard*, Gk. *περδ*, H.G. *farz* ; *da-tōr-em* (giver, acc.), Sk. *dā-tắr-am*, Gk. *δο-τῆρ-a*, origl. suff. *tar*, here raised to *tār* ; *quō-rum* fr. st. *quo-* (rel. interrog.), origl. *ka*, etc.

5. *ū* as=origl. *ā* can only be considered a later parallel form from *ō*, since *o* has frequently become *u* ; probably it does not

occur within the root. Hence the suff. -*tūro*-, fem. -*tūra*-, e.g. § 34.
da-tūr-us (about to give), *rup-tūr-a* (breach), Lat. formns. from
stems in -*tōr*, origl. -*tar*, *da-tōr*-, *rup-tōr*-, origl. *da-tār*-,
rup-tār- ; the suff. of gen. pl. -*um*, -*rum* (prob. for -*ūm*, -*rūm*,
cf. Bücheler, Grundriss der Lat. Decl., p. 40) stands for earlier
-*ōm*, -*rōm* (*bou-om* even in Verg.), Gk. -ων, in *-ῶν, Sk. and origl.
-*ām*, -*sām*, e.g. *(is)tarum*=Gk. *ταών, i.e. τῶν, Sk. *tåsām;*
vōc-um=Gk. *Fοπ-ῶν*, Sk. *vāk̇-ȧm.*

2.-*i*-scale. § 35.

In this, as in the *u*-scale, there is a lack of roots which
present all three steps at once. In the *i*-scale, I know only
the √*fid* in *fides* (faith), *per-fid-us* (faithless) beside *con-fid-o*
(trust), i.e. *feid-o* (*di-feid-ens* is vouched for) and *foid-os* (*foedus*,
treaty) : even in roots which appear in two steps, e.g. √*dic*
(Gk. δικ, Sk. *diç*, etc.), in *in-dic-o* (point at), *causi-dic-us*
(advocate) beside *deic-o*, *dic-o* (say) ; and √*i* (go) in *ĭ-tum* beside
ei-s, ei-t, ei-tur=*īs, īt, ītur* (cf. εἶμι, go, Sk. *é-mi*), there is a step
wanting.

The **fundamental vowel** *i* occurs, e.g. in *dic-are* (dedicate),
√*dic*, cf. Sk. *diç*, Gk. δικ (in δείκ-νυμι); *ĭ-tum* (cf. ἴ-μεν, Sk. *i-más*),
√*i* (go) ; *uid-eo* (see), cf. Sk. *vid-más*, Gk. Fἴδ-μεν, Goth. *vit-um*,
√*vid* ; *sci-n-d-o* (slit), *scissus*=*scid-tus* (slitten), cf. Sansk.
k̇hi-n-á-d-mi, σχίζω=*σχιδ-yω, Goth. √*skid* in *skaid-an*, √*scid;*
√*mig*, origl. *migh*, Gk. μιχ, in *mi-n-g-o*, *mic-tus* for *mig-tus*
(past part. pass.) ; √*lig* in *li-n-g-o* (lick), origl. *righ*, Gk. λιχ ;
qui-s (who?), cf. Goth. *his* (dem.), Lith. *szi-s*, f.f. *ki-s*, √*qui*=
ki. In stem-formative elements, e.g. *ou-i-s* (sheep), Gk. ὄF-ι-ς,
Sk. *áv-i-s*, Lith. *av-ì-s*, √*u*, *av*, with suff. *i*, *i* is often lost in
consequence of its position at the end of a word, e.g. *men-s* for
men-tis, men-ts, f.f. *man-tis,* or dulled to *e*, as *men-tem*, cf. sqq.

This genuine *i* is dulled to *e* according to definite laws, e.g.
in-dex, in-dic-is (pointer), √*dic* ; *ig-ne-m* (fire, acc.) for older
ig-ni-m, Sk. *agni-m*, Lith. *ùgni̯.* The earlier forms of this acc.
occur not uncommonly, as *naui-m* (ship, acc.) beside *naue-m* and

§ 35. others.   Also *mare* for **mari*, cf. *mar-i-a* (in similar cases final *i* is lost); so also in *naue-bos, tempestate-bus* (inscrr.), origl. *i* has passed into *e*, stems *nāui-, tempestāti-*.

Note.—Thus here *e* is the newer, *i* the origl. and hence older sound; whilst in the case of the more usual *i* weakened from *a*, when it is interchanged in the earlier lang. with *e*, the latter is the earlier sound. The language, however, no longer felt the difference of derivation, and both *i*-sounds were treated alike. Perh. unorigl. lengthening of *i* to *ī* should not be separated from step-formn. of *i* (to *ei*).

First step : *ei* (*ī, ē*); **deiu-os, dīu-os* (godlike, *deiuae, deiuinus*, occur), Sk. *dēvá-s,* f.f. *daiva-s,* √*div* (shine); *deic-o, dīco* (say), f.f. *daik-āmi,* √*dic; ei-tur, ī-tur* ('it is gone,' impers.), √*i; feid-o, fīd-o* (trust), √*fid; ueiuo-s, uīuo-s* (alive), cf. Sk. *ǵivá-s*, Lith. *gývas,* √*gi*, redupl. *gig, uig, giu, uiu* (*u* for *g*, through intermed. *gu* (vid. sub. "Consonn."), *ueic-us, uīc-us* (hamlet), Sk. *véças,* Sk. *Foîκoς; uīnum* (wine), i.e. *ueinom*, Goth. *vein*, Gk. *Foîνoς;* clearly *īd-us, eid-us* (a fixed day in the month, origly. the day on which the moon shines, the bright day; Corss. Krit. Beitr. 261), √*id*, origl. and Sk. √*idh* (vid. sub. *ai, ae*).

Deus (god) is weakened fr. **dēus, *dēuos, *deiuos*, and is thus a parallel-fm. to *dīuos*, to which *deiuīnus* points; so *ěo* (go) is clearly for **ēo, *ēyo,* f.f. **aiy-āmi* for **aiāmi*, with splitting up of *i* into *iy; uen-dēmia* (inscrr.)=*uin-dēmia* (vintage).

In word-formative elements, *ē* beside *ei, ī*, is common, later generally the rule, e.g. *omneis, omnīs, omnes*, etc.

ai, ae, occur here and there as in Gk., e.g. *aid-e(m), aed-es* (house, hearth), *aid-īlis* (overseer of buildings), *aes-tās* (summer heat) for **aed-tas*, cf. Gk. *αἴθ-ω, αἴθ-ουσα, αἰθ-ήρ*, Sk. √*idh* (kindle); *ae-uo-m*, old *ai-uo-m* (aye, long time) (except in gend.)= Sk. *év-a-s* (course), cf. *ai-Fóν*, √*i* (go), origl. suff. *va; maes-tus* (sorrowful), *maer-eo* (grieve, intr.) beside *mis-er* (wretched); *aem-ulus* (vying) beside *im-itari* (imitate); *laeuos* (left-), cf. *λαιFós; scaeuos* (left-), cf. *σκαιFós; caecus* (blind), cf. Goth. *haihs* (one-eyed, blind).

Second step is *oi, oe, ū;* e.g. *foid-ere,* n. **foid-os (foed-us,* § 35. treaty), √*fid;* *ūber* (fruitful), early Lat. **oib-ri-s,* f.f. *āidh-ri-s,* cf. Sk. *ēdh-atē* (he grows), hence √*idh, über* (neut. subst. fruit-fulness), early Lat. perh. **oib-es,* f.f. *āidh-as,* fr. same root¦ **oinos, oino(m),* occurs, *oenus, ūnus* (one), cf. Goth. *ains; comoinem, comūnem* (common, acc.), cf. Goth. *gamains;* so we find *loidos, loedos, lūdus* (game); *oitier, oetier, ūtier* (use), etc.

Note.—For *oe* we find *ē* written by mistake (cf. Fleckeisen, 5th Art. aus einem Hilfsbüchlein für Lat. Rechtschreibung, Frankf. 1861, p. 22), e.g. *ob-ēdire* for *ob-oedire,* cf. *audire, n-ēnum*=*n-oenum (non).*

3. *u*-scale. § 36.

Very much obliterated in Lat. Exx. are very rare: we can bring forward only *lŭc-erna* (lamp), Gk. √λυκ, Sk. *ruǩ,* f.f. *ruk,* beside *Leuc-esie* (Carm. Sal.), *Louc-ina* (nom. pr.), *lūcem* (light, acc.), *lū(c)-men* (light), *lou(c)-men;* *dŭc-em* (leader) beside *douc-ere, dūc-ere* (lead); *rŭb-er* (red), f.f. *rudh-ra-s,* beside *rūf-us* (red), f.f. *rāudh-as;* *pro-nŭb-us* (marriage-making), *in-nŭb-us* (unwedded), beside *nūb-o* (marry— of the woman); *rūp-es* (rock, cliff) fr. √*rup,* in *ru-m-p-o* (break); *trūd-o* (thrust) beside *trŭd-i-s* (thrusting-pole).

The fund. vowel *u,* e.g. in *rup-tus* (broken), *ru-m-p-o* (break), cf. Sk. *lu-m-p-ámi,* √*lup,* origl. √*rup;* *us-tu-s* (burnt), √*us,* Sk. √*uš;* *tu-tud-i* fr. pres. *tu-n-d-o* (thump), cf. Sk. *tud-ámi,* √*tud;* *rub-er* (red), for **ruf-er, *ruf-ro-s,* √*ruf*=ρυθ,Sk. and origl. √*rudh;* *iug-um* (yoke)=ζυγ-όν, Sk. *yug-ám,* √*yug;* *fu-i* (was), *fu-turus* (about to be), cf. φυ-τόν, origl. and Sk. √*bhu* (in Sk. lengthened *bhū*). In stem-formn. (not in stem-formative particles), e.g. *pec-u* (cattle, pl. *pecu-a*), cf. Goth. *faihu,* O.H.G. *vihu,* Sk. *paçú-s.*

This genuine *u* was also weakened to *i* (*ŭ*) [like that which arose from *a,* cf. § 32], e.g. *lub-et, lib-et* (it pleases), Sk. and origl. √*lubh* (desire), Goth. *lub* (in *lub-ō,* beloved, *liub-s,* love; *ga-laubs,* dear); *cli-ens* (hearer), √*clu,* √κλυ, origl. *kru* (hear);

§ 36. **manu-bus,* and hence *mani-bus* (*manu-s,* hand), *u* is noticeably preserved in many cases; *fructi-fer, corni-ger,* fr. **fructu-fer, *cornu-ger* (fruit-bearing, horn-carrying).

Note 1.—Genuine *u* does not change to *o* except in *fŏ-re* fr. *fŭ-se,* √*fu.*

Note 2.—*ū* as lengthening from *ŭ* is prob. not to be separated fr. *ū=ou,* 1st and 2nd step-formn. of *u.* In *tū* (thou), we have an unorigl. lengthening, f.f. is *tŭ,* for in Sk. *tv-am,* Gk. τύ, σύ, Goth. *thu,* Scl. *ty,* there is no step-formn. We cannot decide between lengthening and step-formation in cases like *sū-s* (boar), ὗς, O.H.G. *sū; mūs* (mouse), μῦς, O.H.G. *mūs,* etc., where Gk. vouches for the hypothesis of the lengthening.

The first step-formn. (acc. to analogy of all Indo-Eur. langg.)—sounded of course precisely as in Gk.—was *eu;* but it was lost very early, since the only remaining instance of this archaic step-formn. is in *Leuc-esius* (n. prop.), cf. λευκ-ός (white), also *Loucetius, Lucetius;* f.f. is prob. **Leuc-ent-ios,* a further formn. fr. a particp. st. **leuc-ent-* (as *Prudent-ius* fr. *prudent-*), of a pres. **leuc-o,* √*luc,* as φεύγ-ω fr. √φυγ. In consequence of the sound-law mentioned § 33, (*e* before *u, v,* changed to *o*), there will arise fr. *eu* an *ou,* coinciding with 2nd step, and later becoming *ū.* Hence from *dūc-o* (lead), *douco,* we must infer an older **deuco,* f.f. *dauk-āmi,* √*duk* (because pres. stt. of this kind were formed by the 1st step); *ūro* (burn), **ouso* for **euso=εὔ-ω* for **εὐσ-ω,* Sk. *ŏ́s--āmi,* f.f. *aus-āmi,* √*us;* in roots which end in *u* we find *ov* for **ev= eu,* e.g. **plou-ont,* thence *pluu-ont, plu-ont* (they rain); **plou-ont,* however, is for **pleu-onti,* cf. Gk. πλέϜ-οντι (πλέ-ουσι), f.f. *plav-anti;* so *flu-ont=flou-ont,* fr. **fleu-onti,* and other similar pres. fms.; *ious, iour-is* (*iūs, iūr-is,* right), is for **iou-os, *iou-es-is,* and formed like **gen-os, *gen-es-is* (gen-us, gen-eris), fr. √*iu* (iungere), by the first step, as is usual in this kind of noun st., **iou-os* is thus for **ieu-os,* formed fr. √*iu* like κλέϜ-ος fr. √κλυ, and corresponding Sk. *çráv-as* fr. √*çru; iŭs, iŭr-is* (broth)= **iou-s, *iour-is, *iou-os, *iou-es-os, *ieu-os, *ieu-es-os,* f.f. *yav-as, yav-as-as,* fr. another √*yu,* Gk. √ζυ (in ζύ-μη, yeast), cf. Scl.

iu-cha (broth); *pūs* (*pūr-is*, matter)=**pous*, **pou-os*, **peu-os*, f.f. § 36.
pav-as, Sk. and origl. √*pu* (be foul), cf. Goth. *fu-ls*, perh. *fŭ-ls*,
O.H.G. *fū-l*, N.H.G. *fau-l*, f.f. *pau-ra-s*, Lith. *pú-ti* (be foul).
Also *Iou-em*=*Diouem* (acc. n. pr.) must be referred to **dyev-em*,
and clearly *Iū-piter* stands for **dyū-piter*, **dyou-piter*, and the
latter for **dyeu-piter*, st. *dyeu-*=ζευ-, which is merely a sound-
variation fr. *dyeu*, √*dyu*=*div* (shine, as noun-st. ' heaven ' and
' god of heaven '; Sk. nom. *dyā-us* (2nd step) does not correspond with the Lat.): here the 1st step is much commoner than
the 2nd, so that Lat. *ū* must generally be referred hither as=
Old-Lat. *ou*.

Note.—*neu, seu*=*neue*, **seue*, do not belong here strictly, any
more than *ne-uter, ne-utiquam* (also *nutiquam* like *nullus*).

au, as in Gk., is a first step long since unused, and in Lat.
the only diphth. retained, and not yet given up (it occurs still
in Ital. and in more isolated cases in other Latin lang.),
although even in early times it was weakened, esp. in popular
dialects, to the sound *ō;* further *au* is contr. into *ū* (prob.
through intermed. *ō*), e.g. *raud-us*, *rōd-us*, *rūd-us* (crumb of
earth), √*rud*, elsewh. *rub, ruf*, √*rudh* (be red). Exx. of *au:*
aur-ōra (dawn), f.f. prob. *aus-āsā*, √*us* in *ūr-o, us-tus*, cf. Sk.
st. *uš-ás-* (aurora), without step-formn. in root and suff. (the
latter occurs in certain cases only); *aug-eo* (I increase), cf. αὔξω,
αὐξάνω, prob. fr. **aὐγ-σω*, **aὐγ-σανω*, Lith. *áug-u* (I wax), √*ug;*
the above-mentioned *raud-us* (neut. pl. *raud-era*), √*rud*, Sk.
√*rudh*, Gk. √ῥυθ, etc.

Note.—*au* can also arise through a secondary process, e.g.
nauta (sailor), *auceps* (bird-catcher), *gaudeo* (am glad), fr. *nāu-i-ta*,
*au-i-ceps, **gāu-i-deo*, etc.

The second step of *u*, viz. old Lat. *ou*, later *ū*, is equally
wanting with the 1st step, and it is only by the aid of the
cognate langg. that we can detect whether *ou*, *ū*, represent
origl. *au* or *āu:* the latter is certain only in rare instances,
e.g. *rūf-us* (red)=Kelt. *rúad*, Goth. *raud-s*, f.f. *rāudh-as*; clearly

§ 36. here belongs *über* (udder), on acct. of Gk. *οὖθαρ*, f.f. of both *áudhar*, though Sk. *údhas*, O.H.G *útar* (H.G. *euter*), show other degrees of the scale: perh. also *lūc-em*, *Louc-ina*, *lū(c)men*, √*luk*, origl. √*ruk*.

> *Note.*—*ū*, *ou*, are here and there secondary products through falling-out of sounds, as e.g. **councti*, *cuncti* (all together), fr. *co-iuncti*; *noundinum* (S.C. de Bacc.), *nūndinum*, fr. **nouendinum*, cf. *nundinae* (period of 9 days), *prūdens* fr. *pro-uidens*.

§ 37.   VOWEL SOUND-LAWS.

Accurate statement of the extraordinarily variable vowel sound-laws of the Lat. must be left to the special-grammar of the lang.: a general view only can be given here.

Hiatus. In case of vowels coming into contact with one another, hiatus is often obviated by means of contraction. This occurs regularly, when the first vowel is *a*, thus *amo* (1 sing.) fr. **amao*, *amas* (2 sing.), fr. **amais*, f.f. of termn. *-ayāmi*, *-ayasi*; *amarunt* (3 pl. pf.) fr. *ama(u)erunt*; *equae* and *equā* fr. *equāi* (d. sing); *diē*, *fidē*, fr. *diēi*, *fidēi*, etc. Other exx. are found in *sīs* fr. *siēs*, *sīt*, earlier *seit*, fr. *siēt*, f.f. *syāt*; *tibī*, *tibei*, fr. *tibie*, f.f. of termn. *-bhya(m)*; so too in *uōbeis*, *uōbīs*, f.f. of termn. *bhya(m)s*; *senatūs* (gen. sing.) fr. *sena-tuis* (*-tuos*), *senatu* (d. sing.) fr. *senatui*, *cōgo* fr. **co-igo*, *equo* (d. sing.) fr. *equōi*, etc. Both vowels, however, remain in many cases, esp. *u* and *i* with its kindred *e* make no hiatus with follg. vowels, e.g. *fui*, *lues*, *fluunt* (*fluont*); the noun-termns. *-io*, *-ia*, *-ies*; *fieri*, *tenuia* (*tenviā*), *eunt*, *eo*, *meae*. In combination even *co-actus*, *de-esse*, *co-optare*, but also medially, *boo* (*boare*), etc. Hiatus in the middle of a word is almost always brought about by loss of consonn., e.g. *fluunt* fr. *flouont*, *boo* fr. *bouo*, etc. The laws of hiatus in Lat. need a further and more accurate settlement.

§ 38.   Assimilation exercises a wide-spread influence; vowel as-similates vowel, both forwards and backwards, and also in case of indirect contact of vowels (passing over consonn.), causing both

partial and complete similarity; and the same effects are produced § 38.
by consonants upon vowels (relationship between particular con-
sonantal- and vowel-sounds). And, moreover, by this means
immediate contact betw. like vowels is avoided, and dissimilation takes place.

Thus *aureolus*, *gladiolus*, even *vinolentus*, etc., stand for
*aureulus, *gladiulus, *vinulentus, fr. *aureu-s*, *gladiu-s*, *uinu-m*, cf.
longulus, *turbulentus*; *duritie-s* beside *duriti-a*, etc.; cf. *siēm*,
siēs, *siēt*, with Sk. *syām*, *syās*, *syāt*. In these and similar cases
we see an assimilating influence of foregoing vowels on those
follg.; consequently *o* is nearer to *e* and *i* than *u*, and *e* more
akin to *i* than *a*.

A reflexive assimiln. passing over cons. occurs, e.g. in *ex-ul*
but *exil-ium*, *facul-tas* but *facil-is*, *sta-bulum* but *sta-bilis*; *mihi*,
tibi, but Umbr. *mehe*, *tefe*; *bene* but *bonus*.

For relation between *o* and *u*, vide § 33, 2; *u* has a special
affinity for labials, and above all *m* and *l*. Hence from
weakened *a* we get, not *i*, but *u*, in cases like *oc-cup-o*,
au-cup-ium, bes. *capere*, *con-tubernium* (chummage) beside *tab-erna*
(hut), *op-tum-us* (later only, *optimus*), etc.; bef. *l* older *o* became
u, e.g. *poculum* fr. *pocolom*, *consul* fr. *cosol*, *epistula* fr. *ἐπιστολή*;
through this weakening of *a*, before *l*+cons. we find *u*, not *i* or
e (the regular representative of *i* before 2 consonn.), e.g. *salsus*,
insulsus, *sepelio*, *sepultus*, etc.; further, *u* has remained before
n+cons., e.g. *ferunt*, *homunculus* (cf. supr. § 32). Throughout, it
represents here too an earlier *o*, wh. maintained itself intact in
the popular diall., as later inscrr. and Ital. (e.g. *sepoltura* as
early as 558 A.D., cf. Ital. *sepolcro*, *colomna*, Ital. *colonna*) prove.

Even origl. *i*—not weakened fr. *a*—gives way to *u* in cases
like *testu-monium* (witness) beside *testi-s*; *carnu-fex* (flayer) beside
st. *carni-* (n. *caro*, flesh), and the like; where, nevertheless, the
analogy of the commoner cases may have had some influence.

e is retained by preference in final syll. bef. nasals, e.g. *septem*,
cf. *ἑπτά*, *nōmen*, Sk. *nắman-*, *cornicen*, √*can*, *ouem* fr. *oui-m*, and

§ 38. so in most *i*-stems; in acc. sing. of *a*-stem nevertheless we find
o, *u* (*nouo-m*, *nouu-m*); but above all *e* is found bef. *r*, e.g.
camera fr. *καμάρα, operis* beside *nominis; stetĕrunt* for *steti-sonti,
cf. *stetis-ti; ueher-is* fr. *uehis-is*, cf. *uehit-ur; peperi* for *pepiri, fr.
pario, like *cecini* fr. *cano; affero*, not *af-fir-o, wh. we might look
for acc. to analogy, comparing such cases as *colligo* fr. *lego*.
    r has also a preference for *o* (=*u*) preceding, e.g. *fo-re, fo-rem*,
fr. √*fu* (*fu-turus*); Lat. *ancora* fr. Gk. *ἄγκῡρα*; but *robur, ebur*
with *u*, perh. on account of preceding *b*.
    Further, *e* occurs bef. two or more consonn. interchangeably
with *i* bef. one cons., e.g. *iudex* but *iudicis; eques-ter* for *equet-ter,
*equit-ter but *equit-em; asellus* fr. **asin(u)lus*, cf. *asinus; consecro,
abreptus*, etc. (but it remains *i* bef. *ng* in *attingo, infringo* and
the like).
    The sound-combinations *ent, end*, and *unt, und*, are weakened
forms, e.g. *fer-ent-em* beside *e-unt-em* fr. *e-ont-em, where the
earlier sound *o, u*, has been kept in consequence of dissimiln., beside *e, uolunt-arius; faciendus* and *faciundus*, both fr. *faciondus,
remain in ' *sacris faciundis*,' ' *iure dicundo*,' and the like. After
u, e is invariable: *tu-endus, restitu-endus*. *a* is throughout the
origl. vowel in these cases.
    i has a special affinity to *n* and *dentals*, and is the commonest
weakening fr. *a*, e.g. *μηχανή* but *māchina; nominis, hominis, cecini*,
fr. stems *gnāman-, ghaman-, ka-kan-*, etc.
    By dissimiln. is prevented the combn. of two like vowels,
e.g. *ueri-tas* fr. *ueru-s*, but *pie-tas* (*piu-s*), *ebrie-tas* (*ebriu-s*),
etc., not *pii-tas, etc.; *equit-is* (*eques*) but *abiĕt-is, ariĕt-is, pariet-is*
(*abies, aries, paries*); *diuinus, diuo-s*, but *aliēnus* (*aliu-s*); *lēui-gare*
(*lēuis*) but *uarie-gare* (*uariu-s*), etc.   The first vowel is changed
in *mēio* fr. *mĭg-yo, **mĭio: ei, dei*, are older and more correct than
ii, dii, etc.   Through dissimiln. *o* kept ground longer after *u, v*,
e.g. *equos, equom, nouom, mortuos*, etc.
§ 39.   Through loss of consonants vowel-change takes place, viz.
1. C o m p e n s a t o r y   l e n g t h e n i n g ; 2. C o n t r a c t i o n.

1. **Compensatory lengthening,** e.g. *pēs, ariēs*=*pĕd-s*, § 39. *ariĕt-s;* a regular shortening has here taken place later (§ 41), e.g. *pedĕs* fr. *pedēs*=*pedĕt-s, patĕr* fr. *patēr*=*patĕr-s; ferēns* =*ferĕnt-s* (cf. φέρων=φεροντ-ς); *sāl* (salt)=*săl-s* (gen. *săl-is*), cf. ἅλς, etc.; esp. often through loss of nasal bef. *s*, e.g. acc. pl. of *a*-st. *-ōs* (*nou-ōs*)=*-ons* (f.f. *nav-ans*); in compar. *-iŏr, -iŏrem,* fr. *-yans, -yansam*, etc.; further, *pōno* (place)=*pos-no* (cf. *pos-ui*), *quini* (by fives)=*quĭncni, exāmen* (swarm)=*exăg-men* (*ăgo*); thus *g* falls out esp. bef. *y*, e.g. *māior* (greater)=*măg-ior*, cf. *mag-nus* (great), *āio* (say)=*ăg-io* (cf. *ad-ăg-ium*, proverb), *mēio* (urino) =*mĭio*=*mĭgyo*, etc.

2. **Contraction** (vid. supr. § 37), e.g. *amārunt, amāsti, nōrunt, amō* (fr. *amao*), *docēs, audīs* (fr. *doce-is*, *audi-is*); *nouīs*=*nouo-is,* *noua-is* fr. *nouo-bios*, *noua-bios* (v. Decl.), etc. In redupl. perff. this case is very clear, e.g. *fēci* fr. *fĕfĭci*, cf. *cecini*, likew. *iēci, frēgi*, etc.

Note.—Cases like *inuītare* (invite)=*uicitare*, √*uŏc; conuītium* (wrangle)=*conuĭcitium* √*uŏc; suspītio* (suspicion)=*suspicitio,* etc. (on the last ex. cf. Fleckeisen, Rhein Museum, viii. 227; on the other side Corssen, Kritik. Beitr. s. 12 sqq., who writes *suspīcio, conuīcium*, and derives them accordingly, but assigns *inuītare* to an ambig. Sk. √ *vi*). Cf. § 77, 1. a. sub fin.

Weakening (lightening of vowels by change of quality § 40. with and without shortening) is very common in Lat., and throughout not exclusively confined to unaccentuate sylls., whence probably too the analogy of this weakening arose (cf. supr. § 32, 2; on the question cf. G. Curtius, das dreisilbengesezt der Gk. u. Lat. betonung, in Kuhn's Zeitschrift, ix. 321 sqq.). Esp. regular is the occurrence of weakg. in **sylls. of word-formation; in composition and in reduplication,** but also in root sylls. Nevertheless, that the weakening did not invariably occur in the second member of a compound is proved by exx. such as *com-paro, per-agro, per-actus*, etc. (Corss. Kuhn's Zeitschr. xi. 370). **Through weakening**

§ 40.   *a* becomes *e*; *fall-o fe-fell-i, parc-o pe-perc-i, fac-tus per-fec-tus,* etc.

a becomes *u*; *cap-io, oc-cup-o;* here belongs the *u* of the un-accentuated final sylls., e.g. *da-tu-s* f.f. *da-ta-s;* early Lat. *oper-us,* Sk. and f.f. *ápas-as,* etc.: the change fr. *a* to *u* is through in-termed. *o.*

a becomes *i*; e.g. *fac-io con-fic-io, pa-ter Iupi-ter, cad-o, ce-cid-i, can-o, ce-cin-i,* etc.; the change must be through intermed. *e.*   *e* occurs for *i* acc. to the above-stated rule, in cases like *tubi-cen, pe-per-i, oper-is* for **opis-is* (*opos-os* f.f. *apas-as*), etc.   Cf. § 38.

ā becomes *ē*; *hāl-o an-hēl-o.*

ae becomes *ī*; *quaer-o in-quĭr-o, caed-o ce-cīd-i con-cīd-o, aequos in-īquos,* etc.

au becomes *ō, ū*; *caus-a ac-cūs-o, fauc-es suf-fōc-o, plaud-o ex-plōd-o,* etc.

Even long vowels and diphths. became *ĭ* (*ĕ*) by more marked shortening, e.g. *gnō-tus co-gnĭ-tus, iouro* (*iūro*), *pe-iĕro, de-iĕro* (*-yĕro* for **-yiro,* with *e* for *i* bef. *r,* cf. § 38).

Before secondary suffixes, and as 1st member of compds., stems in *o, u,* weaken their stem-termns. before consonn. to *i,* e.g. *duri-tas, duri-ties,* st. *duro-* (*durus*); *corni-culum, corni-cen, corni-ger,* st. *cornu-,* etc.

Bef. vowels *u* remains, e.g. *fructu-arius fructu-osus,* st. *fructu-*; it also keeps ground bef. labials, e.g. *locu-ples, quadru-pes, quadru-plex.*

§ 41.   Also shortening of vowels in unacc. final sylls. prevails very widely.

Thus *ă* in fem. is origl. *ā* (Sk. *ā, η*), hence kept long some-times in earlier Latin; *ĕ,* in abl. sing. of *i*-st. and of conson. stems, following their analogy, is origl. *-ait,* thence *-aid, -eid, -ēd, ĭd,* later *-ei, -ē, -ī* (so *patrē,* tit. Scip. Barb.); *ē* of the vb. sometimes appears short, e.g. *cauĕ, iubĕ; ĭ* in *mihĭ, tibĭ, ubĭ,* etc., is fr. earlier *ī, ei* through shortening, *mihei, tibei, ubei,* occur not seldom: final *ō* always represents origl. *ŏ,* e.g. *homō=*homon-s;*

agō cf. *ắγω*, f.f. *ag-āmi*, next step *ag-ā* by loss of *mi; egō* cf. § 41. *ἐγώ*; in these cases the nasal may have caused the dulling of *ā* to *ō; duo, ambo, octo*, cf. δύω, ắμφω, ὀκτώ.

Shortening occurs regularly bef. final *t; amă-t* for *-āt*=*-ait*, *-aat* fr. *-ayati*, cf. *amā-mus;* so *-et, -it*, in the derived vbs. and in opt. fr. *-ēt, -ĭt*, earlier *-eit :* also *-it* in pf. was sounded *-eit* in earlier times, and the like.

Similarly bef. other consonn., e.g. *-ĭs* of opt. (*feceris*) for and beside *-īs* (*fecerīs*); *pa-tĕr* fr. *pa-tēr* (cf. πα-τήρ) for **pa-ters; -ŏr* in nom. sing. fr. *-ōr*, e.g. *censōr* (tit. Scip.) fr. **cens-tor-s*, and many more such.

Evaporation in unacc. sylls. brings us to total loss, final and § 42. medial loss of vowels (§ 32).

Final loss of vowels is partly of late date only, e.g. *animal* for and beside *animale, dic* for and bes. *dice, hoc* for and bes. *hoce, ut* for and bes. *uti*; partly older, e.g. *uehis* for **uehisi*, f.f. *vaghasi; est, uehit*, for **esti, *uehiti*, f.f. *asti, vaghati* (*tremonti* has remained, Bergk. index lect. Marburg, 1847–8), etc.

Medial loss of weakly-accented vowels is esp. common in Lat., and occurs (1.) bef. vowels, e.g. *minor, minus*, for **minior, *minius; nullus* for *ne-ullus*, etc.; cases can be produced where no contraction has taken place, e.g. *un-ŏculus* (*uno-oculus*), *sem-ănimus* (*semi-animus*), *nŭtiquam* (*ne-utiquam*). (2.) bef. consonn., the commonest case, e.g. *alumnus, uertumnus*, for **alumenus, *uert-umenus*, suff.=Gk. -μενο-, Sk. -māna-; *stella* for **sterla* fr. **sterula; puella* for **puerla* fr. **puerula; misellus* for **miserlus* fr. **miserulus; patrem* for **pater-em*, st. *pater-; rettuli* fr. **re-tetuli; reppuli* fr. **re-pepuli; repperi* fr. **re-peperi*, and so on. Thus the loss of medial vowels is chiefly approved betw. like consonn. (as in Mid.H.G., Zeitschr. x. 160). Unacc. *i* may altogether disappear, e.g. *dixti* fr. *dixisti, ualde* fr. *ualide, gaudeo* fr. **gauideo* (cf. *gauisus*), etc.

Of special importance in treatment of declension is the medial loss of origl. *a* and *i*, i.e. *o* or *u* and *i* before the *s* of nom. sing.

§ 42. Thus arises *puer*, etc., fr. *puers, which comes fr. *puero-s*, *puerus*
(in existence), *uir* fr. *uirs, *uiros, *acer* (§ 43) fr. *acris*, etc.
This is noticeably regular after *r* with short syll. precedg.;
hence *quatuor* stands for *quatuors, *quatuores, cf. τέσσαρες, Sk.
katvăras; after the vowel had been lost, the *s* also fell off from
the *r*. Such forms as *famul* (Enn. Ann.) are obsol.; it stands
for *famuls fr. *famulos*, *damnas* for *damnats fr. *damnatos; alis*
for *alios* (vouched for more than once); *Sallustis*, *Clodis* (Inscrr.)
for *Sallustios*, *Clodios*, etc.; *alid* for *aliod, *aliud*.

Loss of *i* in *i*-st. is remarkably common, whereby its Lat.
nom. has become thoroughly confused with that of conson.
stems, thus e.g. *primas* for older *primatis*, *gens* fr. *gents and
this fr. *gen-ti-s, *mors* for *morts fr. *mor-ti-s, fr. √*gen*, origl.
gan (gignere), and √*mor*, origl. *mar* (mori), f.f. therefore
gan-ti-s, *mar-ti-s*, and the like. Further *acer* for and bes. *acris*,
uigil fr. *uigilis*, etc.

Note.—The occasional omission of vowels in the text of Inscrr.
which could not take place in the spoken lang. (e.g. *dcumius*, *fect*,
uixt for *Decumius*, *fecit*, *uixit*) has been pointed out by Ritschl.
(Rhein. Mus. n. Folge xvi. p. 601 sqq.; xvii. p. 144 sqq.).

§ 43.   Insertion of a helping-vowel likewise sometimes occurs
in Lat., e.g. *s-u-m* fr. *es-mi, *es-u-mi, origl. *as-mi; s-u-mus* fr.
*es-mus, *es-u-mus, origl. *as-masi; uol-u-mus* fr. *uol-mus, f.f. *var-
masi*, cf. *uol-t*, f.f. *var-ti; teg-u-mentum* (hence *teg-i-mentum*) bes.
teg-mentum, and the like belong likewise here; *u* is here the
helping-vowel on account of *m* following, cf. *drach-u-ma* (Plaut.)
fr. δραχ-μή, since in general a similar vowel-insertion was ad-
mitted in foreign words, as e.g. *tech-i-na* (Plaut.) from τέχνη, etc.

Bef. *r*, *e*=*i* (§ 38), e.g. *um-e-rus* (shoulder) bes. Sk. *ắsa-s* för
*amsa-s, *rub-e-r* (red) for *rubr fr. *rubrs, *rub-ro-s=ἐ-ρυθ-ρό-ς,
Sk. also with helping-vowel *rudh-i-rá-s*, origl. *rudh-ra-s; gener*
(son-in-law) for **gen-r(o-s)*, cf. γαμβρός for **γαμ-ρό-ς; ager*
(field) for **ag-r(o-s)*, Gk. ἀγ-ρό-ς; *caper* (he-goat) for **cap-r(o-s)*,
a form like κάπ-ρ-ος (boar), etc.

The common helping-vowel *i* may generally be regarded as § 43.
a weakening of an older *u* or *e* : it occurs rather irregularly
(cf. Ritschl. Rh. M. n. F. 1862, 607 sqq.) in e.g. *mor-i-turus*
bes. *mor-tuos, or-i-turus* bes. *or-tus*, etc.   After the analogy of
consonl. roots this *i* is found also in the case of roots ending in
a vowel, e.g. *ru-i-turus, di-ru-i-tus* bes. *diru-tus, tu-i-tus* bes.
tu-tus, etc.

B. CONSONANTS.

§ 44. CONSONANTS OF THE INDO-EUROPEAN ORIGINAL LANGUAGE.

The consonn. in Indo-Eur. are specially distinguished from the vowels, setting aside their physiological conditions, in that they are fixed and invariable in roots (we may pass over the changes which they undergo in consequence of sound-laws that are always secondary), but cannot, like vowels, raise themselves in a definite scale of gradation. Whilst the nine origl. vowel-sounds of the Indo-Eur. can be reduced to three fundamental vowels, the consonn. are collectively independent of one another. Whilst the vowels by means of their step-formation according to meaning thereby serve for the expression of *relation*, consonn. are merely elements of expression of *meaning;* no relationship is expressed in Indo-Eur. by the use of root-consonn.

The Indo-Eur. origl. lang. has fifteen consonn., which in § 1 are classed according to their physiological conditions, viz. three momentary mutes, three mom. sonants, three mom. son. aspirates, three spirants, and three so-called liquids, i.e. two nasals and *r*. The existence of *b* (mom. son. labial) in the origl. lang. cannot be authenticated by any perfectly certain example: but it is highly probable that it did exist, as the origl. element of the frequent aspirate *bh*. The number of origl. consonn. is also much greater than that of the vowels (prob. 3×3, but certainly 2×3 existed).

The aspirates, as double sounds, seem to be foreign to the most original condition of the lang., and to have developed only in later times: but they certainly existed before the first splitting-up of the origl. lang., for they are found in the three divisions of the Indo-Eur., or at least they can be detected;

that is, they occur in Aryan and in S.-European; in N.-Euro- § 44. pean likewise they must once have existed: the Teutonic has them, it is true, like the other northern langg., changed to *sonants*, but the origl. *sonants* are distinguished from them by becoming *tenues*.

Consonantal sound-laws had not arisen so early as the origl. lang.; consonn. can be placed anywhere, and in any combination which the organism of the lang. required, because these combinations (e.g. *vāk-bhis* inst. pl. fr. st. *vāk, voice*) were not yet so close that those consonn. which are brought together by word-formation exercised any influence on one another (thus e.g. in *vāk-bhis* the influence of *bh* on *k* produces as early as Sk. the fm. *vāg-bhis: k* has here changed bef. sonant *bh* into its corresponding son. *g*: on the improbability of origl. interchange of *i, u,* with *y, v,* cf. § 3).

EXAMPLES. § 45.

Momentary mute unaspirated consonants.

1. *k.* *ka-s* (who), *ka* (-que, and.), *katvār-as* (four), *kankan* (five), *kard* (heart), √*kak* (cook), √*ka* and *ak* (be sharp, quick), √*ki* (lie), √*kru* (hear), *kru-ta-s* (heard), *kvan-s* (dog), √*skid* (cut), √*vak* (speak), √*dak* (bite), √*dik* (show), √*ruk* (light), *ak-man-s* (stone, heaven), *dakan* (ten), *varka-s* (wolf); sf. *-ka,* etc.

2. *t.* *ta-t* (that), *tu* (thou), √*ta, tan* (stretch), *tri* (three), √*sta* (stand), *stag.*(cover), √*pat* (fly, fall), √*prat* (broad), √*vart* (turn); common in stem- and word-formative particles, e.g. sf. *-ta* (pf. pt. pass.), *bhara-ti* (fer-t), *ragh-is-ta-s* (ἐλάχιστος), etc.

3. *p.* √*pa* (drink), √*pa* (protect, rule), thence *pa-ti-s* (lord) and *pa-tar-s* (father), *par* (fill), hence *paru-s* (many) and *par-na-s* (full), √*pad* (go) as noun-st. n. sing. *pad-s* (foot), *pratu-s* (πλατύ-ς), √*pru* (flow), *prav-ati* (he flows), √*spak* (see, look), √*sarp* (creep, serpere), √*tap* (burn, heat), √*svap* (sleep) thence *svap-na-s* (sleep, n.), etc.

§ 46. Momentary sonant unaspirated consonants.

1. *g.* √*ga* (go), 1 sing. pres. *ga-gā-mi,* √*ga, gan* (be born), √*gan* (know), √*ag* (agere), *ag-ni-s* (ig-ni-s), √*grabh* (grasp), √*yu-g* (iungere), thence *yug-am* (yoke, iug-um), etc.

2. *d.* √*da* (dare), 1 sing. pres. *da-dā-mi,* √*dak* (bite), √*dam* (tame, domare), *dama-s* (domus), √*dik* (show), √*div* (shine), st. *dva-* (two), √*ad* (eat), √*sad* (sit), √*vid* (uidere), 1 sing. pres. *vaid-mi,* etc.

3. *b.* I know of no certain example of this sound.

Note.—The Teutonic and Gk. forms of those words that show *b* in the Aryan and S.-European langg. point partly to *bh*, e.g. Sk. √*bandh* (bind), but Goth. *band,* f.f. therefore *bhandh,* Gk. √πενθ for *φενθ, πενθ-ερός (affinis), πεῖσμα for *πενθ-μα (cable); Sk. *bāhús* (fore-arm), Gk. πῆχυς for *φηχυς, N.-Eur. *bōgr,* O.H.G. *puoc,* origl. initial-sound *bh;* Sk. √*budh* (know), Gk. √πυθ (πυνζάνομαι) for *φυθ, Goth. *bud,* not *pud,* as might be expected fr origl. *b* (moreover the Goth. root, notwithstanding the difference of function, is identical with *budh, πυθ);* if *b* were origl., the Gk. fms. would be *βενθ, *βηχυς, *βυθ. These three roots have a final asp., which was the effect of the disappearance of an origl. asp. at the beginning in Aryan and Gk. (this conjecture has been ably confirmed by Grassmann, Zeitschr. xii. 110). In other instt. we lack decisive representatives in N.-European, e.g. βραχύς, *breuis,* Sclav. *brüzü;* Sk. √*lab, lamb* (labi, delabi; 3 sing. pres. *lámbatē*), Lat. *lab.* (lāb-itur), etc.; κάνναβις (hemp), Norse *hanpr,* O.Bulg. *konoplya,* a doubtful and borrowed form. Grassm. Zeitschr. xii. 122 sqq. shows it to be likely that *b* did not exist in Indo.-Eur., at least at the beginning of a word. Nor have I found any certain exx., ap. Bickell Zeitschr. xiv. 425 sqq., of the origl. existence of lab. son. in Indo.-Eur.

§ 47. Momentary sonant aspirated consonants.

1. *gh.* √*ghar, ghra* (burn, shine; be green, yellow), *ghans-s* (m. f. *goose*), √*stigh* (step), √*agh, angh* (be tight), √*vagh* (uehere), √*migh* (mingo), √*righ* (lick), *dargha-s* (long), etc.

2. *dh.* √*dha* (set, make), 1 sing. pres. *dha-dhāmi,* √*dham* (blow), √*idh* (burn), √*rudh* (be, become red) thence *rudhra-s* and *rāudha-s* (red), *madhu* (honey, mead), *madhya-s* (medius), etc.

3. *bh.* √*bha* (shine, speak), √*bhar* (bear, ferre), 1 sing. pres. § 47. *bhar-āmi*, √*bhu* (be, become), 1 sing. pres. *bhav-āmi*, √*bhug* (bend, flee), *bhrā-tar-s* (brother), √*grabh* (grasp), *nabha-s* (neut. nubes), -*bhi* common case-sf. *bh* is not very common in st.-formative particles.

CONSONANTAL PROLONGED-SOUNDS.　　§ 48.

Spirants.

1. *y.* *ya-s* (which), *yuga-m* (yoke, iugu-m), √*yug*, *yu* (iungere); very common in st.-formative particles, e.g. *mạdh-ya-s* (medius), *as-yā-t* (sit, siēt), *bhāra-yā-mi* (φορέω), compar. sf. -*yans* (prob. also -*yant*); also in word-formative sff., e.g. -*bhyam*, -*bhyams*, sf. of dat. sing. pl. -*sya*, sf. of gen. sing. masc. of *a*-st., etc. As a medial sound, *y* is akin to *i*, cf. § 3.

2. *s.* √*sad* (sit), *saptan* (seven), √*su* (sow), thence *su-nu-s* (son), √*sru* (flow), √*svid* (sweat), √*sta* (stand), √*star* (strew), √*smar* (remember), √*as*, pres. *as-mi* (sum), √*us* (urere), √*vas* (dwell, clothe oneself), √*tars* (torrere, thirst), *sva-star-s* (sister); common in word-formative partt., e.g. *akva-s* (equos), nom. sg. masc., *akvā-sas*, nom. pl. masc., etc.; also in st. forms, e.g. *man-as* (mind), etc.

3. *v.* √*va* (flow), √*vam* (uomere), √*vak* (speak), thence *vāk-s* (voice), √*vagh* (carry, uehere), 1 sing. pres. *vagh-āmi*, √*var* (will), √*vart* (turn, uertere), *aui-s* (ouis), √*vid* (see, know), *naua-s* (new, nouos); in stem-formative partt., e.g. sf. -*vant*, Sk. -*vant*, -*vans*, Gk. -Ϝεντ, -Ϝοτ; rarer in word-formative partt., e.g. loc. pl. -*sva*, etc.; *v* as a medial sound is akin to *u*, vid. § 3.

Nasals.　　　　　　　　　　　　　　　　　　§ 49.

1. *n.* *na, an-* (negation), √*nak* (die), thence *nak-ti-s* (night), *nava-s* (nouos), *nāu-s*, gen. *nāv-as* (nauis), √*gan* (be born, know), st. *ana-* (dem. pron.); *n* is common in st.-and word-formative partt., e.g. *par-na-s* (plenus; past part. pass.), *ak-man-s* (stone), *gnā-man* (name), *bhara-nti* (ferunt), etc.

§ 49.   2. *m.*   √*ma, ma-n* (measure, think), thence *ma-na-s* (mind) and *mā-tar-s* (mother), √*mar* (mori), √*smar* (remember), √*vam* (uomere); common in word-formative partt., e.g. *varka-m* (acc. sg.), *ai-mi, i-masi* (eo, imus, 1 sg. pl. pres.), etc.; in st-formative partt., e.g. *ghar-ma-s* (heat), *gnā-man* (name).

§ 50.   *r.*   √*rak* (shriek), √*ruk* (light), √*rik* (liquere), √*righ* (lick), √*rudh* (rubere), *raghu-s* (light, adj.), √*kru* (hear), √*bhar* (ferre), √*ar* (oriri, ire; arare), √*par* (fill) ; also in stem-formative partt., e.g. sf. *tar, bhrā-tar-, mā-tar-,* and the like, but not in word-formative sff.

§ 51.   SANSKRIT CONSONANTS.

The physiologically-arranged table of Sk. consonn. is in § 4, where also their pronunciation is considered. Whilst the vowel system of Sk. is generally original, its conson. system is mixed in many ways with later elements. Hence arises that large number of conson.-sounds which is unparalleled in other Indo-Eur. langg.

The origl. sounds in Sk. are the mom. mutes and sonants, and the sonant aspp. all of gutt., dent., and lab. quality, thus, *k, t, p; g, d, b* (?); *gh, dh, bh;* further the spirants *y, s, v,* and also *n, m, r.* Thus Sk. still possesses the consonn. of the Indo-Eur. origl. lang. entire. All the rest, nineteen in number, have arisen in pure Aryan words from these fifteen origl. consonn., and are to be treated as parallel fms. of them, which have been called forth according to generally perceptible sound-laws, and through the influence of the non-Indo-Eur. langg. spoken by Dravidian (Dekhanic) peoples who were pressed back by the Aryans, and were the earlier inhabitants of the peninsula of Further India, just as neighbouring langg. very often acquire sounds from one another.

The origin of the so-called Sk. lingual mom. consonn. and ling. nasal (*t, d, th, dh, n*) is due to the latter influence, therefore these sounds are peculiar to Indian, and are unknown in this form to other Indo-Eur. langg. Within the Indian these

sounds gain a still wider sway in the course of the development § 51.
of the lang. (in the Prākrits). In Aryan words they are
variations of their corresponding dentals.

Further the palat. mom. sounds and their nasal are all unorigl. (*k̑, g̑, k̑h, g̑h, ṅ*); they have arisen from the corresponding
gutturals; and so is the pal. mute spirant *ç*, which is a variation
fr. *k*. The law acc. to which the gutt. partly pass into palatals,
partly remain, is hitherto unexplained in particular cases (however, that the change of gutt. into palat. did not occur till late,
is implied by the circumstance that the gutt. were reduplicated
by means of the corresponding palatals).

Unorigl. also are all the tenues aspp. (*kh, th, ph;* in the case
of *kh* and *th* the unoriginality is sufficiently clear from the
nature of the unasp. sound), whose origin is in known cases
mainly caused by foregoing *s* (*kh, kh=sk, sth=st*).

Unorigl. also is *h*, which mostly represents *gh*, sometimes also
other aspp.; *ś* occurs partly acc. to definite sound-laws, partly
without perceptible reason for *s;* ◦ (visarga) is an altogether late
variation of *s*, and confined almost entirely to the termination.

The gutt. and palat. nasals stand only bef. mom. consonn. of
their own quality, by which therefore they are conditioned; the
nasalisation of the vowels (˜) is likewise dependent on the
follg. conson.; it occurs bef. *s* and *h* (bef. other consonn. it is
often merely a way of writing nasal consonn.).

l bes. *r*, is as in other langg., unorigl.; it obviously increases
in the course of the development of Sk.

Besides the sound-laws already explained, Sk. has numerous
laws for medial sounds, but esp. for termn. (these laws however
do not belong here, but rather to Sk. special grammar), through
which the conson.-syst. of Sk. became considerably removed
from the basis of the origl. lang.

The representation of gutt. by palatals occurs only bef. vowels
and sonant mom. prolonged sounds, not bef. mom. consonn.,
mute conson.-prolonged-sounds, and in termin. Yet here also

6

§ 51. occur palatals by no means acc. to fixed sound-laws (e.g.
yu-yóǵ-a iunxi, bes. *yóg-a-s* iunctio), so that it seems that the
lang. has availed itself of the change of gutt. into palatals
(originally merely physiological), in order to express differences
of relation.

EXAMPLES.

§ 52.   Origl. mom. mute unaspirated consonn.

1. Origl. *k*=Sk. *k, ḱ, kh, ḱh, ç, p.*

Sk. *k*=origl. *k,* e.g. in *ka-s* (who), √*kar* (make), *kími-s*
(worm), *vŕka-s* (wolf), st.-formative sf. *-ka,* e.g. *dhārmi-ka-s*
(right, fr. *dharmá-s,* duty), etc.

Sk. *ḱ*=origl. *k, ḱa-kára* (feci), *ka-* is the relic of the most
origl. reduplicated supposed √*kar; ḱa* (-que, and), *ḱatvár-as*
(quatuor); √*ruḱ* (shine), √*vaḱ* (speak), whence *váḱ-mi* (I speak),
váḱ-am (uocem, speech); *ḱ* stands for *k* esp. in √termn., etc.

Note.—Bef. mom. sounds and *s* the gutt. remains, e.g. *vák-ti*
(he speaks), *vák-ši* (thou· speakest, *š* for *s* after *k,* v. § 55, 2),
vag-dhi (speak), *g* for *k* acc. to sound-laws, v. post., etc.

kh and *ḱh* occur for origl. *k* after *s*; this *s* more often than
not is lost in case of *skh,* in case of *ḱh* always. [For aspirating
force of *s,* v. Kuhn, Zeitschr. iii. p. 321 sqq., 426 sqq. Cf.
also Ascoli, Zeitschr. xvi. p. 442 sqq.]

Sk. *kh*=origl. *sk,* e.g. *khaṅga-s* (limping), cf. O.H.G. *hinch-an,*
hink-an, √*hank,* likewise without initial *s,* but Gk. σκάζω (limp),
√σκαγ=Sk. *khaǵ,* f.f. *skag; kháǵa-s* (stirrer), cf. Ang.-Sax.
scac-an, Norse *skak-a* (shake); *khaḱ* (spring forth), cf. Sclav.
skak-ati (spring).

Note.—Most words in *kh* cannot, or at least not certainly,
be reduced to their f.f.

Sk. *ḱh*=origl. *sk,* e.g. √*ḱhid* (split), Zend *çḱid,* Lat. *scid,* f.f.
skid; ḱháyá (cover), cf. Gk. σκιά; *gáḱḱhāmi,* f.f. *gaskāmi* (the
redupln. of *ḱh* to *ḱḱh* is regularly written so after a short vowel),
and in similarly fmd. pres. stt.

Note.—Bef. *t, th, kh* becomes *š*, e.g. *prás-tum* (*t* for *t* after *š*), § 52. infin., √*prakh*, f.f. prob. *prask*, with unorigl. ·*s;* cf. Lat. *prec* (precor), *proc* (procax), Lith. *prasz*, Sclav. *pros*, Germ. *frah* (*frathnan*), Sk. *praç-ná-s* (prayer) for **prak-na-s;* but e.g. *prak-šyáti* fut. with *k* acc. to usual rule.

ç=origl. *k*; √*çi* (*çétē*=κεῖται); *ça* and *aç* (acuere), pres. *(a) ç-yáti, çā-tá-s, ci-tá-s* (acutus), whence also *áçman-* (n. *áçmā*, stone); √*çru* (hear); *çvan-*, n. *çvā* (hound); √*diç* (show); √*daç* (bite); *´dáçan-* (ten), etc. *ç* is a favourite sound esp. bef. liq. consonn. and *v*; further in √termns., in place of *k*; it is however not uncommon at the beginning of roots.

In verb stt. *k* remains bef. *s*, though *ç* was produced from it in other circumstances, e.g. *á-dik-šat* (ἔ-δεικ-σε, after *k*, *š* stands for *s*, v. post.), so in certain noun stt., e.g. *dik-šú*, loc. pl. fr. st. *diç-* (n. sg. *dik* for *dik-s, gen. *diç-ás*, quarter of the compass), dat. pl. *dig-bhyás* acc. to sound-laws (v. post.) for *dik-bhyas. Other noun. stt. let their *ç*, however, interchange with *t, ḍ*, unoriginally. Bef. *t, th, ç* becomes *š*, which *t, th*, then become lingual, e.g. √*darç* (Gk. δερκ, see), but *drš-tá-s* (past part. pass.) for *drç-ta-s, f.f. *dark-ta-s*.

Sk. *p*=origl. *k* occurs only sporadically. This change fr. *k* to *p* is seen in all Indo-Eur. langg. except Lat. and Erse; e.g. √*pak* (cook) for origl. *kak*. Whilst Lat. √*coc* preserves both gutt., which evidently arose fr. redupln. of origl. √*ka*, Gk. has in πεπ permitted labials to arise in both cases, Sk. *pak* and Scl. *pek* have only changed the initial, and Lith. *kep* contrariwise the final. This ex. is specially full of information, and points unmistakably to the originality of the *k*, hence the √fm. is in these cases *kak*. Further *pánkan-* (five) for **kankan;* √*sap* (sequi, Vēdic) seems to be a bye-fm. of *sak* (sequi), f.f. *sak*, so that in this root also two variations fr. origl. *k* are to be seen ; st. *ap-* (water) must stand bes. Lat. *aq-ua*, Goth. *ah-va* (river), for origl. *ak-*, Lith. *ùpe* shows likewise the change fr. *k* to *p*, f.f. of *ùpe* is thus *ak-yā, and the root of this word is probably

§ 52. *ak* (be swift). [On the change of origl. *k* to *p*, wh. often does not appear till late in certain words, while in others *k* remains, cf. Beitr. iii. 283 sqq.]

Note.—In the words *hrd-*, *hŕd-aya-m* (heart), *h*=origl. *k*, clearly through intermed. *kh;* origl. *k* is attested by *cord-is*, *καρδ-ία hairt-ō*, Lith. *szird-ìs*, Scl. *srŭd-ĭce.* In √*guh* (hide, 3 sg. pres. *gŭh-ati*, *gŭh-ā*, cairn) *g* is softened fr. *k*, f.f. of root therefore is *kudh*, as Gk. κεύθ-ω (hide), Lat. *cus-tos* for **cud-tos*, Ang.-Sax. *hyd-an*, prove.

2. Origl. *t*=Sk. *t*, *th.*

Sk. *t*=origl. *t*, e.g. *ta-t* (that), origl. id.; *tv-am* (thou) ; √*ta*, *tan*, 1 sg. pres. *ta-nŏmi* (stretch) ; *pát-ati* (3 sg. pŕes.), √*pat* (fly, fall) ; *várt-atē* (3 sg. pres. med), √*vart* (uertere); sf. of past part. pass., e.g in *yuk-tá-s* (√*yug*, *yuǵ*, iungere), cf. *iunc-tu-s*, ζευκ-τό-ς ; sf. *ti* of 3 pers. vb., e.g. 3 sg. *bhára-ti*, 3 pl. *bhára-nti*, cf. φέρε-(τ)ι, φέρο-ντι, *fer-t*, *feru-nt*, Goth. *bairi-th*, *baira-nd*, etc.

Sk. *th*=origl. *t*, esp. after *s*, e.g. √*stha* (stand), e.g. *sthi-tás*, origl. *sta-ta-s* (status) ; √*sthag* (cover), cf. Gk. στεγ, Lith. *steg;* superl. sf. *-ĭṣṭha*, e.g. *lágh-iṣṭha-s*, cf. ἐ-λάχιστος (here *th* has become *ṭh* acc. to sound-laws after *ṣ*). Sometimes *th* stands for *t* without being caused by preceding *s*, thus *tha*, termn. 2 sg. pf., e.g. *babhár-tha* (thou hast borne) could hardly have had an *s* inserted bef. it; as a √termn. in √*prath* (be wide, broad), 3 sg. *práth-atē*, *prth-ús* (πλατύς) ; √*math*, *manth* (move), 1 sg. pres. *math-nămi*, *mánth-āmi*, where origl. *st* must not be assumed.

Note 1.—The unoriginality of *th* is shown by the fact that it does not appear at the beginning of words (except in the few onomatopoëtic or unused and unorigl. words given in Lexx.).

Note 2.—It appears that after *k* (in those cases where *t* though part of a sf. was not felt to be such) this *t* passed into *s;* *s* however in these instances becomes *ṣ* (v. post. § 55, 2), e.g. *ŕkṣa-s* (bear)=ἄρκτο-ς, *ursu-s* for **urctus* (cf. post. sub Lat.) ; st. *tákṣan-* (carpenter)=τέκτον- ; √*kṣan* (slay) further fmn. fr. *kṣa*, cf. κτεν in κτείνω ; √*kṣi* (dwell), Gk. κτι (ἀμφι-κτί-ονες, dwellers-around, κτί-ζω, build), etc. Contrariwise, e.g. *uktá-s* (said), past part. pass.; *vák-ti*, 3 sg. pres. √*vak̑*, origl. *vak* (say, § 52. speak) ; st. *çak-tár-* (fut. part.), *çak-tá-* (past part.), √*çak* (know, be able), etc.

3. Origl. *p*=Sk. *p, ph*.

Sk. *p*=origl. *p*, e.g. √*pa* (drink, protect), whence *pá-ti-s* (lord), *pi-tár-* n.sg. *pi-tá́* (father); √*par* (fill), 3 sg. pres. *pi-par-ti*, whence *pūr-ṇá-s* for *par-na-s (plenus) ; √*spaç* (see, spy) in *spaç-a-s* (spy), *vi-spaṣṭá-s* (perspicuos) for *vi-spaç-ta-s (past part. pass.) ; √*tap*, 3 sg. pres. *táp-ati* (heat, burn) ; √*sarp*, 3 sg. pres. *sárp-ati* (serpere, ire), etc.

Sk. *ph*=origl. *p*, esp. after *s*, e.g. *sphaṭī* (alum), *sphāṭika-s* (crystal), cf. German *spat;* √*sphur*, 3 sg. pres. *sphur-áti* (shake, in Vēd. the root means 'strike, push'), clearly fr. *sphar, cf. σπαίρω, ἀ-σπαίρω, O.H.G. *sporo* (spur), *spor* (track) ; *phéna-s* (foam), cf. Scl. *pĕna*, Lith. *pĕna-s* (milk); Lat. *spūma*, provided it comes fr. *spoi-ma, would here also point to *sp*, in *phĕ-na-s* etc. we must therefore assume a root *spi*, etc. For the rest, *ph* is not frequent in initio.

The aspiration of tenues after *s* is not, however, by any means universal, as is shown by the common combinations *sk* (*skánd-ati*, scandit), *st* (*str-ṇắti*, sternit), *sp* (*spr̥ç-áti*, touches).

Origl. mom. sonant unasp. consonn. § 53.

1. Origl. *g*=Sk. *g, ǵ* (*h*).

Sk. *g*=origl. *g*, e.g. √*ga* (go) in *ǵá-gā-ti*, *ǵi-gā-ti*, 3 sg. pres., *ga-tá-s* (past part. pres.), *á-gā-t* (3 sg. aor.) ; *yugá-m* (iugum) ; *grabh*, *grah* (seize), etc.

Sk. *ǵ*=origl. *g*, e.g. *ǵi-gā-mi* (βίβημι), 1 sg. pres. √*ga* (go) ; *yu-ná-ǵ-mi*, 1 sg. pres. √*yuǵ* (iungere), cf. parallel *yug-á-m* with *g* preserved; √*ǵan* (gignere), e.g. *ǵán-as*=Lat. *gen-us*, 1, 3, sg. ind. pf. *ǵa-ǵắn-a*=γέγονα, γέγονε; *ǵñā-tá-s*=*(g)nō-tus*, √*ǵñ́a* fr. *ǵan*, origl. *gan*, etc.

Note.—Bef. *t* in many cases we find not the gutt. but an un-origl. *ś*, e.g. *sr̥ṣ-ṭá-s*, past part. pass. √*sarǵ* (do) ; *mā́rṣ-ti*, 3 sg. pres. √*marǵ* (cleanse, wash away). Sometimes also *ǵ* is inter-changed with *ḍ* and *ṭ*, acc. to the quality of the following sounds.

§ 53.   In more cases in Sk. *h* (=*gh*) stands where Gk. and the other langg. point to origl. *g*, so that in Sk. we must assume an unorigl. aspiration, e.g. st. *mah-ánt-*, i.e. **magh-ant-* (big), but parallel to it *maǵ-mán-* (strong), cf. Gk. μέγ-ας, μέγ-ιστος, Goth. *mik-ils* (big), Lat. *mag-nus;* indeed beside it stands Sk. √*mah*=*magh* (to wax), which exactly corresponds to Goth. √*mag* (can, be able); *hánu-s* (jaw)=Gk. γένυ-ς, Goth. *kinnu-s* (chin), cf. Lat. *gena*, and (dens) *genu-inus; ahám*, i.e. *agham=ἐγώ, Goth. *ik*, Lat. *ego; gha, ha*=Gk. -γε, Dôr. -γα, Goth. -*k* (in *mi-k*=*μe-γε). In all these cases Gk. γ=Goth. *k* are in favour of origl. *g*.

2.   Origl. *d*=Sk. *d*, e.g. √*da* (dare), 3 sg. pres. med. *dá-da-tē*, 2 sg. imper. med. epic *dá-da-sva*, 1 sg. pres. act. *dá-dā-mi* ; √*dam* (domare), e.g. *dam-á-s, dám-ana-s* (domans, coercens), 3 sg. pres. *dām-yá-ti* ; √*vid* (uidere), e.g. 1 sg. pres. *véd-mi*, 1, 3, sg. pf. *véd-a*=Foîδa, Foîδe ; √*sad* (sidere, considere), e.g. 3 aor. sg. *á-sad-at*, etc.

Note.—*d* in *pīḍ* (press) and *nīḍá-* seems to have arisen from *sd*, namely in case of *pīḍ*, which is proved unoriginal through *ī* and *ḍ*, comes fr. *pisd, *pi-sad=*api-sad*, cf. πιέζω=*πι-σεδψω= *ἐπι-σεδ-ψω ; bes. *nīḍá-s, nīḍá-m*, stands Lat. *nīdu-s*, which may very likely be for *nisdus (cf. *iu(s)-dex, i(s)dem*; v. sub Lat. 'consonn.'), to which Teutonic *nest* points ; *nisda-s would then have arisen from *ni-sada-s, and mean "down-sitting," unless it belong to √*nas*, on which point v. Curt. Gr. Et.² no. 432, p. 282.

3.   Sk. *b* (cf. § 46, 3), which may be held unorigl., occurs, e.g. in *bala-m* (force), with which is usually classed O. Bulg. *bolij* (greater) ; √*lab, lamb* (labi), 3 sg. pres. *lámb-atē*, Lat. *lab*.

§ 54.   Origl. mom. sonant asp. consonn.

1.   Origl. *gh*=Sk. *gh, h.*

Sk. *gh*=origl. *gh*, e.g. √*agh* in *agh-ám* (ill, sin, origl. prob. anguish) ; √*stigh*=στιχ (step), 3 sg. pres. *stigh-nuté* ; *mégh-á-s* (clouds), cf. √*mih*, sub '*h*'=*gh* ; *dīrghá-s* (long)=δολιχό-ς, etc.

Sk. *h*=origl. *gh* ; e.g. *hãsá-s* (goose), cf. χήν, Germ. *gans*, Lith. *żąsìs*, Pol. *gęś* ; √*āh*=*angh* in *āh-ú-s* (snake), *áh-as, āh-atìs* (pain) ; √*vah* (uehere), 3 sg. pres. *váh-ati*, for *vagh*, cf. Goth.

√vag; √mih (pour out, mingere), 3 sg. pres. mḗh-ati for migh, § 54.
cf. supr. mēghás, Gk. √μιχ; √lih (lick), 3 sg. pf. li-lḗ-ha,
cf. λιχ, etc.

Note 1.—In nakha-s, nakha-m (nail, claw), cf. ὄνυχ-ος, Scl.
nog-ŭtĭ, Goth. *nag-l-s, kh stands most strangely where we should
have expected gh.

Note 2.—ǵh occurs rarely, e.g. ǵhasá-s (fish); in other Indo-
Europ. langg. no similar example is yet known; ǵh occurs most
often in initio in onomatopoëtic words.

2. Origl. dh=Sk. dh, h.

Sk. dh = origl. dh, e.g. √dha (set), 1 pres. dá-dhā-mi, cf.
τί-θη-μι, Goth. √da: √idh (kindle), 3 sg. pass. idh-yátē, cf. Gk.
αἴθ-ω; √rudh (rubere) in rudh-irás (ruber), cf. Gk. ῥυθ, Goth.
rud; mádhu (honey, mead, intoxicating drink), cf. μέθυ, etc.

Sk. h=origl. dh, e.g. in hi-tá-s for *dhi-ta-s fr. *dha-ta-s, past
part. pass. √dha (set), cf. θε-τό-ς; √rah (rah-itá-, forsaken,
bereaved; ráh-as, ntr. secret, hidden) for *radh, cf. √λαθ (λαθ-εῖν,
escape notice; λάθ-ρα, secretly); √guh (hide) for *gudh, cf. √κυθ
(κεύθ-ω, hide); -hi for -dhi, sf. of 2 sg. imper. act., e.g. pā-hí
(tuere), but Vēd. çru-dhi=κλῦ-θι; in Sk. this -dhi occurs after
consonn. only, e.g. ad-dhi, √ad (edere), but -hi after vowels.

3. Origl. bh=Sk. bh, rarely h.

Sk. bh=origl. bh, e.g. √bhar (ferre), 1 sg. pres. bhár-āmi, cf.
Gk. φέρ; √bhu (become, be), 3 sg. pres. bháv-ati, cf. φυ;
bhid (findere), 3 sg. pf. bi-bhḗd-a, cf. Lat. √fid; nábhas (air,
heaven), cf. νέφος; √bha, 3 sg. pres. bhā́-ti (gleam), cf. φα,
φα-ν, etc.

Sk. h=origl. bh, e.g. √grah, Vēd. still grabh (seize); má-hyam
bes. tú-bhyam (dat. sg. pers. pron. 1 and 2), cf. mi-hi bes. ti-bi;
bh has disappeared entirely in instr. pl. of a-st., e.g. áçvāis for
*açva-bhis (v. 'declens.').

In roots which end in aspp. an origl. initial asp. loses the
aspiration; e.g. √bandh (bind), 3 s.g. pres. badh-nā́-ti, pf. ba-
bándh-a for *bhandh, Goth. band, Gk. πενθ for *φενθ; bāhú-s

§ 54. (masc. elbow) for *bhāhu-s, cf. Norse bōgr, Gr. πῆχυ-ς for *φηχυς;
√budh (learn, know), 3 sg. pres. budh-yátē, bódh-ati, cf. Goth.
√bud, Gk. πυθ for *φυθ; √druh (hurt), 3 sg. pres. druh-yáti for
*dhrugh, Zend drug, druǵ, druž, but O.H.G. trug, i.e. earlier
drug, are in favour of initial dh. Cf. the reduplication-law
(§ 59, 3).

CONSONANTAL PROLONGED SOUNDS.

§ 55.   Spirants y, s, v.

1. Origl. y=Sk. y, e.g. pron. √ya (rel.), n. sg. masc. ya-s;
ya is further a frequent st.-formative element, e.g. mádh-ya-s=
med-iu-s; the same part. fms. the opt., e.g. s-yā-t = s-iē-t;
further, as one part of the pres. stem which comes fr. as (esse),
and serves to form the fut., e.g. dā-s-yá-ti=δώσει fr. *δω-σ-ye-τι;
ya forms derivative vbs., e.g. bhárá-ya-ti, 3 sg. pres. vb. causat.
√bhar (ferre)=φορεῖ fr. *φορε-ye-τι; √yu, yuǵ (iungere), cf. Lat.
√iug, whence yugá-m=Lat. iugu-m; yúvan-, acc. sg. yúvān-am,
cf. Goth. juggs (same meaning), Lat. iuuenis: yákṛt (liver), cf.
Lat. iecur (id.).

The connexion between y and i is treated in § 14, 1, d; the
splitting up of y to iy, īy, in § 14, 1, c; change fr. y to iy, īy,
v. § 15, 2, b.

2. Origl. s=Sk. s, ś.

Sk. s=origl. s, e.g. √sad (sedere), e.g. sád-as ntr., sád-ana-m
(sedes); sáp-tan-, Vēd. saptán-=septem; √su (beget, sow), e.g.
su-tás, past part. pass.; √sru (flow), 3 sg. pres. sráv-ati: svásar-,
acc. sg. svásār-am (sister); √svid (sweat), 3 sg. pres. svid-yáti;
√star (sternere), 3 sg. pres. str-ṇáti; √smar (remember), 3 sg.
pres. smár-ati; √as (esse), 3 sg. pres. ás-ti; √vas (dwell), 3 sg.
pres. vás-ati; √vas (clothe oneself), 3 sg. pres. vas-tḗ; in st.-
and word-formative particles, as mán-as (ntr. mens)=μέν-ος; -s
is an element of nom. masc. and fem., e.g. vṛ́ka-s, pl. vṛ́kā-sas
(wolf, wolves), etc.

Sk. ś=origl. s, e.g. √uš (ur-ere), cf. us-tus, 3 sg. pres. óš-ati;

√*tarš* (thirst), 3 sg. pres. *trš-yáti*, cf. Lat. *torr-eo*=*tors-eo, § 55.
Germ. *durs-t*; *š* also sporadically after *a*, e.g. √*bhāš* (speak),
3 sg. pres. *bhā́sate*, further fmn. of √*bha*=Gk. *φa* in *φá-τι-ς*,
φá-σι-ς (speech), *φη-μί* (say); bes. *bhās*, 3 sg. pres. *bhā́sate*
(shine, gleam), further fmn. of a similarly sounding √*bha*=Gk.
φa in *φaίνω* (show, make clear)=*φa-ν-yω, *φá-σι-ς* (showing); *š*
thus stands to *s* as palatal to gutt.; it is initial in *šaš* (sex) only,
but cf. Zend *khašvs*, a fm. which renders doubtful the originality
of the initial sound of this numeral in the other langg. of our stock.

Origl. *s* has moreover undergone many more changes in Sk.;
these changes, however, did not occur generally till a relatively
late period; *s* before *t* (*th*) and *p* (*ph*) and after *a* (except in fine)
remains fixed; after *k* and *r*, *š* stands for *s*; likewise after *i, u*
(and their diphthongs, generally after other vowels, as after *a, ā*);
medially bef. most sounds (bef. all vowels and *y, v, m, t, th*;
̥ and ̄ bef. *s* do not break this sound-law); fr. st. *bhūti-*
(=*φυσι-*) thus comes loc. pl. *bhū́ti-šu* for *bhūti-su; *nē-šyáti* (3 sg.
fut. √*ni*, lead) for *nai-syati; *é-ši*, f.f. *ai-si* (2 sg. pres. √*i*, go);
vák-ši (2 sg. pres. √*vak̓*, speak) but *át-si* for *ad-si (2 sg. pres.
√*ad*, eat) and *tá́-su* (loc. fem. pl. *ta*, pron. dem.); st. *dhánus-* (bow),
loc. pl. *dhánu̥-šu* or *dhánuš-šu* for *dhanus-su; with sf. *mant*,
dhánuš-mant-, n. sg. *dhánuš-mān* (provided with a bow).   Betw.
s and *š* there is nevertheless great vacillation (particulars must
be relegated to Sk. special. gr.; it is enough to note here that *š*
=origl. *s*).

̥, *r*, *ç*, occur, like *š*, acc. to definite sound-laws, in place of *s*;
yet mainly in termn. alone, in which case *-as* also may pass
into *ō*, and *s* be lost, e.g. *vrkḁ* for *vrka-s* at end of a sentence, or
bef. *k, p*; *avir ēti* for *avis ēti* (ouis it); *r* occurs for *s* bef. all
sonant sounds unless *a* or *ā* precede; *-as*, however, bef. sonants
becomes *ō*, and *-ās* becomes *ā*; this latter also medially, e.g.
çā-dhi for *çās-dhi, 2 sg. imper. fr. √*çās* (rule), but 3 sg. imper.
çás-tu; *aviç k̓arati* (the sheep goes); *vrkṓ bhavat* for *vrkas abhavat*
(the wolf was); *vrka āstē* for *vrkas āstē* (the wolf sits), etc.

§ 55.   In stems ending in -*s* these changes take place before case-sff.
also which begin with a conson., e.g. st. *mánas*-, g. *mánas-as*,
without change; but instr. pl. *mánōbhis* for *manas-bhis, loc.
pl. *mána°̥-su* for *mánas-su*, which also occurs, *dhánur-bhis* for
*dhanus-bhis, st. *dhánus-* (bow).

š bef. *s* passes into *k*, e.g. √*dvis* (hate), 2 sg. pres. *dvék-ši* for
*dvěš-ṣi; also the change to *ṭ*, *ḍ* occurs, as in the case of *ç*, e.g.
dviḍ-ḍhí, 2 sg. imper. act. √*dviš* for *dviš-dhi. Cf. Sk. grammars.

Note.—In *çváçura-s* (father-in-law), *çvaçrū-s* (mother-in-law),
ç stands in initio (by assimiln. to follg. *ç*), instead of *s*, cf. Zend
qhaçura- i.e. **svaçura-*, ἑκυρό-ς, Lat. *socer, socrus*; similarly in
st. *çúška-* (dry) for **suska-*, cf. Z. *huska-*, O.Bulg. *suchŭ*, f.f.
sausa-s, Lith. *saúsa-s*; *ç* for *s* occurs besides in other single cases
bef. *v* and *u*.

3.   Origl. *v*=Sk. *v*, e.g. √*vid* (perceive), 3 sg. pres. *vét-ti* for
*vēd-ti; √*va* (blow), 3 sg. pres. *vá-ti*, cf. Goth. √*va*; √*vah*
(uehere), 3 s.g. pres. *váh-ati*, cf. Lat. *ueh*, Goth. *vag*, Sclav.
vez, etc.; √*var* (cover), 3 sg. pres. *vr-ṇóti*, whence *úr-ṇā* (wool)
for *var-nā, cf. Gk. Fέρ-ιον, Sclav. *vlŭ-na*, O.H.G. *wol-la*, etc. ;
√*var* (will), cf. Lat. *uol* (uelle), Goth. *val* (will), etc. ; *ávi-s*=Lat.
oui-s, ὄFι-ς; *náva-s*=Lat. *nouo-s*, νέFo-ς, etc.

On the connexion betw. *v* and *u*, v. § 14, 1, c, d.

§ 56.   Nasals.

1.   Origl. *n*=Sk. *n*, e.g. *na*, *an-* (negation); √*naç* (perish),
3 sg. pres. *náçyati*, cf. νεκ; st. *nar-, nara-*, n. sg. *nā* for *nars,
nara-s (ἀ-νήρ); *nāu-s*=ναῦς; *ná-man-*=Lat. *nō-men-*; *dánta-s*
(dens); often *n* is changed into another nasal, e.g. *pūr-ṇá-s*
(plenus, cf. supr. *ū*=*a*, § 8), f.f. *par-na-s*, *ṇ* for *n*, since *r* precedes,
v. post.; *gñā-tás*=*gnō-tus*, origl. fm. of √*gña* is gan, on *ń* for *n*,
v. post.; *yuṅgánti* (iungunt), √*yug*, with inserted nasal, but
yuṅkté, 3 sg. med. with *ń*, since *k* follows, v. post.; *lump-áti*=
rumpit, has nasal *m* because *p* follows; *hāsá-s*, cf. *hanser*, Germ.
gans; *mā-si*, 2 sg. pres. act., *mā-syátē*, 3 sg. fut. med. √*man*
(mean), with ˘ for *n* acc. to Sk. sound-laws, etc.   All these
changes must have been wanting in Indo-Eur. origl. lang.,

because clearly either the nasal was not yet within the root, but § 56. stood after it, acc. to the formative principles of Indo-Eur. (v. Introduction, 2), and so the fms. in question were still perh. *yug-nanti, yug-natai,* or else *n* and *m* remained unchanged, e.g. *man-si,* etc.

Bef. case-termns. which begin with consonn., *n* as a noun-st.-termn. disappears, e.g. st. *nắman-* (nomen), loc. pl. *nắma-su* for **nāman-su (*nāmā̃-su).* This sort of loss of *n* takes place in other like cases also.

2. Origl. *m*=Sk. *m,* e.g. √*man* (mean, think), whence *mán-as* (mens)=μέν-ος; *mā-tár-*=*mā-ter-*; √*smar* (remember), cf. Lat. *me-mor* with lost *s;* √*vam,* Lat. *uom-ere,* 3 sg. pres. *vám-ati;* in st.- and word-formative particles thus sf. *man,* e.g. *nắ-man-*; *m* as sign of acc. case, e.g. *áçva-m*=*equo-m;* *-mi, -masi, -mas,* 1 sg. pl. e.g. *ế-mi,* pl. *i-más,* earlier *i-mási*=εἰ-μι, ἴ-μεν, etc.

The nasals *n, m* have, as the above exx. show, undergone many variations in Sk. because they always adapt themselves to the quality of the succeeding consonn. Accordingly bef. gutt. mom. *ṅ* only is found; bef. palatals is found *ñ,* this sound occurs also immediately after *k̂, ĝ;* bef. lingg. and (acc. to distinct soundlaws) where ling. sounds *ṣ, r,* precede in a word, *ṇ* is found; *n* has its place bef. dentt. and vowels; *m* bef. labb. and vowels (these two origl. nasals only are found in the beginning of a word); bef. *s* and *h,* ˘ is found. Particulars belong to Sk. special-gr.

r- and l-sounds.   § 57.

r was softened to *l* in many cases at an early date; sometimes the earlier lang. retains *r* where the later already has *l.*

Sk. *r*=origl. *r,* e.g. √*ram,* 3 sg. pres. *rámatē* (he is pleased); √*rik̂* (separate), 3 sg. pres. *ri-ṇá-k-ti* (with inserted *na*); √*ruk̂* (shine), 3 sg. pres. *rốk̂-atē;* √*mar* (mori), e.g. *mr-tá-s,* past part. pass. (mortuos); √*par* (fill), 3 sg. pres. *pi-par-ti;* st. √*krp-* (fem. appearance, beauty), √*karp,* cf. *corp-us,* Z. *keref-s;* in sff., e.g. *rudh-i-rá-s*=ἐ-ρυθ-ρό-ς; sf. *tar,* Lat. *tor;* *tra-m,* Lat. *tru-m,* etc.

§ 57.   *Note.*—In termn. *r* was treated like *s*; at the end of a sentence it becomes ꞅ, etc., cf. § 55, 2.

Sk. *l*=original *r*, e.g. *lŏk*, 3 sg. pres. *lŏk-atē* (see), doubtless akin to *ruk* (shine), cf. λευκ-ός and λεύσσω = *λευκ-yω; √*lup* (break), 3 sg. pres. *lumpáti*, cf. Lat. √*rup;* √*kalp* (be in order), 3 sg. pres. *kálpatē*, cf. *krp;* √*lih*, λιχ, Lat. *lig*, Erse *lig*, Goth. *lig*, Lith. *liž*, Scl. *liz* (lick), but in earliest Indian still *rih*. Also where the kindred langg. show no *r*, we must yet assume an origl. *r*, because we notice that *l* is continually spreading, whilst *r* becomes rarer; if we suppose this process to have been going on continuously in pre-historic times, *r* will remain as the older by elimination; cf. Zend. Such instances are found in e.g. *plu* (float), Lat. *plu*, Gk. πλυ, Scl., Lith. *plu*, Germ. *flu* (in *flu-ž*, in diall. *fleu-e* (wash); here precisely it happens that *l*—so frequently interchanged with *r*— occurs throughout; whilst in Sk. there is still a root *pru* (go) in existence, which origly. was prob. identical with *plu*, and must be considered as its earlier fm.

§ 58.   Sketch of some sound-laws important for comparative grammar (so far as they are not contained in foregoing sections).

Between the various ways in which the Indo-Eur. sounds make their appearance in particular Indo-Eur. langg. (i.e. those changes of origl. sounds through which this or that distinct lang. arose from their common fundamental lang., e.g. Sk. *vák-am*, Gk. *Fóπ-a*, Lat. *uŏc-em*, fr. f.f. *vāk-am*), and the variations which the sounds undergo during the separate existence of the lang. thus produced, namely sound-laws, we can draw no sharp line of demarcation. The distinction between sound-representation and sound-law is chronological, and therefore indeterminate, and the exact definition of the date at which a sound-change occurred is generally difficult. For this reason, and also in order not to break up the subject too much, I have often above left the boundary between sound-correspondence

and sound-law ill-defined; moreover, sound-laws—as peculiar to § 58.
the separate-life of a lang.—belong here only in so far as they
bear upon our knowledge of older word-forms.   The numerous
laws, e.g. in Sk., which come into play only when words
are composed into sentences, may here be mostly omitted, since
we are treating of words taken separately.

We find, esp. in written lang., forms of different periods
beside each other, e.g. Sk. *yuk-tá-s* for *yug-ta-s, √*yuǵ* (iungere),
after an earlier mode of formn. than *iš-ṭá-s* for *ig-ta-s, *ik-ta-s,
f.f. *yag-ta-s*, √*yaǵ* (open, v. § 53, 1, n.); here the sound-law by
which *ǵt* becomes *sṭ* is clearly later than the preservation of the
origl. combination *gt*, i.e. *kt* (bef. *t*, *k* must naturally occur for *g*).

Generally speaking we may call the Sk. very rich in conson.
sound-laws; its conson. system is thus manifoldly unorigl. from
this point of view also.   Consonn. often exercise influence on
one another, not only in the middle of words, but also between
the end of one word and the beginning of another when they
are combined in a sentence, a process which we can scarcely
attribute to the lang. at this early condition; the laying-
down of these laws belongs, as we have said, in a great measure
elsewhere.

MEDIAL SOUND-LAWS.

1. Assimilation.   § 59.

a. Medially also sometimes occurs complete assimilation of a
preceding to a follg. sound, e.g. *bhinna-* for **bhid-na-*, past part.
pass. √*bhid* (split); *panna-* for **pad-na-*, likewise fr. √*pad* (go,
fall), and so often in similar cases.

b. Lightening of conson.-groups by loss of one sound is like-
wise not rare, e.g. *kašṭē* for *kakš-tē (*ṭ* for *t* on acct. of *š*, v. sqq.),
3 sg. pres. med. √*kakš* (see), etc.; *á-tut-ta*, 3 sg. med. aor.
compos. √*tud* (push) for *a-tut-s-ta, and so frequently in case of
s betw. two mom. consonn. in like cases.

c. Bef. sonant mom. sounds sonants only, bef. mutes mutes

§ 59. only, are found, e.g. st. *vāk* (voice), instr. pl. *vāg-bhis*; *yu-ná-ǵ-mi*, 1 sg. pres. √*yuǵ* (iungere), but 2 sg. *yu-ná-k-ši*, 3 sg. *yu-ná-k-ti* for *yunag-si, *yunag-ti (cf. § 53, 1); *ád-mi*, 1 sg. pres. √*ad* (edere), but *át-si*, 2 sg. pres. *át-ti*, 3 sg. pres. for *ad-si, *ad-ti, ; *bhárad-bhis*, instr. pl. fr. st. *bhárant-* (ferens) for *bharat-bhis fr. *bharant-bhis, etc.

The influence of spirant *s* on follg. mom. sounds has been already handled under '*s*.' In the case of the combination of *š* with a follg. *t*, *th*, the latter becomes assimild. to *s* because it is a lingual, e.g. superl. sf. origl. *is-ta*; fr. *yans*, compar. sf. shortened *is+ta*, arises next *is-tha (§ 51, sqq.), and since after vowels other than *a*, *ā*, *š* must occur for *s*, *iš-tha, whereby also *th* becomes *ṭh*, so that in Sk. *ištha* stands for *ista*, e.g. st. *áç-ištha*=Z. *āç-ista-*, Gk. ὤκ-ιστο-, origl. *āk-ista-* (fr. *āçú-*, origl. *āku-*, swift). For the group *çt* occurs *šṭ*, e.g. st. *dršṭá-* for **drç-ta-*, past part. pass. √*darç*, origl. *dark* (see); st. *ašṭa-*, *ašṭan-* (eight), for **açta-*, **açtan-*, f.f. *akta-* (cf. ὀκτώ, octo); *vášṭi* for *vaç-ti, 3 sg. pres. √*vaç* (will, wish).

For the changes of *s* produced by assimiln. v. § 55, 2; by nasals, § 56, 2.

An example of **dissimilation** worth notice is found in the change of *s* to *t* at the end of a root bef. the termn. in *s* of fut. and aor., e.g. √*vas* (dwell), 3 sg. fut. *vat-syáti*, 3 sg. aor. *á-vāt-sīt* for *vas-syati, *á-vās-sīt. Doubled *s* was generally avoided, e.g. *ási*, 2 sg. pres. √*as* (esse), for *as-si*=ἐσ-σί, cf. § 55, 2.

Note.—The *s* of √*vas* (dwell) is origl. and perh. not due to *t*, cf. Goth. √*vas* (remain, be), pres. *ris-a*=*vas-āmi*.

2. The **aspirates** stand bef. vowels and son. prolonged consonn. only, and therefore never in termn. The collision of a sonant gutt., dent., or lab. aspirate with follg. *t* (*th*) is common. In this case the aspp. throw their aspiration on follg. *t*, which in its turn becomes like the preceding sound in that it assumes vocal-sound; fr. sonant aspp.+*t* arise therefore son. unasp. consonn.+*dh*;

accordingly $gh+t=gdh$; $dh+t=ddh$; $bh+t=bdh$, e.g. √$budh$ § 59. (learn, know), step-formed $bōdh+tum$ (infin. termn.)$=bóddhum$; √$labh$ (hold)$+tum=lábdhum$, etc.: h here also often is clearly equivalent in force to gh (cf. § 54, 1), e.g. √duh (milk)$+ta$, sf. past part. pass., composes the fm. $dughdá-s$, further $dug-dhi$ (2 sg. imper.) for *$dugh-dhi$, $dóg-dhi$ for *$dōgh-ti$, 3 sg. pres., collectively formed as sounds from still existing √$dugh$. Other roots (whose initial is not d) also treat their h otherwise, e.g. ruh (increase)$+ta$ (pf. part. pass.) fms. $rūdhá-$; *$lēh-ti$, *$lēgh-ti$, 3 sg. pres. √lih, i.e. $ligh$ (lick), become $lédhi$, etc.; $h+t$, th, dh, here becomes dh, accompanied by lengthening of preceding short vowel: this sound-interchange is accordingly clearly more secondary and later than the change of ht, i.e. ght, into gdh. The aspiration is thus throughout postponed to the follg. consonant.

When the aspiration of a root-termn. cannot remain, e.g. in termn. or bef. s, and the root begins with an origl. sonant un-aspd. conson., the aspn. passes over to the latter, e.g. st. $sarva-búdh-$ (all-knowing), n. sg. should be *$sarva-budh-s$, s is necessarily lost, acc. to termination-laws, dh became t, the aspn. passes over to the b, and the word is $sarva-bhút$; precisely so the loc. pl. $sarva-bhút-su$ fr. *$-budh-su$; h here too was treated like gh, e.g. 3 sg. aor. √duh (milk) is $á-dhuk-šat$, with $š$ for s acc. to rule (§ 55, 2), for *$a-dugh-sat$; likewise where the final aspn. disappears through loss (assimiln.), e.g. $dhēhi$ (2 sg. imper. act.) for *$dhāhi$ (§ 15, e), and this for *$dā-hi$ fr. *$dadh-hi$, *$dadh-dhi$; $dadh-$ for $da-dha-$ is pres. st. of √dha (set), hi, dhi, termn. of 2 sg. imper. act.

3. Law of reduplication. In redupln. the gutt. are changed into palatals: $ka-kára$, pf. √kar (make); of more than one conson. or consonantal double-sounds (aspp.; $h=gh$) only the first was maintained; $dá-dhā-mi$, pres. √dha (set, lay); $gu-hó-mi$, √hu (open; cf. also § 54, 3, sub. fin.); $çu-çráv-a$, pf. √$çru$ (hear); only in case of s+mom. sounds does the second

§ 59. of these sounds remain; *ti-šṭha-ti*, pres. √*stha* (stand), origl.
fm. of pres. is *sṭa-sta-ti*.

In other cases the Sk. still shows a more archaic kind of
redupln. by which gutt. and aspp. remain unchanged; so esp.
in ancient intensive-sts., e.g. *kō-ku* (3 sg. med. *kō-kū-ya-tê*),
√*ku* (raise a cry); *kari-kar-*, √*kar* (make); *bhari-bhar-*, √*bhar*
(bear); *ghani-ghan-*, √*ghan*, *han* (slay, kill); in noun-sts., e.g.
ghar-ghara-s (clatter, crackling), etc. (cf. Benf. G. g. 1864,
st. 39, p. 1539 sqq.).

TERMINATION.

§ 60.   1. In termn. only one conson. is tolerated, of more than one
only the first remains, e.g. st. *vāk* (voice, acc. *vāk-am*) should
be in n. sg. **vāk-s*, or rather (acc. to § 52, 1) **vāk-s*, or (acc.
to § 55, 2) *vāk-š*, wherefore *vāk* is now seen. Since aspp. are
double-sounds, they must lose their aspn.; thus we find, not
*sarva-budh, but **sarva-bhud*, with aspn. transferred (acc. to
§ 59, 2), for which, acc. to the follg. law (no. 2), *sarva-bhút*
with *t* for *d* occurs.

Only *r* + mom. conson can stand *in fine*, a case which nevertheless occurs but seldom; moreover bef. follg. *k*, *t*, *ṭ*, and *kh*,
th, *ṭh*, the combn.˜s stands with their representatives, e.g. *áçvān*,
acc. pl. of n. sg. *áçva-s* (equos), f.f. is **açvāns* or **açvāms*,
hence e.g. *açvās tatra* (equos ibi); *çrí-mān* (pleasant), n. sg.
masc. f.f. **çrī-mant-s*, hence e.g. yet *çrīmāç karati* (felix it; ç
for *s* acc. to § 55, 2); *ásan*, 3 pl. impl. √*as* (esse) fr. **āsant*,
*āsans, *t* is esp. often subject to a change into *s*, as in stems in
-ant, which are interchanged with fms. in *-ans*, further in termn.
of 3 pl. *-us* for *-ant*, hence e.g. *āsās tatra* (erant ibi) for origl.
*āsant tatra. In all other cases, however, *n* only remains acc. to
the general rule.

2. As only mute mom. consonn. (when no distinctly influenc-
ing clearer sound follows upon it; in pausa) could stand *in fine*, the
son. consonn. pass over into the mutes of their quality; hence

for *sarva-búdh, not *sarva-bhud, but sarva-bhút is found.   h, § 60.
i.e. gh, becomes ṭ in termn., earlier k (for g, gh) has been retained in such roots only as begin with d, e.g. fr. lih (licking)
comes in nom. (f.f. ligh-s) liṭ (liḍ bef. sonants), but fr. duh
(milking), dhuk (dhug).

Note.—That palatals are not retained in termn. was remarked
above in § 51, sub. fin.

CONSONANTS OF GREEK.   § 61.

v. Table in § 16.

The consonl. system of the Gk. has retained 1. the origl.
aspirates, not, however, as sonants, but as mutes: χ=kh, θ=th,
φ=ph, these can be proved to be the oldest equivalents of the
Gk. sounds; the pronunciation of χ, φ, as spirants, i.e. χ=
Germ. ch, φ=f, and that of θ as a sibilant (nearly like ts), is of
later origin, and arose first partially and afterwards in all cases.
The passing of origl. sonant aspp. into Gk. mute aspirates is not
inexplicable according to the physiology of sounds. Arendt
(Kuhn und Schleicher, Beitr. ii. 283) conjectures, prob. rightly,
that the un-sonant h of the origl. aspp. gh, dh, bh, changed the
preceding sonants g, d, b, into the mutes κ, τ, π, and indeed no
one will deny that kh, th, ph, are much easier to pronounce than
gh, dh, bh. Thus the Gk. already permits of an assimilation.
Change of sonn. to un-sonn. is seen also in Teutonic (origl. g, d=
Germ. k, t). The agreement of the Indo-Eur. langg. collectively,
and also of those langg. which are nearest of kin to the Gk.,
prevents us from accepting the supposition that the Gk. alone
has preserved the oldest equivalents for the Indo-Eur. aspirates
(that the sounds kh, th, ph, existed in the origl. lang. instead of
gh, dh, bh; cf. esp. G. Curtius, Gr. Etym.² p. 369 sqq.). 2.
Gk. shows a dislike of the origl. spirants; y even, in the earliest
accessible state of the lang., is found merely remaining in its
effects, but lost as a separately existing sound; v is retained

7

§ 61. as F in the archaic lang.; *s* stands its ground only in terminations and bef. and after mutes (ξ, ψ); moreover, when another
sound has assimilated itself to it (*s*); before vowels it becomes
h, and generally falls out between vowels. In Gk. as in all
other Indo-Eur. langg., except Zend, *l* already occurs often
beside *r*.

Generally, therefore, the consonantal-system of the Gk. is
nearer to that of the origl. lang. than that of the Sk. or of
most other Indo-Eur. langg.

As for consonl. sound-laws, the loss of origl. spirants and the
variations which arise through this loss, and through the effects
of origl. spirants on neighbouring sounds, bring about a considerable deviation from the older system of sounds. Assimilation has already acquired a widely extended sway:
dentals generally have fallen away before *s*, *n*, mostly with a
lengthening of preceding vowel. The palatal sounds (*y*, *i*)
already show their influence in many cases (zêtakismos).
Further, but few consonn. are tolerated in termn.; in short,
in its consonantal sound-laws Gk. much resembles a lang.
which is already in a comparatively late stage of existence.

§ 62.   EXAMPLES.

Origl. momentary mute unaspirated consonants.
1. Origl. *k*=Gk. κ, γ, π, τ (*ky*=σσ, cf. sound-laws).

Gk. κ=origl. *k*, e.g. καρδ-ία (heart), cf. Lat. *cord*-, Lith.
szird-is, Scl. *srŭd-ĭce*, Goth. *haírt-ō*, Indo-Eur. lang. collectively
presuppose an initial κ,. Sk. *hrd*- thus stands for *khard-, origl.
kard-; κεῖ-μαι (I lie), κοί-τη (bed), √κι, Sk. çi, Scl. and origl.
ki; κύων, κυν-ός (hound), Sk. st. *çvan*-, origl. *kvan*-; κλυ-τός
(famed), √κλυ (hear), Sk. *çru*, Goth. *hlu*, origl. *kru;* δάκ-νω
(bite), √δακ, Sk. *daç*, origl. *dak;* δείκ-νυμι (show), √δικ, Sk.
diç, Goth. *tih*, origl. *dik;* δέκα (ten), Lat. *decem*, Sk. *daçan*-,
Goth. *taihun*, origl. *dakan*-; λευκ-ός (white), ἀμφι-λύκ-η (morn-
ing-twilight), √λυκ, Sk. *ruk*, origl. *ruk*, etc.

Note.—ξ is merely a character for *ks*, e.g. δείξω (I will show) § 62.
=*δείκ-σω; δεξιός (right)=*δεκ-σιος, *δεκ-τιος, cf. *dexter*, Sk.
dákš-iṇas, etc.

Gk. γ is sometimes a later softening fr. κ, which often
remains beside it (cf. G. Curtius, Gr. Et.² 467 sqq , 600 sqq.),
e.g. √φραγ in ἐ-φράγ-ην bes. pres. φράσσω (fence in)=*φρακ-yω
(v. sound-laws), Lat. *farc-io* (on the difference of meaning
v. G. Curt. Zeitschr. xiii. 399); √μαγ in ἐ-μάγ-ην, μάγ-ειρος
(cook), μαγ-εύς (pastry-cook), but μάσσω (knead)=*μακ-yω,
cf. *mac-erare*, Lith. *mìnk-yti* (knead) bes. *mank-sztýti* (soften),
root therefore *mank* fr. *mak;* μίσγω, μίγνυμι (mingle), bes. Lat.
misceo, Sk. *miçráyāmi;* √πλαγ in πλαγ-ή (blow), ἐξ-ε-πλάγ-ην
bes. πλήσσω (strike), i.e. *πληκ-yω, cf. Lith. *plák-ti* (strike),
pres. *plak-ù*, f.f. *plak-āmi*, etc. (cf. Lat. post).

Gk. π=origl. *k* (cf. G. Curt. in Kuhn's Zeitschr. iii. 401 sqq.),
e.g. √πεπ (cook) in πέ-πεπ-ται, πέψω, i.e. πέπ-σω, πέπ-ων (ripe),
bes. πεκ in πέσσω (cook)=*πεκ-yω, origl. *kak*, Lat. *coc;* πέντε
(five), Aiol. πέμπε, πέμπ-το-ς (fifth), πεμπ-άζειν (count by fives),
Lat. *quinque*, origl. *kankan;* √πο in ποῦ (where), πῶς (how),
πότερος (whether, uter), Iôn. still κοῦ, κῶς, κότερος, Lat. *quo-,*
Goth. *hva-*, Sk. Lith. Sclav. and origl. *ka-;* √ἐπ in ἔπ-ομαι
(follow), origl. *sak*, Lat. *seq;* √Fεπ in Fέπος (word), εἶπον
(I said)=*FεFεπον, *Fοπ-ς (voice)=*uōc-s*, origl. *vak* (speak),
in ὄσσα (voice)=*Fοκya (v. sound-laws), *k* has remained;
√λιπ in λείπ-ω (leave), λοιπ-ός (left over)=Lat. *lic* (linquo),
Sk. *rik*, origl. *rik;* √ὀπ in ὄψομαι (I shall see), ὄμμα (eye),
Aiol. ὄπ-πα=*οπ-μα, Lat. *oc* in *oc-ulus*, Lith. *ak-ìs* (eye), etc.,
but dual ὄσσε=*οκyε, fr. a st. *ὀκι- (eye), Lith. and origl. *aki-*
with *k* retained. Acc. to G. Curt. Gk. π is in 17 cases=
origl. *k*, whilst in 104 cases it remains *k*, thus about one-sixth
of origl. *k* has been changed to π.

Gk. τ=origl. *k* occurs mostly in pronl. and num. stems, thus
τί-ς (who), Lat. *quis-s*, Sk. *ki-s* (in *na-kis*, no one, *mā-kis*, O Bulg.
mā-kis, ne quis), origl. *kis;* τε (and), origl. *ka*, Sk. *-ka*, Lat.

§ 62. -*que*, Goth. -*u-h* for *-*ha*, cf. πό-τε (when), Dôr. πό-κα, ἄλλο-τε
(another time), Dôr. ἄλλο-κα; πέντε (five) bes. Aiol. πέμπε
(see ab. π=k), origl. *kankan*, cf. *quinque;* τέσσαρες (four),
origl. *katvāras*, cf. Lat. *quatuor(es)*, Sk. *katvár-as*, Lith. *keturì*.
This correspondence of sounds occurs but rarely in other roots,
e.g. √τι in τί-ω (honour, valuate), τῖ-μή (honour), τί-νω, τί-νυμι
(punish, fine), Sk. *ki* in *káy-ē* (I punish), *apa-ki-ta-s* (honoured),
origl. therefore *ki*.

2. Origl. *t*=Gk. τ (τy=σσ, v. sound-laws), e.g. τό(τ) origl.
and Sk. *ta-t* (nom. acc. sing. dem. pron. st. origl. *ta-*); √τα,
τεν in τέ-τα-κα, τά-νυ-μαι (stretch myself), τείνω (stretch,
lengthen)=*τεν-yω, origl. and Sk. *ta, tan;* st. τρι- (three) in
τρεῖς, origl. and Sk. *tri-;* √στα (stand), in στα-τός (placed),
στά-σις (setting, revolt), ἵ-στη-μι (set up), origl. and Lat. *sta*,
etc.; √στεγ in στέγ-ος (roof), στέγ-ω (cover), cf. Lith. √*steg*,
origl. *stag;* √πετ in πέτ-ομαι (fly), πί-π(ε)τ-ω (fall), origl. and
Sk. √*pat* (fly, fall); πλατύς (broad), origl. *pratus*, Sk. *prthús;*
suff. το of pf. pass. part., origl. and Sk. *ta*, etc.

The combination κτ is in most cases preserved only in Gk.,
while in other langg. it is softened to *ks*, e.g. st. τέκτον-
(carpenter), Sk. *tákšan-*, cf. O.H.G *dëhsa, dëhsala* (axe); ἄρκτος
(bear)=Lat. *ursus*, by Lat. sound-laws for *urcsus fr. *urctus,
Sk. *r̥kšas*, f.f. *ark-ta-s.

Note.—Upon the very uncommon softening of τ to δ in
Gk. cf. G. Curt. Gr. Et.² p. 469 sqq. It occurs almost without
exception in obscure etymologies, not in words accurately corresponding with their kindred langg.

3. Origl. *p*=Gk. π (cf. π=origl. *k*), e.g. √πο, πι (drink),
in πό-σις (draught), πέ-πο-μαι, πέ-πω-κα, πί-νω (drink); πό-σις
(husband), f.f. and Sk. *pá-tis* (lord); st. πα-τέρ- (father), origl.
pa-tar-, fr. √*pa* (protect); √πλα, e.g. in πίμ-πλη-μι, πιμ-πλά-ναι
(fill), origl. *pra* fr. *par*, e.g. Sk. *pi-par-mi* (1 sing. pres. act.);
πλατύς (broad), origl. *pratus*, Sk. *prthús;* √πλυ in πλέϝ-ω
(sail), πλόϝ-ος (voyage), πλυ-τός (washed), Sk. *plu*, origl. *pru;*

√ἑρπ in ἑρπ-ετόν (creeping thing), ἕρπ-ω (creep)=Sk. and § 62.
origl. *sárp-āmi*, Lat. *serp-o*, origl. *sarp*; ὕπ-νος (sleep), origl.
and Sk. *sváp-nas*, cf. *som-nus=*sop-nus*, etc.

Note 1.—The softening of π to β, likewise uncommon, and
only found in words of obscure etymology, has been treated
of by G. Curt. elsewh. p. 471 sqq.

Note 2.—On unoriginal aspiration of tenues caused by operation of sound-laws, v. 'sound-laws.' Sometimes in Gk. as
in Sk. aspirates make their appearance without visible reason.
This occurs comparatively frequently in the case of π, cf.
ἀ-λείφ-ω (anoint), ἀ-λοιφ-ή (ointment), bes. λίπ-α, λίπ-ος
(grease), λιπ-αρός (greasy, shiny), cf. Sk. √*lip* (anoint), O.Bulg.
lĕp-ŭ (plaster), Lith. *lìp-ti* (cleave to); βλέφ-αρον (eyelid) bes.
βλέπ-ω (glance); κεφ-αλή (head) bes. Lat. *cap-ut*, Sk. *kap-ālas*,
kap-ālam (shell, skull); σαφ-ής (clear), σοφ-ός (sap-iens), cf.
Lat. *sap-io* (smack, am wise), O.H.G. √*sab* (understand; in pf.
int-suab, **ant-suob*, he understands, notices), etc. Moreover,
μόθ-ος (bustle) must not be coupled with Sk. √*math, manth*
(i.e. *mat, mant*, stir, move), and O.Bulg. *męt-ą* (trouble), *męt-ežĭ*
(uproar, tumult). In ἔ-τυχ-ον (I chanced), τυχ-ή (chance),
τεύχ-ειν (prepare), and Iôn. τε-τύκ-οντο (they prepared), τύκ-ος
(mason's tool), we cannot suppose different roots; so too δέχ-ομαι
(receive) bes. Iôn. δέκ-ομαι, δοκ-ός (beam), δοκ-άνη (fork) has
the look of an unorigl. asp. In the perf. this unorigl. asp. has
developed into a kind of medium for stem-formation, v. sub.
Perf. G. Curt. Gr. Et.² p. 439 sqq. has treated at length of
Unorigl. Aspiration in Gk.

Momentary sonant unaspirated consonants.   § 63.

1. Origl. *g*=Gk. γ, β.

Gk. γ=origl. *g* (on ζ=γy, v. sound-laws), e.g. √γεν in γέν-ος
(race), γί-γ(ε)ν-ομαι (I am born, become), Sk. *ģan*, origl. *gan;*
√γνο=*gna* fr. *gan* in γι-γνώ-σκω (I learn), γνώ-μη (thought,
opinion); γόνυ (knee)=Sk. *ģānu*, cf. Lat. *genu*, Goth. *kniu;*
√ζυγ, origl. *yug* (iungere) in ζεύγ-νυμι (I yoke), ζυγ-όν (yoke);
√ἀγ in ἄγ-ω (lead)=Sk. *áģ-āmi*, Lat. *ag-o*, O.Norse inf. *ak-a*,
1 sing. pres. *ek*, pf. *ōk*, etc.

Note 1.—It is only in quite detached cases that Gk. δ seems=
origl. *g* (like τ=origl. *k*); thus prob. δελφ-ύ-ς (uterus) must be

§ 63. placed beside Sk. *gárbh-a-s* (id.), esp. since a form ἀδελφειός corresponds perfectly to Sk. *sa-garbhyas* (co-uterinus) in its formn. It is worthy of note that βρέφος, too (v. sq.), stands close to Sk. *gárbhas*.

Note 2.—On Gk. γ and Sk. *h*, cf. § 53, 1.

Gk. β=origl. *g* (cf. § 68, 1, e) ; √βα in βί-βη-μι, βά-σκω (go) =Sk. and origl. *ga* (go), in Sk. *ǵi-gā-mi*, origl. *ga-gā-mi*, Sk. *gá-kkhāmi*, origl. *ga-skāmi* ; βαρύς (heavy)=Sk. *gurús* for origl. *garus*, βάριστος=Sk. *ǵarišthas*, origl. *garistas* (heaviest), cf. Lat. *grauis*=*garu-i-s, Goth. *kaúrs* (heavy, earnest) for *kaúri-s, and this prob. for *kurv-i-s fr. *karv-i-s; βρέφος (neut. offspring, child), Sk. *gárbha-s* (masc. matrix, offspring), O.Bulg. *žrěbę̇*, *žrěbĭcĭ* (to foal), Goth. *kalbō* (fem. cow-calf) ; Boiôt. βανά =γυνή (wife) with root vowel *a* retained, f.f. of both *ganā*, √*gan* (gignere) ; βάλανος (acorn), cf. Lat. *glans, gland-is* (acorn); βίϜος (life)=Sk. *ǵīvás*, Lith. *gývas*, Goth. *kvius*, f.f. prob. *gigvas* (lively) ; βοῦς (bull)=Sk. and origl. *gāus*; βι-βρώ-σκω (eat), βορ-ά (food), √βορ, βρο, origl. *gar, gra*, Sk. √*gar* (swallow); Lat. *(g)uor-are*, Lith. *gér-ti* (drink), Scl. *žrě-ti* (swallow); ἔ-ρεβ-ος (gloom of lower world), cf. Sk. *rág-as* (gloom, dust), Goth. *rikv-is* (neut. darkness) ; √νιβ in χέρ-νιψ (water for washing hands) for *χερ-νιβ-ς, *χερ-νιβ-ος, Sk. √*niǵ*, origl. *nig*, in Gk. retained in νίζω (wash)=*νιγ-γω.

2. Origl. *d*=Gk. δ (on ζ=δy, cf. § 68) ; √δο, origl. *da* (give), pres. δί-δω-μι, origl. *da-dā-mi*; √δακ (bite), pres. δάκ-νω, Sk. √*daç*, origl. *dak*; √δαμ in δαμ-άω, δάμ-νημι (tame, bind), Sk. and origl. *dam* (domare); δόμος (house), Lat. *domus*, Sk. *damás* or *damám*, Scl. *domu*; √Ϝιδ (see), origl. √*vid* (uidere), pf. Ϝοῖδα (knew), Goth. *vait*, f.f. *vi-vāida*; √ἑδ, origl. and Sk. √*sad* (sedere) in ἕζομαι=*sed-yo-mai; √ἑδ, origl. and Sk. √*ad* in ἔδ-ω, ἔδ-ομαι (eat, shall eat), Lat. *ed-o*, Goth. *it-a*, etc.

3. Gk. β, whose origl. existence can be proved, is found very rarely (cf. § 46), e.g. βλη-χή (bleating), βλη-χάομαι (bleat), Lat. *bāl-are*, Scl. *ble-yǫ*, O.H.G. *blā-ʒan*; βραχύ-ς (short), Lat.

breu-is, fr. *bregu-is, Scl. *brŭz-ŭ; βδέ-ω* (pedo), Bohem. *bzdi-ti*, § 63.
Lith. *bezd-ěti*, Germ. *fist* (flatus uentris sine crepitu), thence
fist-en (flatum uentris emittere), Scl.-Germ. thus with spirant
bef. *d* (whether this spirant was inserted in Germ. or lost in
Gk., H.G. *f* does not correctly correspond to *b* of other langg.),
the f.f. of the root is thus *bda* or *bsda=bad* or *basd*.

Note.—*χ, θ, φ*, instead of *γ, δ, β*, in Gk., is barely seen in one
single certain ex.; even the cases which G. Curt. (Gr. Et.[2]
p. 449 sqq.) allows are more or less doubtful. *Θεός* (god) is
in no way related to *ΔιF-ός* (gen. fr. *Ζεύς*), *δῖος* (godlike), Lat.
deus, diuos, but, as G. Curt. makes probable, to √*θες* (Gr. Et.[2]
p. 450) (pray), in *θέσ-σεσθαι, πολύ-θεσ-τος* (much-implored),
Πασι-θέη (implored by all), *θέσ-φατος* (said by god), *θέσ-κελος*
(godly), *θεῖος* for *θεσιος fr. st. *θεο-*, **θεσο-*, with regular loss of
o bef. origl. suff. *ya*, and loss of *s* (cf. *ἀλήθεια*, i.e. *ἀληθεσια
fr. st. *ἀληθέσ-*), Lat. *fes* in *fes-tus; μέθη* (drunkenness) does
not belong to Sk. √*mad* (be drunk), but to *μέθυ* (n. intoxicating
drink, wine), Sk. and origl. *mádhu* (honey-mead, intoxicating
drink), etc. Only in pf. act. we see in later formations *χ* and
φ bes. *γ* and *β* (*εἴ-λοχ-a* fr. *λέγ-ω, τέ-θλιφ-a* fr. *θλίβ-ω*, etc.,
v. post).

Original momentary sonant aspirated consonants. § 64.

1. Origl. *gh*=Gk. *χ* (on *χy=σσ*, cf. § 68), e.g. *χήν* (goose),
cf. Germ. *gans*, f.f. *gansis*, Sk. *hāsá-s*, i.e. *ghansas, Lith. *ząsìs*,
Scl. *gąsĭ;* √*χυ* in *χέF-ω* (pour), *χύ-σις* (pouring), Goth. √*gu-t*,
H.G. *gu-ſs* (gieſs-en); √*ἀχ, ἀγχ* in *ἄγχ-ω* (throttle), *ἄχ-νυμαι*
(am grieved), *ἄχ-ομαι* (id.) *ἄχ-ος* (pain, grief), *ἄχ-θος* (burthen),
ἄχ-θομαι (am burthened), origl. *agh*, Sk. *āh*, Lat. *ang*, Goth.
aggv; √*στιχ* in *στείχ-ω* (go), *στίχ-ος* (rank), *στοῖχ-ος* (rank,
file), Sk. and origl. √*stigh*, Goth. *stig* in *steigan* (step vb.),
staiga (path, the Sclavo-Lith. do not regard aspirates); √*λιχ*
in *λείχ-ω* (lick), Sk. *lih*, earlier *rih*, i.e. *righ* (lick), Goth. *lig* in
bi-laig-ōn (*ἐπι-λείχ-ειν*); √*μιχ* in *ὀ-μιχ-έω* (urino), *ὀ-μίχ-λη*
(mist), Sk. *mih*, i.e. *migh* in *méh-āmi* (urino), *mégh-ás* (cloud),
Germ. *mig*, e.g. Dutch *mīge* (urina); *δολιχός* (long), Sk. *dīrghás*,
f.f. *darghas*, etc.

§ 64.   In ἐγγύς (near)=Sk. ắhús, i.e. *anghus (narrow),—the Goth. aggvus (narrow) corresponds to the aspirated fms., which we hold to be origl. in this case, since we assign ἐγγ-ύς to √ἀχ, origl. agh, in ἄγχ-ω, ἄχ-ομαι, etc. (so G. Curtius). Other isolated cases in which Gk. sonants, mostly after nasals, stand for origl. aspp., are treated by G. Curtius (Gr. Et.² p. 460 sqq.).

Note.—In νίφ-α (acc. snow), νιφ-ετό-ς (snow-storm), νίφ-ει (it snows), φ stands for χ, cf. Lat. *nix, niu-is,* for *nig-s, *nigu-is, (v. post), *ning-it;* the root had an initial *s* lost in Graeco-Italic, cf. Lith. *snìg-ti* (to snow), *snĕg-as* (snow), O.Bulg. *snĕg-ŭ* (snow), Goth. *snaiv-s* (snow), Zend √çniž (çnaēž-enti, 3 pl. pres. 'it snows,' lit. 'they snow'), Sk. √snih (be damp), f.f. of root is therefore *snigh.*

2. Origl. *dh*=Gk. θ (on θy=σσ, cf. § 68), e.g. √θε, origl. *dha* (set), pres. τί-θη-μι, Sk. and origl. *dá-dhā-mi,* Goth. √da, (do), H.G. *ta,* e.g. in 1 pres. *tuo-m* fr. *ti-tō-mi=dhadhāmi;* μέθυ (intoxicating drink), Sk. and origl. *mádhu,* O.H.G. *mëtu* (mead); √ἰθ in αἴθ-ω (kindle), Sk. and origl. √idh; ἐ-ρυθ-ρός (red), √ῥυθ, Sk. *rudhirás,* origl. *rudhras,* √rudh, Goth. √rud in *raud-s,* H.G. *rut* in *rōt,* Lat. *rūf-us,* etc.

Note.—In θερμός, Sk. *gharmás* (heat), Lat. *formus,* cf. Scl. *grĕ-ti* (to warm), Germ. *warm* fr. *gwarm,* √θερ, θέρ-ομαι (am warm), θέρ-ος (neut. summer), origl. and Sk. *ghar,* θ stands where we should expect χ.

3. Origl. *bh*=Gk. φ; √φα (shine) in φα-ίνω (show), φάσ-ις (a 'showing), √φα (speak) in φη-μί, φά-σκω (say), φά-τις (speech, rumour), φω-νή (voice), Sk. and origl. *bha,* Sk. *bhắ-mi* (shine), *bhā-s* (give light, shine), *bhā-š* (speak), Lat. *fa-ri;* √φερ, 1 sing. pr. φέρ-ω (bear), Lat. *fer, fero,* Sk. and origl. *bhar, bhár-āmi,* Goth. *bar, baira;* √φυ in φύ-ω (bring forth), φυ-τόν (plant), Lat. *fu* in *fu-turus, fu-i,* Sk. and origl. *bhu,* O.H.G. *pi* in *pi-m,* weakened fr. *pu, *pi-um;* νέφ-ος (cloud), νεφελη (a cloud), Sk. *nábhas* (a cloud), O.H.G. *nëpal* (cloud); ὀ-φρύς (eyebrow), Sk. *bhrūs,* O.H.G. *prāwa,* etc.

Note 1.—In √λαβ (λαμβάνω, ἔ-λαβ-ον, take, seize) bes. § 64.
λάφ-υρον (booty), ἀμφι-λαφ-ής (clasping), Sk. √labh (keep, get),
β is very prob. a representative of origl. *bh*, caused perh. by
the nasalized pres. λαμβάνω, cf. supr. ἐγγύς fr. √agh; also
βρέμ-ω (roar) has β for origl. *bh*, cf. Lat. *frem-o*, Sk. *bhrám-āmi*
(swarm, rove). On other isolated exx. cf. G. Curt. Gr. Et.²
p. 460 sqq., Grassmann, Kuhn's Zeitschr. xii. 91 sqq.).
Note 2.—√Fραγ in ῥήγ-νυμι (break, tear), ῥῆγ-μα (rent),
διαρρώξ (broken through) for *δια-Fρωγ-ς has F for origl. *bh*
(as in case-sf. origl. *bhi* the *bh* may even be entirely lost, v. sub.
declens.), cf. Lat. √frag in *frang-o*, *frag-men*, *frag-ilis*, Goth.
√brak in *brik-an* (break), pf. *brak*. The same change occurs
in √Fαγ, ἄγ-νυμι (break), ἀ-αγ-ής (unbroken), cf. Sk. √bhag
in *bha-ná-ǵ-mi* (I break), *bhaṅgi-s* (breakage). It is uncertain
whether the roots *bhag* and *bhrag* are akin.

Roots which origly. began and ended with an asp. also lose
in Gk. their initial asp., whereby there thus arises a tenuis
(cf. sup. § 64). Thus e.g. πῆχυ-ς (fore-arm) stands for *φηχυ-ς,
cf. Norse *bōg-r*, O.H.G. *buoc*, like Sk. *bāhú-s* (arm) for *bhāghu-s;
πυθ-μήν (base) for *φυθ-μην, like Sk. *budh-nás* (floor) for
bhudh-na-s, cf. O.H.G. *bod-am*, Lat. *fu-n-d-us;* πενθ-ερός
(father-in-law), πενθ-ερά (mother-in-law), πεῖσ-μα (bond, halser)
for *πενθ-μα fr. √πενθ for *φενθ (bind), like Sk. *bandh* for *bhandh*
(in Sk. also 'relationship' derived fr. 'bonds,' e.g. *bandh-u-s*,
a relation); so too the Goth. fm. *band* points to this (pres.
bind-a, pf. *band*); √πυθ for *φυθ in πυνθ-άνομαι, πεύθ-ομαι
(learn, ask), Sk. *budh* for *bhudh* (be awake, know, be wise),
Lith. √bud (*bud-ěti* be awake, *bud-rú-s* wakeful), O.Bulg. *bŭd*
(*bŭd-ěti* be awake, *bud-iti* wake), Goth. *bud* (*biud-an* bid,
though with a considerable change of meaning). A perfectly
analogous phenomenon is seen in redupln.-laws (§ 68); cf.
Grassm. Kuhn's Zeitschr. xii. 110 sqq.

CONSONANTAL PROLONGED - SOUNDS. § 65.

Origl. spirants; *y*, *s*, *v* (the changes of origl. *y*, *v* have been
treated at length by G. Curt. Gr. Et.² pp. 491–611).

§ 65.　1. Origl. y=Gk. ι, ε, ζ, ʽ, is lost (on y in ζ, σσ, cf. § 68, 1 b, d, e). From assimiln. of y to other consonn. (κερρω for *κερ-yω, ἐλάσσων for *ἐλαχyων, etc.), it follows that it was not lost till late in Gk. To the existence of y in Gk. evidence is given by the operation of the consonantal beginning of Hom. ὥς (as)=origl. $y\bar{a}t$ (abl. of st. ya-), and that of ἵετο, ἱέμενος, etc., origl. √ya (go); even the writing of F for y in Fότι and Τλασίαϝο proves it, on which point we may follow G. Curt. Gr. Et.² no. 606, p. 354.

a. Gk. ι=origl. y, e.g. in the common st.-formative sf. origl. ya, Gk. ιο, thus πάτρ-ιο-ς (fatherly), origl. $patar$-ya-s; τελείω, thence τελέω (finish), for *τελεσ-yω, pres. fm. in ya fr. st. τελες- (τέλος, neut. end), etc., vid. § 26.

Here there occurs also a transposition of origl. y after a liquid cons. to Gk. ι before the liquid, e.g. φθείρω (destroy) fr. *φθερ-yω, etc., v. § 26, 3.

b. Gk. ε=origl. y, e.g. κενεός (empty) for *κενyος, as is shown by Aiol. κέννος fr. Sk. çūnya-s beside *κενyo-ς we may infer an origl. $kvanya$-s common to both; στερεός = στερρός (hard, solid) fr. *στερ-yος; θυρεός (door-stone, door-shaped shield) fr. *θυρyος, with origl. sf. ya, fr. θύρα, door. v. § 26, 2.

c. Gk. ζ=origl. y, e.g. √ζυγ in ζεύγνυμι (bind), ζυγόν (yoke), Lat. iug-um, Sk. $yugám$, etc., Lat. Sk. origl. √yug (iungere); ζέω (seethe, intr.), √ζεσ, cf. ἔ-ζεσ-μαι, ζεσ-τός, O.H.G. $jës$-an (H.G. $gären$), f.f. of root is yas; ζέϝα (spelt), Lith. $yávas$, pl. $yavaí$ (barley), Sk. st. $yava$- (grain).

Note.—A d has been here developed bef. origl. y, for ζ=dz or dy, precisely as in other langg. we find a change fr. y to dy, and further to $d\check{z}$, e.g. Lat. $maiorem$, middle-Lat. $madiorem$. It. $maggiore$, i.e. $mad\check{z}ore$; Prākrt $\acute{g}utta$-, i.e. $d\check{z}utta$-=$yukta$-. G. Curtius (Gr. Et.² p. 550 sqq.) compares this dy for y with gv for v, which appears not unfrequently in later periods of speech (e.g. It. $guastare$ fr. Lat. $uastare$). Curt. also adds δι =origl. y, in sf. διο- (e.g. κρυπτά-διος, secret)=origl. ya, and δε=*δy=origl. y in sf. δεο- (e.g. ἀδελφί-δεο-ς, nephew), and further δ=origl. *y* by entire loss of *y* after the δ wh. it pro- § 65. duced, through intermed. step. *δy. This case is indisputable in Boiôt. δυγό-ν (yoke)=*δyυγο-ν=ζυγό-ν=origl. *yuga-m* (yoke) ; further G. Curt. assumes it in δή (iam) for *dyā, *yā, perh. an instr. pron. st. origl. *ya*, cf. Lat. *iam*, Lith. *yaú*, Goth. H.G. *ju*, and others fr. same st.; it then becomes evident that the δ of apparent sf. -ιδ- is nothing but *iy* for *i*, e.g. μή-νι-ος and μή-νιδ-ος fr. μῆ-νι-ς (wrath ; √*ma*, think, also be wroth, sf. *ni*) θέ-τι-ος and θέ-τιδ-ος (each case formed by sf. *ti*), also φρον-τίδ-ος, ἔριδ-ος bes. ἔρι-ν, etc. ; everywhere therefore we must presuppose in these cases a Gk. f.f. such as *μη-νιy-ος, *θε-τιy-ος. Also the sf. αδ and others with δ are due to origl. *y* acc. to Curtius. Though we cannot treat in detail of the deductions of G. Curtius, we may remark in general on his opinion, that whilst *y* is remarkably common in st.-formation of Indo-Eur., *d* is a rare element, so that we see scarcely any other possibility of bringing the above-named Gk. fms. into harmony with those of the kindred langg. The assumption of so many termns. in special cases of later Gk. forms is, however, not perfectly certain; nevertheless that *y*=δ in δυγόν is beyond doubt. Further the dental certainly corresponds to origl. *y* in χθές=*χδές, *χδγες, *χγες=Sk. *hyas* (yesterday), f.f. *ghyas*, cf. Lat. *her-i*, *hes-ternus*, Goth. *gis-tra-dagis*. What we admit in these cases is possible in others too.

d. Gk. ʽ =origl. *y*, e.g. ἧπαρ (liver), cf. Lat. *iecur*, Sk. *yákrt;* ἅγιος (holy), Sk. *yaǵyas* (to honour, worship), origl. √*yaǵ;* ὥρα (season), cf. O.Bulg. *jāre* (n. year), Goth. *yēr*, O.H.G. *jār;* ὑσ-μίν- (retained only in loc. sg. ὑσ-μῖν-ι), ὑσ-μίνη (combat), √ὑς bef. μ for ὑθ=Sk. *yudh* (fight), e.g. in *yudh-ma-s* (fight, fighter), *yudh-māna-m* (fight), which agrees with the Gk. in the sf. also ; ὑμε-ῖς (you), cf. Sk. *yuṣmá-t* (abl. ; it here depends of course from the stem only), Lith. *jūs* (you), etc.

e. In Gk. *y* is entirely lost (cf. § 27), e.g. initial *y* in Aiol. ὕμμε-ς (you), cf. Sk. *yuṣmá-t* (abl.) ; ὅττι in Sappho fr. st. ὁ- =origl. *ya*-. In the middle of words this loss is more frequent; after consonn., e.g. in termn. of fut. -σω for *σyω, cf. Dôr. fm. -σίω=Sk. and origl. *-syā-mi;* betw. vowels the loss of *y* is commonest of all, as in the termns. of derivative vbs. -έω, -άω, -όω, which alike represent the origl. and Sk. *-ayāmi*, e.g. φορέω

§ 65. (bear)=Sk. and origl. *bhār-áyāmi;* in cases like τελέω fr. τελείω,
for *τελεσ-γω, with origl. sf. *ya* fr. st. τελες- (τέλος neut. end),
in -υω for *-υγω (φύω earlier φυίω, f.f. *bhuyāmi,* etc.); in gen.
sg. masc. and neut. of *o*-st., origl. *a*-st., e.g. ἵππου fr. ἵπποο,
and this certainly fr. ἵπποιο, which stands for *ἵπποσγο, origl.
akvasya; πλέον (more) bes. πλεῖον, f.f. *pra-yans,* comp. fr. √*par,*
pra in πολ-ύ- (many), f.f. *par-u-.* Thus in most cases, before
y entirely disappeared, it became *i.*

Note.—The assimiln. of *y* to other consonn., e.g. λλ=λy and
the like, and its combination with gutt. and dentt. as ζ, σσ, is
treated of under ' sound-laws,' § 68.

2. Origl. *s*=Gk. σ, ', is lost.

a. Gk. σ=origl. *s* in termn. and bef. mutes, more rarely
bef. vowels, e.g. √ἐς, origl. *as* (esse), ἐσ-τί, Sk. and origl. *ás-ti*
(he is); st. μενες- n. μένος (might, strength), origl. and Sk.
mánas; sf. of nom. sg. masc. fem. -*s,* e.g. πόσι-ς, ὄψ=Fόπ-ς,
Sk. and origl. *páti-s,* origl. *vāk-s;* sf. gen. sg. -*os,* origl. -*as,*
e.g. Fοπ-ός, origl. *vāk-as,* Sk. *vāk-ás,* etc.; √στορ, Sk. and origl.
star, e.g. in 1 sg. pres. στορ-έννυμι, στόρ-νυμι (spread), Sk.
str-ṇómi, origl. *star-naumi,* etc.; √στα, ἵστημι (set), origl.
sta-stā-mi, Lat. and origl. *sta;* σῦς bes. ὗς (swine), Lat. *sūs,*
O.H.G. *sū;* σέβ-ομαι (be in awe of), σεμ-νός (awful) for *σεβ-νος,
σοφ-ός (wise), and others show likewise init. *s* bef. vowel;
σιγάω (am silent) bes. O.H.G. *swīgēn* has exceptionally σ for
older *sv,* which regularly should become '; it is also found in
σελ-ήνη (moon), fr. origl. √*svar* (shine), and perh. in some
other instt., cf. σέλ-ας (sheen), ἑλ-άνη (torch), with usual
sound-change, fr. same root (cf. G. Curt. Gk. Et.² p. 625).
This σ bes. ', we must prob. consider to be an archaïsm, which
has been partially retained.

b. Gk. '=origl. *s,* when it is initial before a vowel or origl.
v, e.g. √ἑδ, ἕδ-ος, ἕδ-ρα (seat), ἕζομαι (set myself, sit) for
*ἑδ-γομαι, Lat. *sed,* origl. and Sk. *sad* (sit); ἑπτά (seven), Lat.
septem, origl. and Sk. *saptán-;* √ἑπ in ἕπ-ω, ἕπ-ομαι (follow),

Lat. *sequ-or*, Sk. √*sak̃*, origl. *sak;* ὕπνος (sleep), origl. and Sk. § 65. *svápnas;* ἡδύς (sweet), f.f. Sk. and origl. *svādús;* pron. √ἑ, ὁ, in οὗ, οἷ, ἕ (sui, sibi, se), ὅς (suos), origl. and Sk. *sva-;* ἑκυρός (father-in-law), f.f. *svakuras*, Sk. *çváçuras* for *sváçuras*, Lat. *socer*, Goth. *svaíhra*, etc.

Note.—It is not probable that the ' (which regularly represents *s*) in words which origly. began with *sv* compensates for the *v*, and that *s* afterwards entirely disappeared from before it. If the earlier lang. shows F even then, we may prob. assume that the sign of the asp. was not written bef. F, and that we must theref. read Fέ and the like as *hve;* the long duration of *s* in Gk. seems proved by parallel fms. in diall., such as σφός.

Not uncommonly we find medial ' after vowel transferred to initial ' bef. vowel; e.g. ἱερός (strong, holy) fr. *ἰέρος, *ἰσερο-ς =Sk. *iširá-s* (strong, fresh); εἱπόμην fr. *ἐ-έπομην, *ἐ-σεπομην, √ἑπ (follow) for *σεπ, origl. *sak̃;* εἱστήκειν fr. *ἐ-ἑστηκειν, *ἐ-σεστηκειν, √στα (stand), redupld. *sa-sta*, *σε-στα*; εὕω bes. εὕω (kindle), √ὑς, origl. *us*, Sk. *uš* (burn), f.f. *ausámi*, in Gk. first *εὕσω, *εὕώ; ἑώς (dawn) for *ἑώς fr. *εὑώς, *ἐFώς, cf. Aiol. αὕως for *αὑσως (ἠώς by compens. lengthening for *ἀFως), f.f. of st. is *aus-as-*, cf. Sk. *uš-ás-* (f. dawn), fr. same √*us*, Lat. *auróra* for *aus-ōs-a*, likewise, as in Gk., with stepformn. of root; ἦμαι (sit) for *ἦσ-μαι, cf. Sk. *ás-ē* for *ās-mai*, here in Gk. the init. ' became fixed by analogy throughout, and is added also in ἦσ-ται for *ἦσ-ται=Sk. *ás-tē;* ἡμεῖς (we), cf. Sk. *as-má-t*, ἡμεῖς thus stands by compens. lengthening for *ἀσ-μεις, whence the parall. fm. ἄμμες=*ἀσμες, in which the σ has become assimilated to the μ; in ἡμεῖς therefore the real *s* is doubly represented.

Note.—At first sight ἑός bes. σφός and ὅς seems clearly fr. a Gk. f.f. *σFος, viz. ἑός for *ἑός (*ehos*) fr. *ἕ Fος (*ehvos*), and this fr. *ἐσFος, *ἐ-σFος for *σFος, with the favourite vowel-prefix, which does not occur in σφός and ὅς; but when we recollect the Lat. *suus*, earlier *souos*, i.e. *seuos (§ 33, 2), we are

§ 65. led back to a special Gr.-Ital. f.f. *sevos (cf. Lith. sávo fr. an unused *sava-s suus), which necessarily becomes in Lat. souos, suus, in Gk. ἑϝός; then too we must understand τεός=*τεϝός =tuus, i.e. *tovos, *tevos, Lith. táva-s (tuus). Cf. § 26 n.

Sometimes ʿ appears as a later addition; it seems that the sensibility of the lang. to the distinction betw. ʿ (h) and ᾿ (Semit. ʿelifʾ) began to decay rather early (cf. c.), thus e.g. in ἵππος (horse) fr. *ἰκϝος, cf. the extant fm. ἴκκος, Lat. equos, Sk. áçvas, f.f. akvas; that ʿ occurs here only in later times is proved by forms like Λεύκιππος, Ἄλκιππος, which otherwise would have been pronounced *Λευχιππος, *Ἀλχιππος; ὕστερος (later)=Sk. út-taras; ὑ is so frequently an initial sound, for origl. su, sva, that the more uncommon beginnings which would properly be ὑ, followed the analogy of ὑ; here belongs prob. ὕδωρ (water), cf. Boiôt. οὔδωρ, Lat. unda, Sk. ud-am, ud-akám (water), Goth. vatō, Lith. vandŭ (with earlier vad=ud); ὕφ-η, ὕφ-ος (web), ὑφ-αίνω (weave), cf. Germ. √wab (weave), Sk. ûrṇa-vábh-i-s (m. spider, lit. woolweaver), √vabh, fr. which therefore may arise regularly a fm. ubh, Gk. ὑφ; for *ὑδ, *ὑφ, in these words, we must presuppose an origl. vad, vabh, for which through loss of a arose ud, ubh.

c. In Gk. origl. s, or ratherʿ, which arose fr. origl. s, is entirely lost (cf. § 28). This occurs regularly in middle of words betw. vowels, and more rarely in initio bef. vowels, whilst it is regular bef. initial ν and ρ; e.g. μένος, gen. μένους fr. μένεος, *μενεσος, f.f. and Sk. mánasas; φέρῃ fr. *φερεσαι, origl. bharasai; μῦς (mouse), gen. μυός=Lat. mus, muris, both fr. *musas; Ϝιός (poison) for *Ϝισος=Lat. uirus, Sk. viša-s and viša-m; etc. Yet we also find s kept betw. vowels, e.g. δίδο-σαι, τίθε-σαι, ἵστα-σαι.

In initio bef. vowels ʿ has fallen out in ἀ- (for and bes. ἁ-), ὁ=origl. and Sk. sa- (with), e.g. in ἀ-δελφειός, ἀ-δελφός (brother, lit. couterinus, cf. δελφύς uterus); ἄ-λοχος (spouse, consors tori, cf. λέχος, bed); ὄ-πατρος (having the same father, cf. πατήρ), etc., bes. ἄ-πας (all); ἐτεός (true, correct)=Sk. satyá-s; √ἐχ (in ἔχ-ω hold, have)=Sk. *sah* (*sáh-atē*, he holds, carries; this § 65. √ἔχ=*sagh* is confused in Gk. with √*vagh*, uehere); ἰδίω (sweat), Sk. and f.f. *svidyāmi*, bes. ἰδ-ρώς (sweat); ἡδ-ος (pleasure, delight) bes. ἡδ-ύς (sweet)=Sk. and origl. *svād-ús*, √*svad;* οὖλο-ς (Old-Ep. and Iôn.) bes. ὅλος (whole), Gk. f.f. *solvo-s*=Lat. *saluo-s, sollo-s*=Sk. *sárva-s;* ἔ-σταλ-κα, pf. fr. pres. στέλ-λω (place, send) for *ἐ-σταλ-κα, *σε-σταλ-κα; ἔ-σπαρ-μαι, pf. pass. fr. σπείρω (sow)=*σπερ-yω, similarly for *ἐ-σπ, *σε-σπ. We see that the dropping of the *h*-sound, which has taken place throughout in mod. Gk., began even very early (G. Curt. Gr. Et.² p. 612 sqq.). The feeling of the lang. for *h* was weakened even in early Gk. (cf. supr. 2, b.).

Note.—The st. ὀντ- in ὤν=*ὀντ-ς, οὖσα=*ὀντya, ὄν=*ὀντ= origl. *as-ant-*, pres. part. act. of origl. √*as* (esse), only apparently belongs here. The earlier fms. of this part. ἐών, etc., point to a once-existent fm. *ἐόντ-, *ἐσ-οντ-, with √ἐς preserved, fr. which fm. the *s* regularly dropped out, *ἐσ-οντ- thus became ἐοντ-, later the ε fell off, and thus arose ὀντ-.

s falls away bef. *v* in νυός (bride, daughter-in-law), Lat. *nurus*, but O.H.G. *snur, snura*, Sk. *snušā*, O.Bulg. *snucha*, accordingly we must assume also a Gk. f.f. *σνυσο-ς; √νυ in νέϜ-ω (swim), impf. however in Hom. ἔννεον fr. *ἐ-σνεϜ-ον, Sk. and origl. √*snu* (flow, drip).

s is lost bef. ρ in √ῥυ (flow), ῥέω, ῥυτός=Sk. and origl. *sru*, Germ. *stru*, with inserted *t*, in *strōm*, Lith. *sru* and *stru*, Scl. *stru* in *o-strov-ŭ* (περίῤῥυτος, i.e. isle). Also here *s* is preserved by assimiln. to ρ, e.g. ἐῤῥύην, ἔῤῥευσα for *ἐ-σρυ-ην, *ἐ-σρευ-σα.

Also in √μερ in μέρ-μερ-ος (careful), μέρ-ιμνα (care), μάρ-τυς (witness), as in Lat. *me-mor* and Germ. *māri* (felt), the *s* is lost which is preserved in Sk. *smar*, pres. *smárāmi* (I remember, recall). The same loss perh. occurs elsewhere, though σμ was not disliked as an initial sound.

Before other sounds the loss of *s* is rarer, yet cf. ταῦρο-ς (bull), Lat. *tauru-s*, O.Bulg. *turŭ*, with Sk. *sthŭrá-s* (bull), Zend

§ 65. *çtaora-* (larger cattle, draught-oxen), Goth. *stiur* (bull, calf); sts. the interchange betw. στ and τ is prob. merely a dialectical one, e.g. τέγ-ος bes. στέγ-ος (roof), στέγ-ω (cover), Lith. *stóg-as* (roof), *stég-ti* (to cover), Sk. √*sthag*, origl. *stag* (cf. Lat. *teg-o*, Germ. *decken*, √*dak*, without initial *s*). For further exx. of this phenomenon, which is hard to decide upon, vid. G. Curt. Gr. Et.² p. 621 sqq.

The assimiln. of *s* to other consonn. is treated,́ § 68; the loss of *s* with compens. lengthening, § 28.

3. Origl. *v*=Gk. υ, F, which was lost in the later langg.; origl. *v* is expressed by᾿.

a. Gk. υ=origl. *v*, e.g. δύω, δύο, which bes. δώδεκα proves an early Gk. st. δϜο-=Sk. *dva-*; the same holds good in κύων (dog), bes. Lat. *canis* for *quani-s*, Sk. *çvā* (nom. sing. for *çvan-s*, st. *çvan-*, *çun-*), and in some other cases. It is very hard to decide whether *v* or *u* was the origl. here; perh. *uv* (Engl. *w*) is the earliest.

On the Aiolic vocalisation of *v* between vowels (χεύω=χεϜω, etc.), so too on the transposition of *v* near liquid consonants, as e.g. γουνός=Aiolic γόννος from *γονϜος, st. γουυ- (knee), with -ος of the gen. sg., before which υ, that is *u*, passes over into F, δουρός, δούρατος, fr. *δορϜος, *δορϜατος, from which are explained also δορός, δόρατος, by loss of *v*, cf. nom. δόρυ (spear), v. supra § 26 b, 1, 3.

b. Gk. F,[1] which was lost in the later stage,=origl. *v* (cf. § 27), e.g. Foîνος (wine), cf. Lat. *uīnum*, O.Lat. *ueinom*, f.f. of st. *vaina-* (or, acc. to Gk., *vāina-*); Foîκος (house), Lat. *uīcus*, i.e. O.Lat. *ueicos*, Sk. *vēça-s*, origl. *vaika-s*; Fέργον (work), √Fεργ=Sk. *vrǵ*, *ūrǵ*, Germ. *vark* (work, to work), origl. *varg*; √Fιδ (see, know), origl. Sk. *vid*, Lat. *uid*, Germ. *vit*, e.g. in Fίδ-μεν=Sk. and origl. *vid-mási*, Foîδα=Sk. *vēda*, Goth. *vait*,

---

[1] J. Savelsberg, "de digammo eiusque immutationibus dissertatio," pars i. Aquisgrani, 1864; pars ii. 1866.

f.f. *vivāida* ; √*Feπ*, speak=Lat. *uoc* for *uec, Sk. *vak̆*, origl. *vak*, § 65. e.g. in *Féπ-ος* (word)=Sk. *vák-as* (speech) ; *ŏFις* (sheep)=Lat. *ouis*, Lith. and origl. *avìs* ; *ὦον* for *ὠFιον, f.f. *āvya-m*, fr. origl. *avi-s*, Lat. *aui-s* (bird) ; *νέFος* (new)=Lat. *nouus* for *neuos, Sk. and f.f. *náva-s* ; *πλέF-ω* (sail), √*πλυ*=Lat. *plou-o for *pleu-o (pluo), Sk. and origl. *pláv-āmi* ; *ῥέF-ω* (flow), √*ῥυ*, origl. and Sk. *sráv-āmi*, √*sru*, cf. *ῥεῦ-μα* (stream) ; sf. *-Feντ-* = Sk. and origl. *-vant-* (e.g. in *στονό-Feσσαν*=*-Feτ-yαν*, with loss of nasal) ; *ναῦς* (ship), gen. *νᾱFός*=Sk. and origl. *nāus*, gen. *nāv-ás* ; after consonn. e.g. in *δώδεκα* (twelve), *δίς* (twice), for *δFω-δεκα *δFι-ς, st. *δFo-*, *δFι-*, origl. *dva-* (cf. *δύο*) ; *δορός, γόνατος*, fr. *δορFος, *γονFατος, cf. *δόρυ* (spear), *γόνυ* (knee), etc.

Note.—Thus *vy* can disappear in medio betw. vowels ; this occurs in sf. *tav-ya*, formed by *ya* and step.-formn. of stem termn. of abstracts in *tu*, sounded in Gk. as *τέο*, e.g. *δοτέος* (dandus)=Sk. *dātávyas* ; *θετέος* (ponendus)=Sk. *dhātávyas*.

c. Gk. *ʻ*=origl. *v* in *ἕσπερος, ἑσπέρα* (evening), cf. Lat. *uesper*, *uespera* ; *ἴσ-τωρ* bes. *ἴσ-τωρ*, a fm. which we expect according to *Fἴδ-μεν*, st. *Fιδ-τορ-* (knowing, witness), thence *ἱστορ-ία* (questioning, history), √*Fιδ* ; *ἕννυμι* (clothe), *εἷμα* (garment), Aiol. *Féμμα*=*Féσ-ννμι, *Feσ-μα, √*Feς*, cf. Lat. *ues-tire*, Sk. and f.f. of √*vas* : ʻ may, however, here have arisen also fr. *s*, and then been transposed : cf. supr. 2 b.

Note.—In isolated exx. *β*=origl. *v*, *βούλομαι* (I will), which we hold stands for *βολνομαι (cf. Sk. *vrṇė*, f.f. *var-na-mai*) ; to which Aiol. *βόλλομαι* and *βόλλα*=*βουλή* (will, council) seem to bear evidence ; *ου* would thus arise fr. *o* by compensatory lengthening, in place of the lost *ν* ; √*βολ* for *Fολ corresponds to the Lat. *uel, uol* (in *uel-le, uol-t*), Sk. and origl. *var* (choose, will) ; *ὄροβο-ς* (vetch) bes. Lat. *eruo-m*, O.H.G. *araweiʒ*, cf. H.G. *erb/se*. For other exx. of this correspondence of sound v. G. Curt. Gr. Et.² p. 514 sqq. Dialectically *β* for origl. *v* occurs more often, e.g. Lakôn. *βέργον, βιδεῖν*, for *Féργον* (work), *Fιδεῖν* (see), origl. √*varg*, √*vid* ; Lesb. Aiol. *βρίζα* (root), *βρόδον* (rose), for *Fρίζα, Fρόδον*, etc. Yet it is not unlikely that here (except in comb.

§ 65. βρ=Fρ) β is practically only a character representing the v-sound instead of F.

Quite beside the ordinary rule we find σφ=earlier sv in pron. st. σφε-, σφο- (σφεῖς, you, σφέ-τερος, σφό-ς, your)=Sk. and origl. sva-; in σφώ (you two) for *σϜω, *τϜω, fr. σύ, Dôr. τύ, origl. tu (thou); here σφ arises, prob. early, for sp, in consequence of the aspirating force of s (v. sub. § 68); so, too, σφόγγος bes. σπόγγος, σπογγία, which corresponds in root to the Goth. svamms, st. svamma- (Lat. fungus is perh. borrowed fr. Gk.); sp here occurs exceptionally for sv, as takes place sometimes in Zend; in Hom. φή (as) for *σφη, cf. Goth. svē (as), the initial s has been lost (G. Curt. p. 387).

Origl. v is said to be=μ in ἀμνός (lamb) for *ἀϜι-νο-ς, fr. origl. avi-s, Gk. ὄϜι-ς (sheep), and in other single instt. more or less doubtful (G. Curt. p. 521).

Still more doubtful is the change from v to γ (G. Curt., p. 527 sqq.).

On the assimiln. of v to other consonn. e.g. τέσσαρες= *τεσϜαρες, *τετϜαρες, v. 'sound-laws.'

§ 66. Nasals.

1. Origl. n=Gk. ν (cf. sound-laws for medial and final loss of origl. n in Gk.); e.g. νέϜος (new)=Sk. and origl. návas; ναῦς (ship)=Sk. nāus, Lat. nauis; ἀ-νήρ (man), st. νερ-=Sk. and origl. nar-; ἐννέϜα (nine), Lat. nouem, Sk. and f.f. návan-; √νεκ in νέκ-υς, νεκ-ρός (corpse)=Lat. nec in nec-are, Sk. naç, origl. nak; neg. ἀν-=origl. and Sk. an-; √ἀν, origl. and Sk. an (blow) in ἄν-εμος (wind)=Lat. an-imus, cf. Sk. an-ilás (wind); √γεν in γέν-ος (race), γί-γ(ε)ν-ομαι (become)=Lat. gen, origl. gan; √μεν, origl. and Sk. man (think) in μέν-ος (mind, might)=Sk. mán-as; 3 pl. vb. -ντι (-νσι)=Sk. and origl. -nti, e.g. φέροντι, φέρουσι=Sk. and origl. bháranti, etc.

Before gutturals in Gk. the nasal becomes guttural, origl. nk, ng, ngh=Gk. γκ, γγ, γχ; bef. labials it is labial. Accordingly the radical nasal, origl. n, which occurs after the root in the case of certain present-forms, remains, as in τέμ-νω (I cut; cf. aor. ἔ-ταμ-ον), is ν bef. dentt., e.g. λανθ-άνω (escape notice), cf. ἔ-λαθ-ον; it becomes μ bef. labb., e.g. λαμβ-άνω (take), cf.

ἔ-λαβ-ον ; γ bef. gutt., e.g. λαγχ-άνω (get by lot), cf. ἔ-λαχ-ον. § 66. The same interchange is seen besides naturally in compds. where συν- is changed to συμ-, συγ-, according to the quality of the following conson.

Note 1.— √γαμ in γάμ-ος (marry), γαμ-έω (marry), is, like Lith. √*gam* (*gim-ti*, am born, *pri-gim-tis*, nature, *gam-in-ti*, beget, furnish), a further fmn. fr. √γα (γε-γα-ώς), developed early to γε-ν (the meang. 'beget' through that of 'marry'); μ is here not fr. ν in γεν. In γαμ-βρός (son-in-law) for *γαμ-ρο-ς we conjecture a 'popular' etymology fr. γαμ-έω, through which an earlier *γαν-ρο-ς = Lat. *gener*, i.e. *gen-ro-s* (son-in-law), may have passed to *γαμ-ρος; cf. Lith. *žén-ta-s* (son-in-law), f.f. *gan-ta-s*, O. Bulg. *zętĭ* (id.), f.f. *gan-ti-s*, similarly fr. √*gan*; cf. § 75, 2, n.

Note 2.—"Αλλος (other)=Lat. *alius*, Goth. *alis*, we hold to be unconnected with Sk. *anyá-s* (other), with G. Curt., and see in it a fmn. fr. origl. pron. √*ar*. That such a root existed is proved by st.-fmative sf. *ra* (v. post). Corss. (Krit. Beitr. p. 295 sqq.) divides them thus: *a-li-s*, *a-liu-s*, *ǎ-λyo-ς*, because he holds the *a* to represent pron. √*a* (dem. e.g. Sk. gen. sg. masc. nt. *a-syá*), *li*, *lyo*, to be sff. *tā-li-s*, *quā-li-s*.

2. Origl. *m.*=Gk. μ, ν (the latter in termn.), e.g. st. με-, μο-, ἐμε-, ἐμο- (pron. pers. 1)=Lat. *me-*, Germ. *mi-* (in *mi-ch*, *mi-r*), Sk. and origl. *ma-*, thence -μι, pl. -μεν, Dôr. -μες, 1 sg. pl. vb. =origl. and Sk. *-mi*, *-masi* (e.g. εἶ-μι=origl. *ai-mi*, Sk. *é-mi*; ἴ-μεν=Sk. and origl. *i-mási*); μέσσο-ς (μέσος)=*μεθ-yος (v. post, § 68, 1, e)=Lat. *mediu-s*, Sk. and origl. *mádhya-s*, Goth. *midji-s*; st. μήτερ- (mother), Sk. and origl. *mātár-*; √μεν, μνα, origl. and Sk. *man* (think), in μι-μνή-σκω (remember), μέν-ος (mind, might)=Sk. and origl. *mánas*; μέθυ (intoxicating drink), Sk. and origl. *mádhu*, O.H.G. *mëtu*; ἅμα (together, with), ὁμό-ς= Sk. *sama-s* (similar, like), sama-m, samā (ὁμοῦ), cf. Lat. *sim-ilis*, *sim-ul*, Goth. *sama* (same); √Fεμ (ἐμέω)=Lat. *uom* in *uom o*, for *uemo, Lith. *vem* (1 sg. pres. *vem-iù*), Sk. and origl. *vam* (spue, 1 sg. pres. *vám-āmi*). Final *m* becomes ν, e.g. sign of acc. ν=origl. *m*, e.g. τό-ν=Sk. and origl. *ta-m*, cf. Lat. *is-tu-m*; ν=*m* as sf. of 1 pers. sing., e.g. ἔφερο-ν=Sk. and origl. *ábhara-m*.

§ 66. *Note.*—The exx. which are intended to prove medial *ν* to be a representative of origl. *m* (cf. Curt. Gr. Et.² p. 476 sqq.) are all doubtful. Thus e.g. βαίνω (go) fr. *βαν-ψω, which must not be assigned to Sk. √*gam*, but to √*ga*, comes fr. the common formatives of the present st. *na* and *ya*; in χθών (earth), st. χθον-, bes. χθαμαλός (lowly, on the earth), cf. χαμαί (on the earth), Zend st. *zem*- (earth), O. Bulg. *zemya, zemlya*, Lith. *zéme* (earth), the *ν* seems to have penetrated inwards from the termn. : so, too, perh. st. χιόν- (χιών, snow) bes. Lat. *hiem(p)s*, Sk. *hima-s* (snow, cold), Zend st. *zim-, zima-* (winter, cold), O. Bulg. *zima-*, Lith. *žёmà* (winter).

§ 67. r- and l-sounds.

Origl. *r*=Gk. ρ, λ.

Gk. ρ=origl. *r*, e.g. in √ρυθ (be red), Sk. and origl. *rudh*; suff. *-ρο*, Sk. and origl. *-ra*, both in ἐ-ρυθ-ρό-ς (red) = Sk. *rudh-irá-s*, Lat. *ruber*, i.e. *rub-ro-s*, origl. *rudh-ra-s*; √ἀρ in ἀρ-όω (plough), ἄρ-οτρον (a plough), cf. Lat. *ar-o, ar-atrum*, Goth. *ar-yan*, Lith. *ár-ti*, Scl. *or-ati* (plough); √ὀρ in ὄρ-νυμι (rise), Lat. *or*, Sk. *ar* in *r-nómi* (orior); √ρυ, Sk. and origl. *sru*, flow, etc.

Gk. λ=origl. *r*, e.g. in √λυκ in λευκ-ός (white), Lat. *luc*, Germ. *luh*, Sk. *ruk*, origl. *ruk* (shine); √πολ, πλε, Sk. and origl. *par* (fill), in πολύς (many), Sk. *purús* for origl. *parus*, πίμ-πλη-μι (fill); ἐ-λαχύς (small)=Sk. *laghús*; δολιχός (long), Sk. *dīrghás*, Zend *dareghō*, origl. *dargha-s*; ὅλος (whole) for *ὁλϝος, Lat. *sollus* for *soluos*, Sk. *sárva-s*, etc.

§ 68.   Some important Sound-laws.

Medial.

1. Assimilation.

a. Perfect assimiln. of a preceding to a following sound; e.g. of *s* to *ν*, *μ* following, ἕννυμι (clothe)=*ϝεσ-νυμι; Aiol. ὄρεννος (mountainous)=*ὄρεσ-νος fr. ὄρος (mountain), st. ὀρες- sf. *-νο*; Aiol. ἔμμι (am)=*ἐσ-μι; εἰ-μί, ὀρει-νός, represent the double cons. by compensatory lengthening. Not unfrequently consonants which were afterwards lost are preserved in such assimilns., e.g. περίρρυτος (sea-girt) for *περι-σρυ-το-ς, √ρυ § 68. (flow, ρέF-ω) for *σρυ, Sk. and origl. *sru*, Germ. *stru* (with inserted *t*), etc.; ἄρρηκτος (unbreakable, unbroken) for *ἀ-Fρηγ-το-ς, √Fραγ (Fρήγ-νυμι, break, Fρῆξις, rent, for *Fρηγ-τι-ς); φιλομμειδής (freely smiling) for *φιλο-σμει-δης, √μι for *σμι, Sk. and origl. *smi*, O. Bulg. *smi*, etc.

The assimiln. of momentary labb. to following μ is well known; e.g. γράμμα (writing) for *γραφ-μα (γέ-γραμμαι for *γεγραφ-μαι, 1 pf. med. fr. γράφ-ω, write), etc., and the assimilns. which perh. occur only in compds., e.g. συλλέγω, συρρέω, and the like.

In the commonest of these cases, i.e. in assimiln. of all the dentals (including ν) to a following *s*, the double *s* so produced was not tolerated in the later form of lang., even when *s* was medial and followed a short vowel: only the archaic (Hom.) lang. shows such forms as ποσσί fr. *ποδ-σι (loc. pl. fr. st. ποδ-, foot); throughout *s* is the only trace of the process of assimiln., not seldom (especially in nom. sing. and where ντ, νδ, νθ, were originally existent) accompanied by compensatory lengthening of precedg. vowels (cf. § 28), in which cases, perh. not common, we must assume an assimiln. of the ν by resolution into a vowel-sound. This is a well-known sound-law, to which belong such exx. as loc. pl. σώμᾰ(τ)-σι, πο(δ)-σι, κόρῠ(θ)-σι, δαίμο(ν)-σι. The *s* which produces the assimiln. is often unorigl., i.e. has arisen, through the action of a previous sound-law (v. infr.), from τ, e.g. πείσις (feeling) fr. st. πενθ- (cf. πένθος, grief) and suff. -σι-ς fr. -τι-ς. Compensatory lengthening occurs in such cases as εἰδώς=*FειδFοτ-ς, δαίμων=*δαιμον-ς, φέρουσι=*φερονσι fr. φέροντι; ν+dent. must both be lost before *s*, e.g. σπείσω fr. *σπενδ-σω, πείσομαι fr. *πενθ-σομαι, τιθείς fr. *τιθεντ-ς, χαρί-εις fr. *χαρι-Fεντ-ς (φέρων, however, fr. *φεροντ-ς, v. § 28, 3; χαρίεσσα fr. *χαριFετ-yα [v. e], without compensatory lengthening, because no ν was originally there).

Moreover, in this place belong the cases in which the assimiln. takes place together with the loss of the former consonant, e.g.

§ 68. διδάσκω (learn) for *διδαχ-σκω, cf. διδαχ-ή (teaching) ; λάσκω (cry out, speak) for *λακ-σκω, cf. ἔ-λακ-ον ; ἔψευκα for *ἐψευδ-κα fr. ψεύδ-ω (tell lies), etc.

    b. Complete assimiln. of a following to a pre-ceding sound.

    This kind of assimiln. is, like the former, an especial favourite in the Aiol. dialects, whilst elsewhere, instead of the double consonn., compensatory lengthening (§ 28) of the preceding vowel, or transposn. of *v* and *y* generally occurs. Thus F, *y*, and σ become assimilated to a preceding liquid, F and *y* some-times to other sounds also, viz. σ, *y*, to τ, δ ; e.g. γόννος=γουνός =*γονF-ος, gen. fr. st. γονυ- (knee) ; st. πολλό- for *πολFο-, a further fmn. through *o*, origl. *a*, fr. st. πολύ- (many), origl. *par-u-* ; ἵππος (horse) fr. *ἰπFος, ἰκFος (cf. sideform ἴκκος), origl. *ak-va-s*; κτέννω (kill) =κτείνω=*κτεν-yω ; χέρρων=χείρων (worse) =*χερ-yων, etc. In the case of λy the assimiln. has been re-tained in other diall. ; στέλλω (send)=*στελ-yω ; ἄλλος (other) =*ἄλyος, Lat. *alius ;* except ὀφείλω (owe) fr. *ὀφελyω, and perh. a few others ; πτίσσω (peel)=*πτισ-yω (ἔ-πτισ-μαι), cf. Lat. √*pis* in *pinso, pis-tor,* Sk. *piš* (e.g. *pi-náš-ṭi,* Lat. *pinsit*) ; this does not often happen, *s* usually is lost, and also *y* at a later period, cf. supr. § 65, 1, a, e ; πόδ-εσσι fr. *ποδεσϜι, -σϜι=origl. -*sva*, is termn. of loc. pl., ποδε- is the noun-st. fr. earlier ποδ- (foot) ; in this case also the later lang. has only one σ, e g. πόλεσι, γλυκέσι, which never disappears from between the two vowels, because it stands for σσ. τέτταρες, τέσσαρες (four), fr. *τετϜαρες (f.f. *katvāras*), and thence *τεσϜαρες is an ex. of F assimild. to a mom. sound. ττ for τy, θy, κy (apparently γy, v. infr. e, β), χy is produced in the same way, since κy first became τy, as this sound-change occurs in many langg., and the aspiration (of θy, χy) becomes lost before y.

    Thus, e.g. ἐρέττω (I row) fr. *ἐρετ-yω, cf. ἐρετ-μός (oar) ; ἥττων (less, worse) fr. *ἥτyων for *ἥκ-yων, cf. ἥκ-ιστος (superl.) ; ἐλάττων (less, smaller) for *ἐλατyων, and the latter for *ἐλαθ-

γων, *ἔλαχ-γων, cf. ἐλάχ-ιστος and ἐλαχύς. (little). These § 68.
forms in ττ have by-fms. in σσ (v. infr. e, β), and have not
arisen through an unparalleled change of σσ into ττ, but one
produced by·a divergence of diall. in the treatment of the same
fund-fms. as underlie the fms. in σσ. Accordingly, since e.g.
πτίσσω (v. supr.) stands for *πτισ-γω, no t-sound ever was in
existence here, and so no parallel fm. *πτιττω occurs.

δδ, initial δ, for δy, γγ, a sound which did not become δy until
late, is likewise dialectic; e.g. Boiôt. Lak. Δεύς for *Δγευς
(Ζεύς); Boiôt. σφάδδω for *σφαδ-γω fr. *σφαγ-γω (σφάζω, cut
the throat), √σφαγ (ἐ-σφάγ-ην); σαλπίδδω for *σαλπιδ-γω,
*σαλπιγ-γω (σαλπίζω, trumpet); st. σαλπιγ- (σάλπιγξ, σάλ-
πιγγ-ος (trumpet). This also is the explanation of Att. Iôn.
ἔρδω (do) fr. √Fεργ (pf. ἔοργα, i.e. FέFοργα, Fέργο-ν, work),
Goth. vark, for *Fερδ-γω, *Fεργ-γω, from which we ought to have
found *Fερζω acc. to the rule, but this form seems to have been
avoided on account of the unpleasant combination ρζ, cf. Iôn.
Fρέζω, Boiôt. Fρέδδω=*Fρεγ-γω, which differs from *Fερδ-γω
merely in transposition from Fεργ to Fρεγ. So also δ fr. δy is
produced in place of origl. y (v. supr. § 65, c, n.).

The same assimiln. occurs, except in archaic remains such as
ἔρσω, ὦρσα, χέρσος (χέρρος), θάρσος (θάρρος), πέφανσαι (which
perh. is hardly authenticated), beside medial combinations, as
λσ, ρσ, νσ, μσ, e.g. Aiol. ἔστελλα=ἔστειλα=*ἔστελ-σα; Aiol.
ὀρράτω=ὀρσάτω; Aiol. ἐγέννατο = ἐγείνατο=*ἐγενσατο; Aiol.
ἔνεμμα = ἔνειμα = *ἔνεμσα; thus ἔφηνα stands for *ἔφαν-σα
ἤγγειλα for *ἤγγελ-σα, etc. Thus χήν (goose), gen. χην-ός fr.
*χεν-ς, *χενσ-ος, cf. Lat. (h)ans-er, Sk. hã-sas, O.H.G. st. gansi-,
Lith. ẓąsì-s, O. Bulg. gąsĭ; μήν (month), Iôn. Aiol. μείς, gen.
μην-ός fr. *μεν-ς, cf. Lat. mens-is, Sk. mās- (origl. ma-nt-, pres.
part. act. √ma, measure); ὄλλυμι (destroy) stands for *ὀλ-νυμι.

c. An assimiln. of preceding to following sounds.
It is well known that τ and σ can be preceded only by mute
mom. sounds (λεκ-τός, λέκ-σις, i.e. *λεγ-σις, √λεγ), δ by none

§ 68. but sonant mom. sounds (γράβ-δην, √γραφ), θ by none but aspp. (λεχ-θῆναι, √λεγ).

Before ν labb. pass into their nasals, e.g. σεμ-νός (awful) for *σεβ-νος, cf. σέβ-ομαι (I dread), yet they are found, e.g. ὕπ-νος (sleep), in opposition to *som-nus (*sop-nus).

Bef. labb. ν notably passes into the lab. nasal μ (e.g. ἔμ-πειρος for *ἐν-πειρος), bef. gutt. into the gutt. nasal γ (e.g. συγ-καλέω for *συν-καλεω), cf. § 66, 1.

Bef. μ the dentt. τ, δ, θ, often pass into their spirants, e.g. ἤνυσ-μαι fr. ἀνύτ-ω (bring to pass, finish), πέ-πεισ-μαι for *πε-πειθ-μαι, etc.; yet Ιόn. ὀδ-μή occurs beside later ὀσ-μή (smell), √ὀδ; ἴδ-μεν (we know) bes. ἴσ-μεν; ἀριθ-μός, ἀτ-μός, κεκορυθ-μένος, and others, do not show the change to σ.

Further, the change of gutt. κ, χ, before μ into γ is well known, e.g. δόγ-μα, √δοκ; τέ-τυγ-μαι, √τυχ; yet χ often remains, e.g. δραχμή. This law was likewise incompletely applied in the earlier (Ιόn.) langg., e.g. ἴκ-μενος, ἀκαχ-μένος.

Sometimes nasals seem to change preceding mom. sounds into aspp., e.g. λύχ-νος (light, torch) fr. √λυκ (λευκ-ός, white), origl. ruk; ἀκ-αχ-μένος (sharpened, pointed), redupl. √ἀκ (be sharp); cf. ἀκ-ωκ-ή (point), and others.

The same influence is exercised by ρ, λ, in many cases, e.g. suff. -θρο, -θλο, bes. origl. tra, Zend thra (here the spirants have the force of aspp.), e.g. βά-θρο-ν (base), √βα (go); κλεῖ-θρον (lock), fr. κλείω, κλήΐω, κλήω (lock); θέμε-θλον (ground-work), etc., bes. ἄρο-τρο-ν (plough)=Lat. arā-tru-m (ἀρόω, I plough), etc.

Before ι in stem- and word-formative particles (except in Dôr. dial.) τ is changed to σ, e.g. φησί (he says), Dôr. φατί; the -τι of 3rd pers. sing. is kept in ἐσ-τί (he is); the abstracts in -σι-ς for -τι-ς, e.g. φά-σις, in Hom. and tragg. φά-τις (speech); πέψις (cookery, √πεπ, f.f. kak, cook) fr. *πεπ-τι-ς, f.f. kak-ti-s; suff. ya, Gk. -ιο, forming -τya, with stems ending in t-, ta- (the stem-termn. a of ta being lost, which is regularly the case bef. suff. ya), Gk. -τιο, and hence -σιο, e.g. fr. πλοῦτο-ς (wealth) is fmd. Dôr. πλούτ-ιο-ς, and hence πλούσιο-ς (rich); fr. ἐνιαντό-ς § 68. (year), Dôr. ἐνιαύτ-ιο-ς, and hence ἐνιαύσιο-ς (yearly); st. γεροντ- (n. sing. γέρων, old man) with sf. *ya*, Gk. *ια*, makes γεροντία, and thence γερουσία (senate); f.f. *(d)vikati*, Dôr. Fίκατι, εἴκατι (perh. fr. *ἐFικατι), Att. εἴκοσι (twenty); from Dôr. φέροντι, τιθέντι (3 pl.), f.f. *bharanti*, *dadhanti*, come *φερουσι, *τιθενσι, and thence by rule (v. supr.) φέρουσι, τιθεῖσι (Ιôn.), etc. Yet in Att. and Ιôn. is found φά-τι-ς (speech), √φα, and the like.

Also bef. *v* this change of *τ* to *σ* sometimes takes place, thus in σύ for Dôr. τύ (thou), cf. Lat. and Lith. *tu*; suff. -συ-νη, f.f. -*tu-nā*, further fmn. of common abstract sf. -*tu* (-*tv-a*).

d. An assimiln. of following to preceding sounds. *y* in the combn. *dy* is so similar to the preceding dent. sonant *d*, that it becomes a dental sonant spirant (French or Polish *z*), *dy* thus becomes *dz* (acc. to Sclav. or French pronuncn.), written ζ, e.g. Ζεύς fr. *Δγευς=Sk. *dyāus* (√*dyu=div*), cf. early Lat. *Diou-is*; Aiol. ζά=*δγα for διά (through); ἕζομαι (sit, seat myself)=*σεδ-γομαι, √ἐδ=σεδ; σχίζω (split) for *σχιδ-γω, √σχιδ; τρά-πεζα (table) for *τετρα-πεδ-γα (four-footed), cf. Lat. st. *ped-* (*pes*, *ped-is*, foot), etc.

Here belongs the aspiration of origly. unaspirated consonn. through influence of preceding prolonged-(liquid) sounds. In Greek this influence is especially exercised by *s*, cf. Sk. § 52: i.e. *σχιδ-γω, σχίδ-η (splinter), √σχιδ, for and bes. √σκιδ in σκίδ-νημι (divide, scatter), cf. Lat. *scid* in *scindo*, Goth. *skid* in *skaida* (cut), Sk. *k̑hid*, i.e. origl. *skid*, in *k̑hi-ná-d-mi* (slit); πάσχω (suffer) for *πα-σκω or perh. *παν-σκω, √πα in πα-θ (ἔ-παθ-ον), and πε-ν, πέν-ομαι (endure, tire myself), further formations in θ and ν; the σ sometimes disappears before the aspp. which it has called into existence, e.g. ἔρχομαι (come), for *ἐρ-σχομαι, ἐρ-σκομαι, √ἐρ (come, go), cf. Sk. *rk̑hāmi*, also *árk̑hāmi=*ἔρχω, origl. 1 sing. act. *ar-skā-mi*, med. *ar-ska-mai*; κρῑθή (spelt) for *χρῑθη (cf. § 64, sub fine, and 2 infr.), and this for *χρισθη, *χριστη, cf. O.H.G. *gërsta*, etc.

§ 68. The nasals also seem to have this aspirating effect sometimes, e.g. Boiôt. -νθι for -ντι, 3 p. pl. act. vb.; ὀμφ-ή (voice) for *Γομπ-η fr. √Γεπ, origl. *vak* (speak); ἐγχ-ος (nt. spear) fr. √ἀκ (be sharp), cf. ἄκ-οντ- (ἄκων, javelin).

Perh. ρ, λ, are the cause of aspiration in τρέφ-ω (nourish), which thus by assumption may be for *τερφω bes. τέρπω (sate, delight, cf. τέρπεσθαι ἐδητύος), Sk. *tarp* (be sated, delighted), Lith. *tàrp-ti* (thrive); πλάθ-ανος, πλαθ-άνη (flat cake), bes. πλατ-ύς (broad), Lith. *plat-ùs*, etc., πλάτ-η (plate, oar-blade). Concerning 'unorigl. aspiration,' cf. G. Curt. Gr. Et.[2] p. 439 sqq.

e. **Mutual assimilation (complete or partial) of two sounds, each affecting the other.**

a. γy becomes ζ=dz (v. d supr.), as γ bef. y becomes d, y after d becomes z, e.g. κράζω (cry), i.e. *kradzō fr. *κραδyω, and this fr. *κραγ-yω, √κραγ, cf. κέ-κράγ-α; ἄζομαι (dread) fr. *ἄγ-yομαι, cf. ἅγ-ιος (holy); μέζων, μείζων (greater), the latter having, moreover, y transferred to the preceding syll. (cf. § 26), fr. *μεγ-yων, cf. μεγ-άλη, μέγ-ας (great), etc.

In νίζω (wash) bes. χέρ-νιβ-ος (χέρνιψ, water for handwashing), νίπτω (wash)=*νιβ-τω, the earlier root-fm. *nig*, Sk. *níǵ*, is retained (cf. § 63). Λάζομαι (grasp) bes. λαμβάνω (take) is obscure, unless it be the unique ex. of ζ=βy, formed perh. on the analogy of the common fms. in -αζω, -αζομαι.

β. τy, θy, κy, χy, become σσ; in τy and θy, y perh. became the dent. mute spir. s, after dental mutes, whereby arose τς, θσ, then the preceding mute dentt. assimilated themselves to this σ; because σσ=τy, θy, also in Dôr., we must not assume that τy (θy) passed next into σy, as τι into σι (v. sup. c), and this σy into σσ by rule (b), for in Dôr. τ remains before ι; κy, χy, became firstly τy, θy, as of course gutt. so often pass into dentt. bef. y, and then these sounds became σσ in the way above described; e.g. ἐρέσσω (row) fr. *ἐρετ-yω, cf. ἐρετ-μός; κρέσσων, κρείσσων (stronger, better), with transposn. of y (cf.

μέζων, μείζων), fr. *κρετ-γων, cf. κράτ-ιστος; κορύσσω (I arm) § 68.
fr. *κορυθ-γω, cf. κε-κόρυθ-μαι; βάσσων for *βαθ-γων, cf. βαθ-ύς
(deep); πίσσα (pitch)=*πικ-γα, cf. pix, pic-is; ἥσσων (less, worse)
for *ἠκ-γων, cf. ἤκ-ιστος; ἐ-λάσσων (smaller) for *ἐ-λαχ-γων, cf.
ἐ-λάχ-ιστος, ἐ-λαχ-ύς, Sk. lagh-ús.

Not unfrequently σσ has apparently arisen from γy : in these
cases thus much is clear, that in the older state of langg. a
fundamental κ is always found still preserved, and that this κ
was not softened to γ till a later period, after κy had been in-
corporated into a fixed group of sounds ; e.g. πλήσσω (strike)
bes. πέπληγον, πληγή (blow), but origl. √πλακ, cf. πλάξ, πλακ-ός
(flat, plate), Teut. flah, Lith. plăk-ti (strike), whence plók-sztas
(flat, adj.) ; φράσσω (inclose)=*φρακ-γω, but ἐ-φράγ-ην with
softening of κ to γ, cf. Lat. farc-io, etc.   Cf. supr. § 62.

Note 1.—βράσσων must be assigned to βραχ-ύς (short), not
to βραδ-ύς (slow) ; so G. Curt. Gr. Et.[2] p. 600.

Note 2.—Likewise we mentioned in § 62, above, that κy
is still preserved in cases such as πέσσω (cook) bes. πέψω,
πέπων (ripe) ; ὄσσα (voice) bes. ἔπος ; ὄσσε (eyes) and ὄσσομαι
(see) bes. ὄψομαι (*πεκ-γω, Sk. pak̄, Lat. coc ; ὄσσα=*Ϝοκγα,
√Ϝεκ, √Ϝοκ, origl. vak ; ὄσσε=*ὄκ-γε, ὄσσομαι=*ὄκγομαι, √ὀκ,
origl. ak, cf. oc-ulus, Lith. ak-ìs).

f. Apparent insertion of a consonant between two
concurrent consonants.   νρ and μρ, also μλ, as in other
langg. (e.g. French gen-d-re fr. Lat. gener, generum, *genrum ;
nombre fr. Lat. numerus, *numrus ; humble fr. Lat. humilis,
*humlis), become νδρ, μβρ, μβλ, i.e. n and m thereby are joined
with follg. r and l, in an easier combination, because they
preserve the extremities of momentary consonn. ; n becomes nd,
m becomes mb, to which the subsequent r- or l-sound was merely
lightly joined ; e.g. ἀν-δ-ρ-ός for *ἀνρ-ος, gen. st. ἀνερ- (man) ;
μεσ-ημ-β-ρία (mid-day) for *-ημ-ρια, cf. ἡμέρα (day) ; ἄ-μ-β-ροτος
(deathless) for *ἀ-μρο-τος, √μρο=Lat. mor (mori) ; μέ-μβλω-κα
(pf.) for *με-μλω-κα, fr. μολ-εῖν (go, come), √μολ, μλο ; in
βροτός the μ has fallen away from bef. β, βροτός stands for

§ 68. *μβροτος (preserved in ἄ-μβροτος), and this for *μρο-τος, past part. from √mar, mra (mori), cf. Sk. mar-ta-s (a mortal, man, Rigved. I. 84, 8, acc. to Kuhn, Beitr. iii. 236); the same process takes place in βλίττω (cut honey) for *μβλιττω, fr. *μελιτ-γω, st. μελιτ- (μέλι, honey); βλώσκω (go, come) for *μβλωσκω fr. *μλωσκω, √μολ in μολ-εῖν, etc.

Note.—In πτόλις, and such like cases, bes. πόλις (city), cf. Sk. puram, purī, √par (fill); πτόλεμος bes. πόλεμος (war), cf. πελεμίζω (brandish), and Lat. pello; πτίσσω (peel)=*πτισ-γω for *πισγω, √πις=Lat. pis (pinso), Sk. piš, πτ stands for π without any visible cause. They seem to be dialectic fms.

g. The ejection of s from between consonn., e.g. τέτυφ-(σ)θε, is well known.

Loss of s between vowels is treated of § 65. In like cases τ also disappears, but not so often; e.g. κέρως for κέρατ-ος (gen. sing. st. κερατ-, horn); φέρει (3 sing. pres. act.) fr. *φερε-τι, origl. bhara-ti. The dent. nasal also is subject to similar decay in known cases, e.g. μείζους for μείζον-ες (n. pl. masc. fem. st. μειζον-, greater).

h. Transposition, as in θάρσος bes. θράσος, δέδορκα bes. ἔδρακον: it is not easy to ascertain which arrangement is here the primitive one.

Note.—τέ-θνη-κα bes. ἔ-θαν-ον, and the like, are primitive deviations from root-fms., and must not be treated according to Gk. sound-laws. Cf. 'root-formation.'

2. Dissimilation. Here belong the known changes of mom. dent. bef. τ and θ to σ, so as to facilitate pronunciation; this change is found in Eran. Lat. and Sclavo-germ. also, e.g. ἀνυσ-τός fr. ἀνύτ-ω; ἀσ-τέον fr. ἄδ-ω; πεισ-θῆναι fr. πείθ-ω; πισ-τός for *πιθ-τος, etc.

Sometimes two consecutive aspp. are avoided by changing the former or latter into an unasp. conson., e.g. ἐ-τέ-θην, ἐ-τύ-θην, for *ἐ-θε-θην, *ἐ-θυ-θην, √θε, θυ, cf. τί-θη-μι, θύω; σώ-θη-τι for *σω-θη-θι, the termn. of 2 p. sing. imp. is -θι, origl. dhi, cf.

κλῦ-θι, origl. *kru-dhi*, etc. This change scarcely ever takes § 68. place except in the case of θ (in φ and χ perh. only in compds., e.g. ἀμπ-έχω, ἐκε-χειρία).

For a similar phenomenon in the case of root-fms., which origly. began and ended with aspp., v. supr. § 64, sub fine).

Moreover, the attempt to avoid pronouncing similar sounds close together causes the contraction of two similar or like consonn. into one, by means of evaporation of the vowel that lies between them, e.g. τράπεζα (table) for *τετρά-πεζα (four-footed) ; τέτραχμον for earlier τετρά-δραχμον (four-drachm piece) ; ἀμφορεύς (two-handled jug) for earlier ἀμφι-φορεύς, etc.

3. The aspirates. Whenever by sound-laws aspp. which terminate a root become unasp. consonn., the aspiration falls back upon the τ which begins the root; the same change takes place when θ follows upon the root-termn., notwithstanding that the asp. remains before θ, e.g. st. τριχ-, cf. τριχ-ός, but *θρικ-ς, i.e. θρίξ (hair); τρέχ-ω (run), but θρέξομαι ; τύφω (fume), but θύψω ; τρέφ-ω (nourish), but ἐθρέφθην, etc. In cases like the last mentioned the aspiration before the θ appeared to the Greek instinct for language to be caused by it (the θ), and similarly also where the aspiration occurs in the case of e.g. π, β; accordingly the sound that ended the root was only characterized as aspirate by the retrogression of the aspiration upon the initial conson.

For the law by which, in the case of roots which origly. began and ended in aspp., the initial consonn. lost their aspiration, v. supr. § 64, sub fine.

4. Law of Reduplication. Of two initial consonn. the former only was admissible into the syll. of redupln.,—hence the aspp. are redupld. through their first element alone (χ, i.e. *kh*, through κ; θ, i.e. *th*, through τ; φ, i.e. *ph*, through π)— e.g. ἵ-στη-μι (set), i.e. *σι-στη-μι for *sti-stā-mi*; γέ-γραφ-α (have written) for *γρε-γραφ-α ; πέ-φυ-κα (have been born) for *φε-φυ-κα ;

§ 68. τί-θη-μι (place) for *θι-θη-μι; κί-χρη-μι (lend, borrow) for *χι-χρη-μι, and this for *χρι-χρη-μι, etc.

In the case of more consonantal combinations, the first consonant also falls away, so that instead of redupln., only a vowel appears, e.g. ἔ-γνω-κα (have learnt) for *γε-γνω-κα; ἔ-κτον-α (have killed) for *κε-κτον-α, etc.   Cf. Sk. redupln., § 59.

§ 69.   TERMINATION.

The only consonn. tolerated *in fine* in Gk. were ς and ν (generally fr. μ; this is also the case in the N. European langg. of the Teut. stem), e.g. πόσι-ς, origl. *pati-s*; πόσι-ν, origl. *pati-m*; and further ρ also, e.g. πάτερ, voc. f.f. *patar*, n. sing. πατήρ, f.f. *patars* (κ is found only in ἐκ, shortened fr. ἐξ 'out,' and in οὐκ 'not,' which likewise is prob. a shortened fm.).   Other conson. were either cast off, or changed into ς or ν.

Thus the frequent final *t* of Indo-Eur. is thrown off in Gk. (cf. Lat. *nouō* fr. *nouōd*, origl. *navāt*, abl. sing.), or changed to ς, e.g. τό (the, neut.), Sk. and origl. *ta-t*, Lat. *(is)-tu-d*, Goth. *tha-t-a*; ἔφερε (3 sg. impf.), Sk. and origl. *ábharat*; ἔφυ (3 sg. aor.), Sk. *ábhūt*; ἔφερον (3 pl. impf.), origl. *abharant*; φέρον (acc. sg. neut. pres. part. act.) for *φεροντ; τέρας (wonder, sign) for *τερατ, cf. gen. τέρατ-ος; εἰδός (neut. pres. part. act. 'knowing') for *εἰδϜοτ, cf. gen. εἰδότ-ος, etc.   In consequence of loss of final ι, θ became final; when this occurred, θ also became ς, e.g. δός (give) fr. *δοθ for *δο-θι, origl. *da-dhi* (imper. aor. √δο, origl. *da*, dare).   δ drops off: παῖ (voc.) for *παιδ (n. sg. παῖς, child); so also κ in γύναι (voc. woman) for *γυναικ (cf. e.g. gen. γυναικ-ός); κτ in ἄνα (voc.) for *ἀνακτ (ἄναξ, gen. ἄνακτ-ος, lord), γάλα (n. acc. milk) for *γαλακτ (e.g. gen. γάλακτ-ος), etc.   From ντ only τ is lost, e.g. γέρον (voc. fr. n. γέρων for *γεροντ-ς, gen. γέροντ-ος, old man) for *γεροντ.

The final *m* so common in Indo-Eur., esp. as sign of acc. and element of 1st sing. of vb., is usually replaced by ν in Gk., e.g. πόσι-ν, Sk. and f.f. *páti-m;* νέϜο-ν, Sk. and f.f. *náva-m;* ἔφερο-ν

(1 sing.), f.f. and Sk. *ábhara-m*, etc. More rarely it coalesced § 69. with the precedg. vowel; this is probably the reason why precdg. *a* was lengthened, and hence also in the above lang. it remained as *ă*, and did not change into *ε*, e.g. πατέρ-α=*πατερ-ᾱ fr. *πα-τερ-αν, f.f. *patar-am*; ἔδειξα (1 sg. aor.)=*ἐ-δεικ-σᾱ, f.f. of termn. -*sa-m*, cf. Sk. *á-dik-šam*; δέκα, cf. Lat. *decem*, Sk. *dáçan-*, etc.

Where there are more than one consonn. of which *s* is the last, the last *s* is cast off regularly, in the n. sing. generally, with compensatory lengthening, e.g. φέρων for *φεροντ-ς, μήτηρ for *μητερ-ς, ποιμήν for *ποιμεν-ς, εὐμενής for *εὐμενες-ς; yet *s* is retained also, as e.g. in τιθείς, διδούς, etc., fr. *τιθεντ-ς, *διδοντ-ς, and, in known cases, the foregoing sounds also, e.g. φάλαγξ (gen. φάλαγγ-ος, phalanx), λύγξ (gen. λυγκ-ός, cough), φλόξ (gen. φλογ-ός, flame), ὄψ (gen. ὀπ-ός, voice); even ἔλμινς for *ἐλμινθ-ς (gen. ἔλμινθ-ος, intestine worm), πείριν-ς for *πειρινθ-ς (gen. πείρινθ-ος, hamper), ἅλς (gen. ἁλ-ός, salt), which end in displeasing combinations.

The well-known ν ἐφελκυστικόν is no relic of an earlier state of the lang., but a peculiar and late phenomenon in Gk., e.g. ἔφερε-ν, Sk. and f.f. *ábharat* (3 sg. impf.); in these cases the ν does not appear, therefore, until the origl. *t* had already been lost, and the feeling for lang. had become accustomed to treat the form as ending in vowel; φέρουσι-ν, Sk. and f.f. *bháranti* (3 pl. pres.); ποσσί-ν, f.f. *pad-svi* (loc. pl.).

On the 1st pers. pl. of the vb. this ν has taken firm hold; the f.f. of this termn. is -*masi*, hence rose -*mas*, which is kept in Dôr. -μες; through the loss of final *s*—which occurs here and there even in Gk. (in Lat. it is notoriously common), e.g. in οὔτω bes. and for οὔτως (thus)—fr. -μες arose *-με, and upon this was grafted ν, at first prob. ephelkustik, and thus was produced -μεν, e.g. Sk. and origl. *bhárāmasi*, hence Sk. *bhárāmas*, Gk. (Dôr.) φέρομες, *φερομε, φέρομε-ν (we must not think of a change of *s* to *n* in this case, any more than elsewhere throughout the range of the Indo-Eur. lang.).

§ 70.   CONSONANTS IN LATIN.

The table of consonn. is to be found in § 30.

The Lat. lang. is esp. characterized by lack of the aspp., which were represented by the corresponding unaspirated sonants, and by unorigl. spirants f, h; the latter in such a way that f (repres. by b, in medio) may stand for any origl. asp., h almost exclusively=origl. gh.

k (written c, q) remains always unchanged, but here and there drops away in initio; it does not become p or t, as in the other Indo-Eur. langg. The origl. spirants y, s, v, are generally retained, though s very often passes into r, and y and v often drop out, and are interchanged with i and u.

The consonn. are subject to numerous sound-laws: assimilation; dissimilation; change from t to s; from s to r; medial, initial, and final loss (the latter in a still higher degree in archaic Lat.)—all remove the consonantal system of Lat. widely from the origl. condition of the Indo-Eur. lang.

§ 71.   EXAMPLES.

Origl. mom. mute unaspirated consonn.

1. Origl. k=Lat. k, i.e. c, q. Origl. k often attaches to itself a v, by a sound-law not yet understood (cf. Goth.). The written character, with a few archaic exceptions, represents k by c; before u (when other vowels follow $= v$) k is represented by its equivalent q (at an earlier period also before the u which forms the syll., e.g. *pequnia*), e.g. √*coc* in *coc-tus*, *coqu-o* (cook), origl. *kak*, cf. Gk. πεπ, Sk. *pak*; *quinque* (five), origl. *kankan*, cf. Gk. πέντε; √*quo* in *quo-d* (which), etc., origl. *ka*, cf. Gk. πο, earlier κο; *-que* (and), Sk. *-ka*, origl. *ka*, cf. Gk. τε; *quatuor* (four) for **quatuores*, origl. *katvāras*, cf. Gk. τέτταρες; st. *cord-* in *cor* (heart) for **cord*, gen. *cord-is*, origl. *kard*, cf. Gk. κραδ-*ία*; √*qui* in *qui-s*, *qui-d* (what), origl. *ki*, cf. Gk. τί-ς, τί; √*qui* in *qui-es* (rest), origl. *ki*, cf. Gk. κι in κεῖ-ται; √*clu* in *clu-o* (hear),

in-clu-tus (famed), origl. *kru*, cf. Gk. κλυ; √*scid* in *scindo* (split), § 71.
origl. *skid*, cf. Gk. σχιδ; *canis* (hound) for *cvan-is, origl. *kvan-s*,
cf. Gk. κύων, κυν-ός; √*dic* in *deic-o*, *dĭc-o* (say), -*dĭc-us* (saying),
origl. *dik*, cf. Gk. δικ in δείκ-νυμι; *decem* (ten), origl. *dakan*, cf.
Gk. δέκα; √*luc* in *lūc-eo* (shine), *louc-em*, *lūc-em* (n. lux, light),
origl. *ruk*, cf. Gk. λυκ; √*loc* in *loc-utus*, *loqu-i* (speak), origl.
rak, cf. Gk. λακ; √*uoc* for *uec in *uŏc-em* (n. uox, voice), *uoc-are*
(call), origl. *vak*, cf. Gk. Fεπ; suff. -*co*, fem. -*ca*, origl. -*ka*, fem.
-*kā*, e.g. *ciui-cu-s*, *uni-cu-s*, cf. Gk. -κο-ς, etc.

In Lat. as in Gk. (cf. § 62) *k* is sometimes softened into *g*,
e.g. *ui-gin-ti*, *tri-gin-ta*, bes. *ui-cen-sumus*, *tri-cen-sumus* (*uigesi-
mus*, *trigesimus*, cf. εἴ-κο-σι, τριά-κον-τα), -*gin-*, -*cen-*, is here a
relic of *(de)cem*, f.f. *dakan*; *neg-otium*=*nec-otium; *gubernator*
bes. κυβερνήτης, etc.

Note 1.—This is prob. the case also in *glōria* (glory) for
*clōria, *clōsia, a further fmn. of st. *clōs- for *clouos-, *cleuos-
=Gk. κλεFεs-, Sk. çrávas- (glory), Sclav. *sloves*- (n. acc. *slovo*,
word), root origly. *kru* (hear), as Sk. çravas-ya- (famous), cravas-yā
(famousness, Kuhn, Zeitschr. iii. 398), yet the *ō* is strange, for
we should have expected *ū*, cf. *in-iūria*=*ious-ia, fr. *ious*, *iūs*, a
further fm. fr. *iouos, *ieuos.

Note 2.—The pronunciation of *c* bef. *i* became, as in other
langg., that of palat. *k* (perh. like Germ. *k* in *kind*): the
preference for *c* before *i*, where another vowel follows, was the
stronger, because in these cases *i* was nearly the same as *y*, so
that the combinations *cio*, *ciu*, etc., were not only sounded like
kio, *kiu*, but tolerably early (precisely as in other langg. also)
were pronounced *tyo*, *tyu* (Ital. *cio*, *ciu*), whence arose the
common fluctuation in writing about the end of the second or
the beginning of the third century A.D. (Corss. Krit. Nachtr.
p. 48). The change of *i*, *y*, after *t*, into *s*, *š* (*tyo*=*tšo*), does not
occur till the Romance period.

Note 3.—In the pronoml. stems, *hi-*, *ho-* (*hi-nc*, *ho-nc*), notwithstanding the regularly corresponding Sk. **ghi-*, *gha-* (in *hi*,
then, *ha*, *gha*, important particles), ought not prob. to be separated from Goth. *hi-*, *hva-*, Sclav. *sĭ-*, *kŭ-*, Lith. *szi-*, *ka-*, i.e.
origl. *ki-*, *ka-*, on account of the perfect similarity of their functions; further, in √*hab* in *hab-eo*, *hab-ēs*=Goth. *hab-a*, *hab-ais*
(I have, thou hast), cf. Osk. *hip-ust* (habuerit), *haf-iest* (habebit),

§ 71. whose initial conson. is, as in Goth., *k* (Goth. √*hab* also corresponds to Lat. √*cap* in *cap-io*) ; Lat. *h* seems to be origl. *k*, a
permutation which is found sporadically in Sk. *hrd-, hĭd-aya-*
(heart)=origl. *kard-* (cf. Lat. *cord-*, Gk. καρδ-ία, Goth.
haírt-ō) [the antiquity of this *h* in Aryan is shown by Zend *zeredhaêm*
=Sk. *hŕdayam*].   With Bopp, therefore, I now hold the Lat.
pron. stems *hi-, ho-*, to be parallel-fms. to origl. *ki-, ka-*, regularly represented in Lat. by *qui-, ci-, quo-, cu-* (*qui-s, ci-tra,
quo-d, cu-ius*, used as interrog. and relat.), and so, too, √*hab* in
hab-ēre, as a parallel-fm. to *cap* in *cap-ere*, for Goth. *b* can be=
origl. *p*, and *b* may possibly arise in Lat. through softening
from *p* (*bibo*, drink,=origl. *papāmi*).   The correspondence of
Lat. *h* to Goth. *h* remains none the less remarkable, but esp. the
conformity of the two langg. as regards *habēre*, whose perfect
identity, nevertheless, no one denies.   But we must not suppose
words were borrowed in either case.   Other views are found in
Corss. Krit. Nachtr., p. 89 sqq.; Comp., 1st ed., p. 715.

Note 4.—Accordingly *p* is not in Lat.=origl. *k* (but cf. Osk.
and Umbr.); words in which *p* seems=origl. *k* are therefore
borrowed.   Thus *Petronius, Epona*, are Keltic, cf. Lat. *quatuor,
equos* ; *popina* is Osk., cf. Lat. *coquina, coquere* ; *palumbes*, bes.
Lat. *columba*, must prob. be derived fr. Osk., and *limpidus*, too,
bes. *liquidus*, must be a dialectic, and not originally a Roman
by-form, in which case both words, as is often maintained, were
identical; if *lupus* is really=Gk. λύκος, it must therefore also
be attributed to Osk., Sab., or Umb., but beyond doubt it belongs to Zend ; *u-rup-i-s, raop-i-s* (name of wild beasts of the
breed of dogs), √*rup*, *lup* (rend, cf. Spiegel, Zeitschr. xiii. 366);
sap-io (taste of), *sap-iens* (wise), does not belong to *sucus*, Gk.
ὀπός (sap), but to O.H.G. √*sab* (understand, pf. *int-suab* ; Mid.
H. G. pres. *ent-sebe*, pf. *ent-suop*), Gk. σοφ-ός (wise), σαφ-ής
(intelligible, clear), with unorigl. asp. (v. supr. § 62, 3, n. 2) ;
saep-io (hedge in), *prae-saep-e* (crib, stall), does not agree with
Gk. σηκό-ς even in root-vowel (Lat. *ae*=*ai*, Gk. η=ā) ; *trepit*
(vertit ; Paul. Ep., 367 ; Curt. Gr. Et.² 411) seems to be borrowed from Gk. τρέπει.

2., Origl. *t*=Lat. *t* ; e.g. in *tu* (thou), origl. *tu*, cf. Gk. τύ,
σύ ; √*to* in *is-tu-d* (dem.), origl. *ta, ta-t*, cf. Gk. τό ; √*ten* in
ten-tus (held, stretched), *ten-or* (holding, length), *ten-eo* (hold),
ten-do (stretch), origl. *tan*, cf. Gk. τα, τεν ; st. *tri-* (three) in *trēs,
trīs, treis*, origl. *tri-*, cf. Gk. τρι- in τρεῖς ; √*sta* (stand) in *sta-tus,*

sta-re, origl. *sta,* Gk. στα; √*teg* (cover), origl. *stag,* Gk. στεγ; § 71.
√*pet* in *pet-o* (make for), *im-pet-us* (onset), *penna* fr. *pes-na,*
**pet-na,* origl. *pat* (fly, fall), cf. Gk. πετ; √*uert* in *uert-ere*
(turn), origl. *vart* ; suff. *-to,* fem. *-ta*=*-tā,* cf. Gk. -τό-, -τη, e.g. in
da-tu-s, origl. *da-ta-s,* Gk. δο-τό-ς; *-t,* 3 p. sing., *-nt,* 3 pl. vb.,
origl. *-ti, -nti,* cf. Gk. -τι, -ντι, e.g. *fer-t, fero-nt(i),* Sk. and origl.
bhára-ti, bhára-nti, Gk. φέρε-(τ)ι, φέρο-ντι, etc.

Note 1.—On final *t,* cf. § 79 : for Lat. *br*=Gk. θρ, origl. *tr,*
§ 77, 1, c.

Note 2.—The change fr. τι bef. vowels to *ts* (*z*) occurs first in
Romance langg.

3. Origl. *p*=Lat. *p,* e.g. √*po* in *po-tus* (drink), origl. *pa,* cf. Gk.
πο in πό-σις; in *bi-bo* (drink), f.f. *pa-pāmi, p* has been softened
into *b,* a change occurring also in other isolated cases (cf. Corss.
Krit. Nachtr. p. 176 sqq.) ; *po-ti-s in *impos, compos, im-po-tem,*
com-po-tem (unable, able), *po-t-est* (he can), *-po-te, -pte* (a no-
ticeable affixed particle, e.g. *ut-pote, suo-pte*), Sk. and origl.
pá-ti-s (lord), Gk. πό-σι-ς, origl. √*pa* (protect) ; *pa-ter* (father),
origl. *pa-tar-s,* cf. Gk. πα-τήρ, same root; √*ple* in *plē-nus* (full),
origl. *par, pra,* cf. Gk. πλε ; *ped-is* (gen.; n. *pes,* foot), Sk. and
origl. *pad-ás,* cf. Gk. ποδ-ός; √*spec* in *spec-io, spic-io* (see), *spec-ies*
(appearance), Sk. *paç* for **spaç,* O.H.G. *spah* (in *spëh-ōn,* espy,
spāh-i, shrewd), origl. *spak* ; √*tep* in *tep-eo* (am warm), *tep-or*
(warmth), Sk. and origl. *táp* ; √*sop* in *sop-ire* (make sleepy),
som-nus (sleep) for **sop-nus,* Sk. and origl. *svap,* cf. Gk. ὑπ-, etc.

Note.—√*flu, flug (fluc-tus),* a later and further fmn. fr. *flu,* in
**flou-o, flu-o* (flow), does not belong to πλυ, Sk. *plu,* Sclav. *plu,*
etc., for Lat. *f* is not=origl. *p* : this root is represented by Lat.
plu (plu-it, i.e. **plou-it,* it rains) ; perh. Lat. *flu* is to be placed
beside Gk. φλύ-ω (swell, overflow), οἰνό-φλυξ, -φλυγ-ος ; so
Curt. Gr. Et.² 271 ; we can scarcely take *flu* for **sflu,* and this
for *sθlu fr. *stru for *sru* (flow), with Ad. Kuhn (Zeitschr. xiv.
223) ; in the latter case Lat. *fluo,* i.e. **flouo,* stands equal to Sk.
srávāmi, Gk. ῥέϝω ; *flu-men* for **sθroumen, *sθreumen,* essentially
=ῥεῦμα for **σρευμα,* O.H.G. *strou-m,* Pol. *strumień* (running
stream).

§ 72. **Momentary sonant unasp. consonants.**

1. Origl. *g*=Lat. *g, gv (gu), v.*

Lat. *g*=origl. *g*, e.g. √*gen* in *gi-g(e)n-o* (beget), *gen-us* (race), *gna* in *gnā-tus* (one born, son), origl. *gan*, cf. Gk. γεν; √*gno* in *gnō-sco* (learn), *gnō-tus* (known), origl. *gna*, transposed fr. *gan*, cf. Gk. γνο in γι-γνώ-σκω; *genu* (knee), cf. Gk. γόνυ, Sk. *g̑ánu*, Goth. *kniu*; √*ag* in *ago* (drive), origl. *ag*, pres. *ag-āmi*, Gk. ἀγ in ἄγ-ω; √*iug* in *iugum* (yoke), *iung-o* (join), Sk. *yug̑, yug*, origl. *yug*, cf. Gk. ζυγ, etc.

Lat. *gv (gu)*=origl. *g*. As origl. *k* developed into *qu (kv)*, so also *g* (=origl. *g* and *gh*, cf. § 73, 1) into *gv*: this *gv* is, however, retained only after *n*; it also occurs after *r*, bes. *g*, in *urgueo* bes. *urgeo* (urge), √*urg*, origl. *varg*, cf. Sk. *varg̑* (shut out), Lith. *vèrž-ti* (urge). Between vowels this *g* has become assimilated to the *v* (without lengthening of a previous short syll.), so that the *v* alone therefore remains. In this way it happens that Lat. *v* betw. vowels may be origl. *g* and *gh*, e.g. √*uig* for **guig*, cf. Germ. *quick* in *uixi* (pf.)=**uig-si*, *uic-tus* (diet)=**uig-tus*, but *uīu-os* (alive), *uīu-o* (live) for **uigu-os*, **uigu-o*. For further exx. of this interchange of sound v. sub '*gh*' (v. Corss. Krit. Beitr., p. 68, on interchange of *g* and *gv* in Lat.).

Note 1.—*fluxi, fluc-tus, con-flūg-es* (confluence), bes. *fluo*, i.e. **flou-o* (flow), show indeed a further fmn. of √*flu* to *flug*, as Gk. φλυ to φλυγ (§ 71, 3 n.); we see, however, no ground for the assumption that *fluo, *flou-o*, together with *fluu-ius* (river), have passed through fms. **flogu-o, *flugu-ium* (Corss. Ausspr. etc., i.¹ 44). In this case the root-fm. is preserved without *g*.

Note 2.—Cf. exx. cited under *gh*, § 73, 1, and sound-laws, § 77, 1. a.

Note 3.—In *bos, bouis* (ox)=Gk. βοῦς, βοϜός=Sk. *g̑āus* (gen. *gōs* prob. represents origl. *gav-as*), cf. O.H.G. *chuō*, *b*=origl. *g*, a correspondence of conson. otherwise foreign to Lat.; accordingly the word is probably borrowed. G. Curt. Gr. Et.² nos. 639, 642, brings forward *super-bus, super-bia* (proud, pride), which he takes to stand for **super-bios*, as=Gk. ὑπέρ-βιος (overween-

ing), -βία (presumption), -βιος however=Sk. *ǵi*, pres. *ǵáy-āmi* § 72.
(triumph), f.f. *gi*; *bo-ere*, *bou-are* (cry, sound), *re-bo-are* (re-
sound), with Gk. βο-ή (call, cry) fr. Sk. √*gu* (let sound), Old
Bulg. *gov-orŭ* (noise); *super-bus* is, however, not precisely similar
to ὑπέρ-βιος, a word compounded according to Gk. principles
(for we should then be obliged to consider it borrowed), but
rather a special Lat. fmn. like *acer-bus*, *mor-bus* (Corss. Krit.
Beitr. 61), and *boare* with βοή need not by any means be referred to Sk. *gu*, O. Bulg. *gov-orŭ*. It seems to me to be a mere
imitative sound.

Note 4.—*c* and *g* were not distinguished in earlier Lat. writing,
but prob. in the spoken lang. only.

Note 5.—Bef. *n* we are now accustomed in pronunciation to
change Lat. *g* to gutt. *ṅ*, i.e. the *g* becomes assimild. to *n*, according to its scale, becoming nasal : instead of *mag-nus*, *dig-nus*,
etc., we say *maṅ-nus*, *diṅ-nus*. This is the same interchange of
sound which is seen quite early in the lang., e.g. in *Sam-nium*
for **Sab-nium*, *som-nus* for **sop-nus*. Spellings such as *singnum*
make it probable that even as early as the times of the later
Cæsars, people had begun to pronounce *signum* as *siṅnum*. Yet
we cannot consider this pronuncn. of *gn* as *ṅn* to be ancient,
because the Roman grammarians do not mention it. From this
later pronunciation of *gn* we must distinguish the principle on
which *gn* was treated in Romance langg., where it became a
palatal *ń*, e.g. Ital. *magno*, *degno* (pron. *maño*, *deño*), Fr. *magne*,
digne (pr. *mań*, *diń*). Therefore the above-named pronunciation
of Lat. *gn* cannot have arisen through Romance influence.

2. Origl. *d*=Lat. *d*, rarely *l*.

Lat. *d*=origl. *d*, e.g. √*da* in *dă-tus* (given), Sk. and origl.
√*da*, cf. Gk. δο; √*dom* in *dom-are* (tame), Sk. and origl. √*dam*,
cf. Gk. δαμ-άω; *dom-us* (house), Sk. and origl. *dam-as*, cf. Gk.
δόμ-ος; *dent-em* (tooth, acc.), Sk. and origl. *dánt-am*, cf. Gk.
ὀ-δόντ-α; √*uid* in *uid-ere* (see), Sk. and origl. *vid*, Gk. Ϝιδ;
√*ed* in *ed-o* (eat), Sk. and origl. *ad*, cf. Gk. ἐδ; √*sed* in *sed-eo*
(sit), Sk. and origl. *sad*, cf. Gk. ἑδ, etc.

Lat. *l* = origl. *d in initio*, and, more rarely, medially bef.
vowels, e.g. *lacrima* (tear) fr. *dacrima* (Festus), cf. δάκρυ, Goth.
tagr, O.H.G. *zahar*; *lēuir* (father-in-law), cf. δαήρ-, st. δαερ-, for
*δαιερ-, **δαιϜερ-* (Ebel, Zeitschr. vii. 272), Sk. st. *dēvár-*, n. sing.

§ 72. *dĕvá*, also *a*-st. *dēvará-s*, O.H.G. *zeihhur*, Lith. *dĕveri-s* (known to me through the Dictionary only), O. Bulg. *dĕverĭ; lingua* (tongue), earlier *dingua*, cf. Goth. *tuggō*, Germ. *tunge; ol-ere* (smell) bes. *od-or* (scent), cf. ὄξ-ωδ-α, ὀδ-μή, ὀσμή. Sometimes both the *d-* and *l*-forms remained extant; thus *im-pel-imentum* bes. *im-ped-imentum* (hindrance), fr. st. *ped-* (pes, foot); *de-lic-are* bes. *de-dic-are* (dedicate), √*dic (dīc-o*, δείκ⸴-νυμι, etc.), etc.

3. Lat. *b* may be origl. *b* (v. § 46, 3), e.g. in *bal-are* (bleat), cf. Gk. βλη-χή (a bleating), βλη-χάομαι, Sclav. *blĕ-ja͟*, O.H.G. *blā-ʒan* (bleat), an onomatopoëtic word; *breuis* (short), corresponding to Gk. βραχύς, Sclav. *brŭzŭ* (quick); √*lab* in *lāb-itur* (glides, sinks), *lap-sus*=*lab-tus* (past part.), Sk. √*lab*, *lamb* in *lámb-atē* (he sinks, falls).

§ 73. **Momentary sonant aspirated consonants.**

Note 1.—*f* may represent any of the aspp., and is placed mainly *in initio;* medially *b* occurs instead of *f;* yet *rūfu-s* (red), *scrofa* (sow), *Afer* (African), *sifilus* and *sifilare* (Fr. *siffler*, Zeitschr. xvi. 382) bes. usual *sibilus* (whistling, piping), *sibilare* (to whistle, pipe), etc., with medial *f* betw. vowels, according to the principles of the other Italian langg., whose influence perh. made itself felt in these words (Corss. Krit. Nachtr. p. 194, sqq.). In *signi-fer, pesti-fer*, and the like, *f* evidently arises from the perceptible connexion with *ferre*, whilst in *ama-bam*, etc., fr. √*fu (fui*, etc.), origl. *bhu* was no longer felt.

Note 2.—*ch, th, ph*, are not Latin but Gk. sounds, which did not come into use till a comparatively late period, and are yet unknown in the earlier lang. Further details as regards the history of these ways of spelling belong to the special gr. of Lat.

1. Origl. *gh*=Lat. *g, gv (gu), v, h, f*.

Lat. *g*=origl. *gh*, e.g. √*ger, gra*, in *ger-men* (bud),=Lith. *żel-mŭ̆*, st. *żel-men-* (sprout), *grā-men* (grass), origly. a side-form of *ger-men*, cf. O.H.G. *gruo-ni* (green), *gra-s* (grass), Sk. *hár-it-*, *har-ita-* (green), Zend *zairita-* (yellowish-green), Gk. χλο-ή (green, grass), O. Bulg. *zel-enŭ* (green), Lith. *żél-ti* (grow green, wax), *žál-ias* (green), *žol-é* (grass, greens), origl. √*ghar, ghra* § 73. (be green, yellow, grow green); *grā-tu-s* (pleasant), cf. Osk. Umbr. √*her* (wish), χάρ-ις (grace), χαίρω, i.e. *χαρ-yω (rejoice), Sk. *har-yāmi* (love, desire), Germ. √*gar* (desire), e.g. in O.H.G. *gër-ōn* (desire), origl. √*ghar, ghra; grando* (hail) bes. Sk. *hrād-unī,* Gk. χάλαζα, i.e. *χαλαδ-ya, *χλαδya (v. § 29, 1), origl. root therefore *ghrad;* except before *r* and in *ger-men* Lat. *g=gh* is confined to the middle of words; √*ang* in *ang-o* (throttle, kill), *ang-ustus* (narrow), *ang-or* (pain), *ang-īna* (quinsy), origl. √*angh,* Gk. ἀγχ ἀχ in ἄγχ-ω, ἄχ-νυμαι, ἄχ-ος, Sk. *ah, āh,* Goth. *agg,* origl. *agh;* √*lig* in *lig-urio, li-n-g-o* (lick), origl. *righ,* Sk. *rih, lih,* Gk. λιχ in λείχ-ω, λίχ-νος, Goth. *lig;* √*mig* in *mi-n-g-o, mēio,* for *migio,* origl. *migh,* Sk. *mih,* Gk. μιχ in ὀ-μιχ-έω, ὀ-μίχ-λη.

Lat. *gv (gu), v=*origl. *gh* (cf. § 72, 1, and § 77, 1, a), e.g. *angu-is* (snake), *angu-illa* (eel), cf. Gk. ἔχ-ις (viper), ἔγχ-ελυς (eel), Sk. *ah-is,* i.e. *agh-is,* Lith. *ang-ìs* (snake), *ung-urýs* (eel), O.H.G. *unc* (snake); in *nix* (snow), i.e. *nig-s* fr. *snigh-s,* gen. *niu-is* for *nigu-is, *snigh-as,* is found—as also we see fr. Lith. √*snig,* in *snìg-ti* (to snow), *snẽg-a-s* (snow), and Gk. νίφ-α (snow, acc.), νίφ-ει (it snows)—an origl. √*snigh* as a basis, which is clearly shown in Sk. *snih* (be moist); *breu-is* (short) for *bregu-is,* Gk. βραχύς; *leu-is* (light) for *leguis,* cf. ἐ-λαχύς, Sk. *laghú-s.* In *breuis* and *leuis* the correspondence of *v* to *gu* ought prob. to be explained as occurring through change of origl. *gh* to *gv,* but rather through the introduction of a secondary *i* into the previously existing stems *bregu-, legu-,=braghu-, raghu-.* Nevertheless even thus the origl. *gh* is involved in the *v,* because the *gh,* or rather its Lat. equivalent *g,* has become assimild. to the *v.*

Note.—Therefore *g* may represent both origl. *gh* and *g;* in such cases as *mag-nus* (great) bes. μέγ-ας, *ego* (I) bes. ἐγώ (§ 64, 1), we must not permit ourselves to determine that Lat. *g* is = origl. *gh,* merely on account of Sk. *mah-ánt-, ahám,*

§ 73. since the corresponding Goth. fms. *mik-ils*, *ik*, show the unasp. conson.

Lat. *h*=origl. *gh*, esp. *in initio*, very rarely *in medio*, e.g. *hiem-ps* (winter), cf. Gk. χιών (snow), χεῖμα (storm), χειμών (winter), Sk. *himá-s* (snow, cold), Sclav. *zima* (winter, cold), Lith. *żëmà* (winter); *homo* (man), earlier *hemo*, st. *homen-*, *hemen-*, cf. Goth. *guma* (man), st. *guman-*, Lith. *żmů*, st. *żmen-* (mankind), which collectively point to a f.f. *ghaman-*; *holus*, *helus*, *heluola* (greens), √*ghar* (be green), cf. χλο-ή, Sk. *hár-ita* (v. sub *g*=*gh*); *haed-us* (he-goat, Cod. Medic. Vergili), cf. Goth. *gaits* (f. she-goat), O.H.G. *geiʒ*, the initial conson. of this word was therefore *gh*; √*veh*, pres. *ueh-o* (carry, draw), √*vagh*, pres. *vagh-āmi*, Sk. *vah*, pres. *váh-āmi*, Zend *vaz*, pres. *vaz-āmi*, Gk. Feχ in Fóχ-ος (waggon), Goth. *vag* in *(ga-)vig-a* (move), *vig-s* (way), Sclav. *vez*, pres. *vez-ą*, Lith. *vez*, pres. *veż-ù*.

The *h* easily comes to be entirely lost, e.g. in *anser* (goose) for *hanser, cf. Sk. *hāsá-s*, O.H.G. *gans*, st. *gansi-*, Sclav. *gąsĭ*, Lith. *żąsì-s*; *olus* for earlier *holus* (v. supr.); *uïa* (way) fr. *ueh-ia, *ueia, *uïa, √*ueh*, cf. the completely analogous Lith. *vëżé* (track), i.e. *veżya, f.f. of Lith. and Lat. word, thus *vagh-yā*; *nēmo* (no man), fr. *ne-hemo, etc.

Note.—*h* is often found where it should not be, by false analogy, e.g. *humerus* for *umerus*, which is warranted by MSS., cf. Gk. ὦμο-ς, Sk. *ása-s* and *ása-m*, Goth. *amsa*, st. *amsan-*; in later times *h* was noticeably often placed bef. initial vowel : *h* must therefore have fallen out of use in many cases tolerably early.

Lat. *f*=origl. *gh*, e.g. *fel* (gall), st. *felli-*, clearly fr. **felti-*, cf. Gk. χολ-ή, χόλ-ος, O.H.G. *galla*, Sclav. *żlŭčĭ*, √*ghar* (be green); *for-mu-s*, *for-midus* (hot), cf. Sk. *ghar-má-s* (heat), Scl. *grĕ-ti* (to warm), *gor-ĕti* (burn), Germ. *warm* for *gwarm fr. *gar-m, all of which point to a √*ghar* (on Gk. θερ-μός, θέρ-ομαι, v. supr. § 64, 2. n.); *fra-gra-t* (*fragrare*, emit odour), provided it really comes from a redupln. of √*ghra*, cf. Sk. *ǵi-ghrā-ti*, *ghrā-ti* (stinks,

Benf. Or. u. Occ. iii. 69) ; *fu-tis* (tub), *fū-tilis* (unstable, cf. Curt. § 73.
Gr. Et.² no. 203, p. 156), √*fu-d*, *fundo* (pour), cf. Gk. √χυ in
χέϝ-ω, Teut. *gu-t*, in Goth. *giut-an* (pour).

Since *f* and *h* correspond to origl. *gh*, and *h* easily disappears
altogether, we can explain such forms as *faedus*, *fēdus*, bes.
haedus, *aedus*, *ēdus* (cf. *geiꝫ*) ; *folus* bes. *holus* and *olus* (√*ghar*) ;
fostis bes. *hostis* (foe ; Goth. *gasts*, guest, points distinctly to
the origl. initial *gh ;* in both langg. the meaning has been
developed in divergent lines, cf. Corss. Krit. Beitr. 217 sqq.) ;
fordeum bes. *hordeum*, prob. for **horteum*, **horsteum*, cf. O.H.G.
gersta, Gk. κρῑθή for **χρῑστη* (§ 68, 1,.d ; on this word cf. Corss.
Krit. Nachtr., p. 104 sqq.) ; *festūca* (stalk, switch) bes. *hasta*
(spear), cf. Goth. *gazds* (thorn), O.H.G. *gart* (thorn), **gartya*
(*gardea*, *kertia*, *gerta*), initial origl. *gh* therefore ; and the like.
Cf. the change fr. *gh* to *f* in cases such as Engl. *enough* (pron.
inŭf), A.S. *genōh* (genug) ; *laugh* (pr. *lāf*)ᵢ A.S. *hleahhan*, Goth.
hlahyan (laugh), etc.

Note 1.—No ex. of *b*=origl. *gh* seems to be found.
Note 2.—The origl. √*ghar* (be green) is found also in fms.
ger (germen), *gra* (grāmen), *hel* (helus), *hol* (holus), *ol* (olus), *fol*
(folus), and *fel* (fel). In the other langg. also the feeling of
relationship of the different words which spring from this root
has been lost.

2. Origl. *dh*=Lat. *d*, *f*, *b*.

Lat. *d* = origl. *dh*, e.g. *mediu-s* (middle-) = origl. and Sk.
mádhya-s, Gk. μέσσος, i.e. **μεθyο-ς*, Goth. *midji-s ;* *aed-es*
(house, origly. fire-place, cf. *aes-tus*, *aes-tas*, fr. **aed-tus*, **aed-tas*),
√*idh*, origl. Gk. αἴθ-ω, Sk. *indh*, cf. O.H.G. *eit* (fire) ; *uidua*
(widow), cf. Sk. *vidhavā*, Goth. *viduvō*.

Hence it arises that the origl. roots *da*, *dha* (give, set), may
become intermixed, e.g. *ab-do* (do away, hide), *con-do* (found),
crē-do (believe), belong not to *da-re* (give), but to a root lost in
its uncompounded fm., corresponding to Gk. τί-θη-μι, Sk. *dá-dhā-*
-mi, O.H.G. *tuo-m*, cf. Sk. *çrad-dadh-āmi* (believe) ; of the coin-

§ 73. cidence of the origl. *da, dha* (as in Zend), we find proof in *uen-di-t* (sells) bes. *uēnum dat* = Sk. and origl. *vasnam dadhāti*, ὦνον τίθησι, *dat* therefore stands here most likely as representative of *dha*, Gk. θε, not of *do*, Gk. δο ; further, *do* which has become like a sf., e.g. in *albi-du-s, ari-du-s, sordi-du-s*, is prob. to be referred to this root, as the similar roots also in Lat. are elsewh. still practically used as suffixes (e.g. *laua-cru-m, ludi-cru-s, ala--cri-s, uolu-cri-s*, cf. √*kar* (make) ; *late-bra, fune-bri-s*, cf. √*bhar*, ferre, etc.). In uncompounded words √*dha* is in Lat. *fa, fe ;* v. post.

Note.—*r* for *d* fr. *dh* is altogether sporadic, in *meri-dies* (mid-day) fr. *medi-dies (*medius=mádhyas*, cf. μεσ-ημβρία, Germ. *mit-tag*, Sk. *madhyāhna-s* fr. *madhya-, medius*, and *ahan-*, day) ; in the case of *ar=ad* (*ar-uorsus*, etc.), the comparison with words of the kindred langg. is not easy (cf. regular change of *d* to *r* in Umbrian).

Lat. *f*=origl. *dh*, e.g. *fŭmus* (smoke), cf. Sk. *dhūmás*, Lith. *dúmai* (pl. n. sing. would be *dūma-s*), Sclav. *dymŭ*, O.H.G. *toum*, Gk. θύ-ος (burnt sacrifice), √*dhu* ; *fores* (pl. door), *foris* (passage), *foras* (outwards), cf. Gk. θύρα, Goth. *daúr*, O.H.G. *tor, turi*, Scl. *dveri*, Lith. *durýs*, Sk., however, *dvāra-m, dvār-*, Ved. *dur-* with *d*, not *dh*, to which the S.- and N.-European langg. point ; *fer-us, fer-a, fer-ox* (wild), cf. Gk. θήρ, θηρ-ίον ; *fir-mus* (fast), *frē-tus* (trusting to), *frē-num* (bridle), *for-ma* (shape), cf. Sk. *dhar-imán-* (id.), √*dhar* (hold) ; *fĭo=*feio* (become), f.f. *dhayāmi*, √*dha* (set, do), Gk. θε, Goth. *da*, from which also the secondary √*fac* is formed (*fac-io*, make), likewise *fă-ber* (wright), st. *fa-bro-*, cf. Sk. *dhā-tar-* (founder, ordainer ; Kuhn, Zeitsch. xiv. 229 sqq.).

In *rūfus* (red)=Goth. *raud-s*, f.f. *rāudha-s*, √*rudh*, medial *f* stands also for origl. *dh*, whilst *rub-er* (red), *rub-igo* (rust), are regular, and show *b* for *f* (v. supr. n. 1), but collateral *raud-us* (clod), origl. √*rudh*, cf. Sk. *rudh-irá-m* (blood), Gk. ἐ-ρυθ-ρός, and hence we find this root in Lat. as *rud, ruf, rub* (for *rutilus*, v.

infr.). Cf. the *f*-like pronuncn. of *th* in Eng. and *θ* in mod. Gk; § 73. in Russian Gk. *θ=f* in pronunciation.

Lat. *b*=origl. *dh* in medio, e.g. *rub-er*, st. *rub-ro-*=*ἐ-ρυθ-ρό-*, Sk. *rudh-i-rá-*, origl. *rudh-ra-*, √*rub*, Sk. *rudh*, Goth. *rud*, O.H.G. *rut*, Scl. *rŭd* (be red); *ūber* (udder), i.e. *ouber, Gk. *οὖθαρ*, Sk. *ū́dhar-*, *ū́dhas-*, *ū́dhan-*, M.H.G. *ūter*, *iuter*, root-syll. origl. *audh;* *ūber* (adj. rich), i.e. *oiber, cf. Sk. *ḗdh-atē* (increases), √*idh* (Walt. Zeitschr. x. 77); *uerbum* (word)=Goth. *vaúrd*, H.G. *wort*, f.f. *vardha-m*, cf. Lith. *várda-s* (m. name); *barba* (beard), stands bes. Norse *bardhr*, H.G. *bart*, Lat. *b*=Germ. *t*, *d*, must be der. fr. origl. *dh*.

3. Origl. *bh*=Lat. *b*, *f*, *h*.

Lat. *b*=origl. *bh* in medio, e.g. *ambō* (both)=Gk. *ἄμφω*, cf. Sk. *ubháú*, earlier *ubhā́*, Goth. *bai*, nt. *ba* (with loss of init. sound), Scl. *oba*, f.f. of st.=*ambha-; lub-et* (pleases), Sk. √*lubh* (desire), Goth. *lub* (in *liub-s*, dear, *-lubō*, love, etc.); *nĕbula* (mist), *nūbes* (cloud), Gk. *νεφέλη*, *νέφος*, Sk. *nábhas* (cloud, sky), O.H.G. *nĕbal*, Scl. *nebo* (sky); *-bī* in *ti-bī*, *i-bī*, *(c)u-bi*, corres. to Sk. *-bhyam*, sf. dat. sg. (only preserved in certain cases, e.g. *tú-bhyam*, *-bhya*=Lat. *ti-bī*); *-bus*, sf. dat. abl. pl.=Sk. *-bhyas*, cf. Gk. *-φιν*, both alike containing particle *bhi :* √*fu* in verb. fms. composed by it begins with *b*, e.g. *ama-bam*, *ama-bo*, for *ama-fam, *ama-fo (v. post. "conjugation").

Lat. *f*=origl. *bh*, e.g. √*fa* in *fā-ri* (speak), *fā-tum* (utterance, fate), origl. *bha*, cf. Gk. *φα* in *φη-μί*, *φω-νή*, *φά-τις*, Sk. *bhā-š* (speak); √*fer*, pres. *fer-o* (bear), cf. Gk. *φερ* in *φέρ-ω*, origl. and Sk. *bhar*, pres. *bhár-āmi*; √*fu* (be) in *fu-turus*, *fu-am*, Sk. and origl. *bhu*, Gk. *φυ* in *φύ-ω*, *φυ-τός*; √*fug* in *fug-io* (flee), *fug-a*, cf. Gk. *φυγ* in *φεύγ-ω*, *φυγ-ή*, Sk. *bhug̓*, Goth. *bug*, pres. *biuga*, origl. *bhug; fráter* (brother), origl. *bhrātar-s*, cf. Gk. *φράτωρ*, Sk. *bhrā́tā*, Goth. *brōthar*, etc.

Lat. *h* is very rarely=origl. *bh ;* e.g. in *hor-da* bes. *for-da* (bearing), √*fer*, origl. *bhar ;* in *mi-hi*, *-hi* stands for *-bi*, which we should have expected, as also in Sk. *má-hyam* for *ma-bhyam,

§ 73. cf. *ti-bi*, Sk. *tú-bhyam;* in both langg. the initial *m* seems to have had a dissimilating influence on the *bh*. We must not hence venture to assign a fm. *ma-hyam* to the origl. lang., for the origl. could only be sounded *ma-bhyam* (or *ma-bhiam, ma--bhiyam*, cf. § 3), a f.f. which diverged later into Sk. *má--hyam*, Lat. *mi-hei*; in dat. pl. of *a*-st., in -*is* fr. -*ois, -ais*, origl. -*a-bhyams, -ā-bhyams* (v. 'decl.'), origl. *bh* has entirely disappeared, perh. through intervening *h* (cf. *mihi*); so too prob. *ama-ui* for *ama-fui, √*fu*, origl. *bhu* (be).

Note.—In some exx. a Lat. tenuis stands apparently for an asp.; these are *rutilus* (fiery red) bes. Sk. √*rudh*, Gk. ῥυθ; *pati* (suffer) bes. Gk. παθεῖν; *pūtēre* (stink) bes. Gk. πύθ-εσθαι; *putāre* (calculate) bes. Gk. πυθέσθαι (learn), otherwise distinct from it in use; *sapiens* (wise) bes. Gk. σοφός; *latēre* (escape notice) bes. Gk. λαθεῖν, Sk. √*rah* for origl. *radh*. Cf. L. Meyer, Gr. of Gk. and Lat. Langg., i. p. 51; G. Curt. Gr. Et.[2] p. 374, Kuhn's Zeitschr. ii. 355; Grassmann ap. Kuhn, id. xii. 86 sqq.; Corss. Krit. Beitr. p. 75. sqq., 79 sqq. Herein we concur in the conclusions of Curt. and Corss., which amount to this,—that in the above-named words also *t* and *p* are not=origl. *dh, bh*, Gk. θ, φ. *ru-tilus* (cf. *fu-tilis, mu-tilus*) seems to have sf. -*tilo*, and to stand peculiarly for *rud-tilus, *rus-tilus (v. post.), like early Lat. *ad-gre-tus, e-gre-tus*, for *-*gred-tus*, *-*gres-tus* (class. *gressus*, √*grad, gred*, in *grad-ior*, step), *pa-tior* however is a later fmn. fr. √*pa*, which is otherwise formed in Gk. πα-θ, πεν-θ (πένθος, suffering, grief); to the origl. existence of the shorter root-fm. *pa*, πα, the fms. πέν-ομαι (am in want), πον-έω (suffer, labour), point; therefore πε-ν, πο-ν, give evidence to πα, just as γε-ν, γο-ν (beget), do to a real pre-existent γα (*n* is a common secondary root-termn.). The same explan. holds good in *puteo*, where *t* belongs to the origl. root as little as does θ in πύ-θομαι; the root is *pu*, which clearly occurs in Lat. *pūs*, gen. *pūris* (matter), i.e. *pou-os, *pou-es-os, f.f. *pav-as, pav-as-as*, cf. πύ-ον (id.), Sk. *pú-yatē* (becomes foul, stinks), *pú-ya-s* (matter), Lith. *pú-ti* (befoul), O.H.G. *fū-l* (foul), f.f. *pau-ra-s*. *Pu-tare* fr. *putus* (pure), lit. = 'make clean, clear,' and has therefore nothing to do with Gk. πυθέσθαι, Sk. √*budh*, etc.; σοφός stands for *σοπος with unorigl. aspn., cf. supr. § 62, 3, n. 2. Thus *latēre* alone remains unexplained bes. λαθεῖν, a solitary instance, for which we must not try to make good a consonantal change which is otherwise unknown.

CONSONANTAL PROLONGED-SOUNDS.

Spirants *y, s, v.*   § 74.

1. Origl. *y* = Latin *j* (written *i*), *i*.

Lat. *j* = origl. *y*, initial and medial, yet not commonly between
vowels, and almost only after long vowels, e.g. *cū-ius, plebē-ius,*
or when a conson. has assimilated itself to the *y*, as in *āio,
māior, mēio* (v. post.), e.g. √*iug*, Sk. *yúǵ*, Gk. ζυγ, origl. *yug*,
in *iu-n-go*, (join), *iug-um* (yoke)=origl. and Sk. *yug-ám*, Gk.
ζυγ-όν, Goth. *yuk*, O.Bulg. *igo* = **jŭg-o* ; pronl. √*ya* in *ia-m*
(already), cf. Lith. *yaú*, Goth. *yu* (already) ; *ius* (broth), cf. Sk.
yūša-s, yūša-m ('pease-soup,' 'the water in which pulse of
various kinds has been boiled ;' Wilson), Scl. *iucha; iuuenis*
(young man), cf. Sk. *yúvan-*, Goth. *yuggs*, Scl. *yunŭ*, Lith. *yaúnas*
(young) ; *āio* (say) for **ag-io*, pres. fmn. in sf. origl. *ya*, √*ag*,
origl. √*agh*, cf. *ad-ăg-ium* (saying), Sk. *ah* (say) ; *māior* (greater)
fr. **mag-ior*, comp. sf. *-ior*, earlier *-ios*, Gk. -ιον, Sk. *-yās, -īyās*,
origl. *-yans* ; *mēio* = **migio*, i.e. **migh-yāmi*, pres. fmn. in origl.
ya, etc.

Lat. *i* = origl. *y* after consonn., e.g. *med-ius*=origl. and Sk.
mádhyas, cf. μέσσος=**μεθ-yος; patr-iu-s* (father-), origl. *patar-
-ya-s*, cf. πάτρ-ιο-ς, Sk. *pitr-ya-s*, st. origl. *patar-*, sf. *ya* ; *siem,
siet* (1, 3, sg. opt. pres.), origl. *as-yā-m, as-yā-t*, cf. εἴην, εἴη, fr.
*ἐσ-yη-μ, *ἐσ-yη-τ, Sk. *syā-m, syā-t,* opt. pres. √*as* (be) ; *capio*
for **cap-yō*, i.e. **kap-yā-mi*, pres. in origl. *ya*, etc.

Not uncommonly *y* disappears entirely, thus regularly betw.
vowels, as, e.g. *moneo* (remind, warn), f.f. *mānayāmi*, causative from
√*men* (*men-tem, me-min-i*), origl. *man* (think) ; *sēdo* (seat, set), fr.
*sēdao, *sēdayo, Sk. and origl. *sādáyāmi*, caus. from √*sed* (sedere),
origl. *sad ;* further before *i* and *e* which stands for *i* (§ 35, § 38),
e.g. *capis, capit,* for **capyis, *capyit,* i.e. *kap-ya-si, kap-ya-ti,* bes. *capio,*
i.e. *kap-yā-mi ; obex* (obstacle, hindrance), gen. *obicis,* for **obyex*
=**ob-yic-s, ob-yic-is,* √*iac* (cf. *iac-io, ob-iic-io, ob-ic-io*) ; yét elsewh.

§ 74. after consonn. also, e.g. *minor, minus* (less), for **min-ior,* **min-ius,* origl. sf. *-yans,* compar.-fmn. ; *ero, eris, erit,* fr. **eso,* **esis,* **esit,* for **esyo,* **esyis,* **esyit,* f.f. *as-yā-mi, as-ya-si, as-ya-ti,* pres.-fmn. through *ya* of √*as,* which expresses fut. meaning, cf. Sk. *s-yā́-mi, s-yá-si, s-yá-ti,* Gk. ἔσομαι for **ἐσ-yo-μαι; -bus* sf. of dat. and abl. pl. origl. *-bhyams,* Sk. *-bhyas,* etc.

2. Origl. *s*=Lat. *s, r.*

Lat. *s*=origl. *s.* Initially, generally also finally, medially betw. mute consonn.; betw vowels *s* passes over into *r* almost always in the class. lang. Before sonant consonn. *s* partly falls out (becomes assimld.), partly likewise becomes *r* (v. 'sound-laws'), e.g. √*sed* (sed-ere), origl. and Sk. *sad,* Gk. ἑδ, Goth. *sat* (sit); *septem* (seven), Sk. and origl. *sáptan,* Gk. ἑπτά ; √*sta* (stand), e.g. in *sta-tus,* origl. *sta,* Gk. στα, Sk. *stha;* √*ster* in *ster-no* (strew), Sk. and origl. *star,* Gk. στορ ; √*es* in *es-t,* origl. and Sk. *as,* Gk. ἐσ in ἐσ-τί ; √*us* (burn) in *ur-o, us-tus,* origl. *us,* Sk. *uš; -s,* sf. of nom. sg., origl. and Sk. *-s,* Gk. -ς, Goth. Lith. *-s,* e.g. *equo-s,* origl. *akva-s,* Gk. ἵππο-ς, Sk. *áçva-s ;* sf. *-os, -es,* e.g. *gen-os, gen-us* (race), gen. *gen-er-us, gen-er-is,* origl. *gan-as, gan-as-as,* cf. Gk. γέν-ος, *γεν-εσ-ος=γένους, Sk. *g͘án-as, g͘án-as-as,* etc.

Lat. *r*=origl. *s* (cf. sound-laws, § 77, 1. f.).

3. Origl. *v*=Lat. *v* (in writing undistinguished fr. *u*), *u.*

Lat. *v*=origl. *v,* e.g. √*vid* in *uideo* (see), Sk. and origl. *vid,* Gk. Ϝιδ; √*vom* for *vem in *uom-o* (spue), Sk. and origl. *vam,* Gk. Ϝεμ ; √*voc* for *vec in *uoc-are* (cry), *uōc-em* (acc. voice), origl. *vak,* Sk. *vak͘,* Gk. Ϝεπ ; √*veh* in *ueh-o* (carry), origl. *vagh,* Sk. *vah,* Gk. Ϝεχ, Goth. *vag* ; √*vol* in *uol-t* (he wills), Sk. and origl. *var* (uelle) ; *oui-s* (sheep), origl. *avi-s,* Lith. *avì-s,* Sk. *ávi-s,* Gk. ὄϜις ; *nouo-s* (new), orig. and Sk. *náva-s,* Gk. νέϜο-ς, etc.

Note.—Though *quis, quod, anguis, suauis* are the usual ways of writing those words, yet here, too, *u* = *v* (thus *qvis, qvod, angvis, svauis*), because this *u* is not metrically=vowel.

Lat. *u*=origl. *v* after mom. consonn. and *n*, e.g. *quatuor* (four), § 74. Sk. *katvãras*, Gk. τέτταρες=*τετϜαρες, Goth. *fidvōr*, origl. *kat-vãras*; this *u* = *v* seems secondarily to have the force of a conson., whence e.g. the lengthening by position of the short *a*, expressed in the spelling *quattuor*; esp. often *u*=origl. *v* in the origl. st.-fmative sf. *-va*=Lat. *-uo*, *-vo*, later *uu*, *vu*, which in Lat. were sounded *-uo* (later *-uu*), fem. *-ua*, after most consonn., except *r*, *l*, *q*, e.g. *al-ŭo-s* ('the nourishing—'), √*al* (*al-o*, nourish); *ar-ŭo-m* ('the ploughed—'), √*ar* (plough); *eq-ŭo-s* (horse), origl. *ak-va-s*, Sk. *áç-va-s* ('the running—'), origl. √*ak* (run), etc.; but *uac-uo-s* (empty), √*uac*; *noc-uo-s* (hurtful), *re-lic-uo-s* (left over) bes. *re-liq-vo-s*, √*noc*, *lic* (altogether usage often wavers betw. *v* and *u*, as *aqüae*, *acuam*, bes. *aqva*; *tenvia*, *genva*, bes. *tenuia*, *genua*, etc.); *con-tig-uo-s* (contiguous), √*tag* (*tango*); *de-cid-uo-s* (falling off), √*cad* (*cad-o*); *in-gen-uo-s* (inborn, free), √*gen* (*gi-gn-o*, *gen-us*); *sūd-or* (sweat), *sūd-are* (sweat), prob. for **suid-or*, **suid-are* (as e.g. gen. *senatus* for *senatuis*), and this for **svid-or*, **svid-are*, √*svid*, cf. ἰδίω for **σϜιδ-ιω, Sk. *svid-yāmi*, O.H.G. *swizzan*, *sweiz̧*, *swiz̧*, earlier *svit*, origl. *svid* (sweat), etc.

Note.—*suŏs* (his) is not=*sva-s*, but was sounded *sovos* in the earlier lang.; accordingly we have also *tuŭs*=*tovos*; in Lat. and in Gk. there is here a step-fmn. of *u* to *eu*, *ou* (ἐός, τεός=**seu-os*, **teu-os*), whilst the other langg. show *v*.

Not unfreq. *v* disappears entirely, thus e.g. *se*, *si-bi* (himself), etc., for **sve*, **svi-bi*, fr. st. origl. *sva-*; *te* (thee), *ti-bi* (to thee), for **tve*, **tvi-bi*, cf. Sk. *tva-m* (n. sg.); for origl. initial *sva-*, *so-* occurs regularly (v. supr. § 33); *canis* (hound) for **cvan-is*, cf. κύων, Sk. st. *çvan*, f.f. *kvan-*; *suadeo* (recommend) for **suadveo*, fr. *suavis* (sweet)=**suadv-i-s*, cf. G. ἡδύ-ς, Sk. *svādú-s*; *deus* (god) =**dēus*, **dēvo-s*, **deivo-s*, **dīvo-s*, f.f. *daiva-s*, cf. Sk. *dēvá-s*, Lith. *déva-s*. The later lang. permits frequent loss of *v* from betw. vowels, e.g. *suus*, *suum*, for earlier (inscrr.) *souos*, *souom* (**suvus*, **suvum*); *fluunt*, earlier (inscrr.) *flouont*; *fui*=**fuvi*, and so, too, in other like cases; *boum* for *bouum*; *prudens* fr. *prouidens*;

§ 74. *nōlo*=*neuolo; amarunt*=*amauerunt*, etc.   Yet *nouos, ouis*, etc., with *v* preserved, are the only fms. found.

Note.—On the alleged change of *v* to *b* in Lat. v. Corss. Krit. Beitr., 157 sqq.   Only in *ferbui*, pf. fr. pres. *ferueo* (boil), *v* after *r* and bef. *u* has become *b*; *bubile* bes. *bouile* (ox-stall) seems caused by the analogy of *bu-bulus* (ox-); *opilio, upilio* (shepherd), stand for **oui-pilio*, cf. *Pal-es, αἴ-πολ-ος, βού-πολ-ος* (Corss. ib. 152; Krit. Nachtr., p. 180 sqq.).

§ 75.   N a s a l s.

1. Origl. *n*=Lat. *n.*   As in other Indo-Eur. langg., so also in Lat., origl. *n* bef. gutt. consonn. becomes gutt., bef. labb. it becomes lab., i.e. *m*, (*ṅ*=gutt. *n*, § 4).   Exx. : *ne* (negation), in *ne-c, ne-fas*, etc., Sk. and origl. *na; in-*, Umbr. *an-*, Gk. *ἀν-*, Sk. and origl. *an-* (neg. in composn.) ; √*nec* in *nec-are* (kill), *noc-ēre* (hurt), Gk. *νεκ*, Sk. *naç*, origl. *nak; st. noc-ti* (night) in *noc-te-m*, origl. *nak-ti-*, cf. Lith. *nak-tì-s*, Gk. st. *νυκτ-*, Sk. *nákta-m* (adv. by night) ; *nāuis* (ship), Sk. and origl. *nāus*, Gk. *ναῦς*; √*gen* in *gen-us* (race), *gi-g(e)n-o* (beget), Gk. *γεν*, Sk. *ǵan*, origl. *gan; n* is common in suff., e.g. origl. *-na* in *plē-nu-s* (full), f.f. *prā-na-s*, origl. *par-na-s*, √*par* (fill), *na* fms. the perf. part. pass., but has also various other functions, e.g. *som-nu-s* (sleep) for **sop-nu-s*, origl. and Sk. *sváp-na-s*, Gk. *ὕπ-νο-ς* ; sf. *-man*, e.g. in **gnō--men, nō-men* (name), Sk. *nā-man-*, origl. *gnā-man- ; -nti, -nt*, fm. 3 pl. vb., e.g. **fero-nti, feru-nt*,=*φέρο-ντι*, Sk. and origl. *bhára-nti*, etc.

Exx. of change of *n* to *ṅ, m*, are found in pres. fmn., e.g. *iu-n-go* (join), √*iug, ru-m-po* (break), Sk. *lu-m-pǻmi*, √*rup*, Sk. *lup*, which in f.f. were prob. *yug-nāmi, rup-nāmi;* only later did the nasal pass into the root, whereby arose *yuṅgāmi, rum-pāmi*, i.e. *iungo, rumpo*.

Note.—On *gn* v. supr. § 72, 1, n. 5.

2. Origl. *m* = Lat. *m*, e.g. √*men* in *me-min-i* (remember), *men-tem, mens* (mind), *moneo* (warn), Gk. *μεν*, origl. and Sk. *man* (think) ; *mā-ter* (mother), *μή-τηρ*, Sk. *mā-tǻ*, origl. *mā-tar-s* ;

√*mor* in *mor-i* (die), *mor-tuos* (dead), Sk. and origl. *mar;* √*uom* § 75. for *uem in *uom-o* (spue) (§ 33), Gk. *Fεμ*, Sk. and origl. *vam*, etc. In sff. also *m* often occurs, e.g. sf. *-men*, origl. *man*, as in **gnō-men, nō-men*, Sk. *nā́-man-*, origl. *gnā-man* ; origl. sf. *-ma*, an intensitive, most often forming superl., esp. in combination with sf. *-ta*, as *ta-ma*, Lat. e.g. in *pri-mu-s, optu-mu-s; -m* 1 pers. sg., *-mus* 1 pl., e.g. *(e)s-u-m* fr. *es-mi, Gk. *εἰ-μί* fr. same f.f., Sk. and origl. *ás-mi; feri-mus*, Gk. *φέρο-μεν*, Dôr. *φέρο-μες*, Sk. and origl. *bhárā-masi; -m* of acc. sing., e.g. *equo-m*, Sk. *áçva-m*, cf. Gk. *ἵππο-ν*, with *ν* for *μ*, acc. to Gk. sound-laws of termn., origl. *akva-m*, etc.

Note.—In *tene-brae* (darkness), prob. for *tenes-brae, *temes-brae, √*tam* in Sk. *tám-as* (darkness), O.H.G. *dëm-ar* (dawn), etc., *n* has arisen by dissimiln. fr. *m*, to avoid the labialism **temebrae ;* in *nōnus* (ninth) for *nōmus, *nouimus, cf. *nouem* (nine), *septimus* bes. *septem, decimus* bes. *decem, primus*, etc., the init. *n* has had an assimilating influence ; *gener* (son-in-law) does not stand for *gemer on acct. of *γαμβρός* (on which cf. § 66, 1, n. 1), because *gemer would have stood its ground like *uōmer* (ploughshare), also Sk. *ǵā́-mātar-* (son-in-law) proves nothing, because it is a compd. of *ǵā* (come after) from √*ga*, origl. *ga* (gi-gn-ere), and *mā-tar-* (bearing, bringing forth) ; *gen-er*, st. *gen-ero-* for *gen-ro-*, is derived rather fr. √*gen* (beget), sf. *ra*, in this case with auxil. vowel *i*, pronounced *e* bef. *r* (§ 38).

r- and l-sounds. § 76.

Origl. *r*=Lat. *r, l*.

Lat. *r*=origl. *r*, e.g. *rex* (king), i.e. *rēg-s, origl. *rāg-s*, cf. Sk. st. *rāǵ-* (id.) ; √*rub* in *rub-er* (red), *rub-ru-m*, cf. *ἐ-ρυθ-ρό-ς*, *ἐ-ρυθ-ρό-ν*, Sk. *rudh-i-rá-m*, origl. *rudh-ra-s, rudh-ra-m ;* √*rup* in *ru-m-p-o* (break), *rup-tu-s*, cf. Sk. *lup* (rumpere) in *lu-m-p-ā́mi*, *lup-tá-s*, Lith. *lup* in *lùp-ti* (flay) ; √*or* in *or-ior* (rise), *or-tus*, cf. *ὄρ-νυμι*, Sk. and origl. *ar;* √*ar* in *ar-o* (plough), cf. *ἀρ-όω*, Scl. *or-ya̜*, *ar-atrum* (plough), cf. *ἄρ-οτρον*, O. Bulg. *or-alo* for **or-adlo ;* √*fer*, 1 sg. pres. *fer-o* (bear), Gk. *φερ*, 1 sg. pres. *φέρ-ω*, Sk. and origl. *bhar*, 1 sg. pres. *bhár-āmi ; frā-ter* (brother), *φρά-τωρ*, Sk. *bhrā́tā*, origl. *bhrā-tar-s*, etc. *r* is frequent in

10

§ 76. stem-formative particles, thus in sff. *ro, ru,* origl. *ra* (*rub-ru-m,* origl. *rudh-ra-m*); *tōr,* origl. *tār* (*da-tōr,* origl. *da-tar-s,* n. sg.); *tro, tru,* origl. *tra;* in word-formative particles, i.e. in case- and person-termns., it does not occur.

    Lat. *l*=origl. *r* (cf. 'sound-laws,' upon Lat. interchange of *l* with *r* for purposes of dissimiln.), e.g. √*loc* (speak) in *loqu-or, loc-utus,* Gk. λακ, Scl. *rek* (*rek-ą,* loquor), origl. *rak;* √*luc* in *luc-erna* (lamp), *lūc-em* (acc. light), Gk. λυκ, Sk. *ruǩ,* Goth. *luh,* origl. *ruk;* √*lic* in *linquo* (leave), *re-lic-tus,* Gk. λιπ (λείπω), Sk. *riǩ,* origl. *rik;* √*lig* in *lingo* (lick), Gk. λιχ (λείχω), Sk. *lih,* origl. *righ;* √*lub* in *lub-et* (it pleases), Goth. *lub* (*liubs,* love), Sk. *lubh* (desire), origl. *rubh; leuis* (light) fr. **legu-is,* cf. Gk. ἐ-λαχύ-ς, Sk. *laghú-s,* origl. *raghu-s; plē-nu-s* (full), f.f. *prā-na-s,* parall. fm. to *par-na-s,* Zend *perenō,* Sk. *pūrṇá-s,* i.e. origl. *par-na-s,* Goth. *fulls* for **ful-na-s; sollus* (whole, Fest.) for **soluo-s,* parall. fm. to *sal-uo-s* (whole), Gk. **ὅλϜος,* Sk. and f.f. *sár-va-s;* √*uol, uel,* in *uol-t* (he wills), f.f. *var-ti, uel-le* (will), for **uel-se* (v. post), Sk. and origl. *var* (choose), etc. In st.-formative particles also *l* is common.

§ 77.   SKETCH OF SOME SOUND-LAWS WHICH ARE IMPORTANT FOR COMPARATIVE GRAMMAR.

MEDIAL.

    1. Assimilation. We omit here the assimilns. which occur in prepositional compds.; they bear a subordinate meaning for Compar. Gr., and belong to the Special Gr. of Latin. Further, except that they are treated as well known, they are not at all, or only briefly, mentioned.

    a. Complete assimiln. of foregoing to following consonn. This occurs after long vowels, after which doubled consonn. cannot easily be made audible, and can scarcely be distinguished from evanescence (ejection) of the former conson.; whilst after short vowels the doubling of the conson. is the distinctive mark of real assimiln. As, however, the evaporation of one conson. bef. another can hardly be conceived of as conditioned in any other way than by assimiln. to the follg. cons., we § 77. likewise treat here of cases where consonn. are lost before consonn.

The doubling of consonn. was not characterized in writing before Ennius; in inscrr. it does not appear in frequent use until after 640 A.V.C.

Note.—Upon the doubled tenuis in Lat. cf. C. Pauli, Zeitschr. xviii. 1 sqq., where many words of difficult etymol. are considered. Acc. to Pauli the doubling is not seldom unorigl., and arises ' through sharpened pronunciation.'

Exx. of complete assimiln. of foregoing to follg. consonn. after short vowels are found in *sum-mu-s* for **sup-mu-s*, cf. *sup-er*, *sup-erior*, *sup-remus*; *flamma* fr. **flag-ma*, cf. *flag-rare*; *serra* (saw), prob. fr. **sec-ra*, cf. *sec-are* (cut); *sella* fr. **sed-la*, cf. *sed-ere*; *lapil-lus* fr. **lapid-lus*, cf. *lapid-em*; *puel-la* fr. **puer-la*, **pueru-la*, cf. *puer*; *asel-lus* fr. **asin-lus*, **asinu-lus*, cf. *asinu-s* (ass); *esse* fr. **ed-se*, cf. *ed-o* (eat); *penna* fr. **pesna*, and this fr. **pet-na*, √*pet*, origl. *pat* (fly), etc.

Complete assimiln. of foregoing to follg. consonn. after long vowels; the spelling does not show the doubling in these cases. The assimiln. (dropping out) of *d*, *t*, and often *n* before *s*, is well known; a foregoing short vowel therefore becomes long, wherein we believe we see an evidence that a doubling of the conson. was once really in existence, e.g. *suāsi* fr. **suād-si*, pf. fr. *suād-eo*, etc.; *pēs*=**pĕd-s*, cf. *pĕd-em*; *milēs*, *milĕs* only later, fr. **milĕt-s*, cf. *milit-em*; *formōsus* fr. **formonsus*, sf. origl. *-vans* fr. *-vant*, whose *v* disappeared; *equōs* fr. **equon-s*, i.e. acc. sg. *equo-m*+pl.-sign *s*; *consul* bes. *cōsul*; *quotiens*=**quotient-s* bes. *quoties*; *censor*, *censeo*, bes. rarer *cēsor*, *cēseo*, etc. Thus the lang. has sometimes decided early in favour of loss of *n*, whilst at others the *n* has stood exclusively for a longer time, and until a later period of written lang.

A follg. *j* assimilates itself not seldom to precedg. *g*; *j* is then written indivisibly, but the foregoing vowel, if short before, now becomes long (cf. § 39, 1), e.g. *mā-ior* fr. **măg-yor*, cf. *mag-nus*, √*mag*, origl. *magh* (wax); *ā-io* fr. **ăg-yo*, cf. *ad-ăg-ium*,

§ 77. √*ag*, Sk. *ah*, origl. *agh* (say); *mē-io* by dissimiln. (cf. § 38) fr. **mi-yo* for **mĭg-yo*, cf. *mi-n-g-o*, √*mig*, Gk. μιχ, origl. *migh* (cf. § 74, 1). Bef. origl. sf. -*ya*, *g* remains, because here *y* changes into *i* (§ 74, 1), e.g. *ad-ăg-iu-m*, *nau-frăg-iu-m*. Cf. the extensive loss of consonn. before *y* with compensatory lengthening in composition, e.g. *se(d)-iungo*, *pe(r)-iero*, *di(s)-iudico*, *tra(ns)-icio*, etc.

Loss of *g* bef. *v* without compensat. lengthening occurs, e.g. in *brĕu-is* for **bregu-is*, cf. βραχύ-ς; *lĕu-is* for **lĕgu-is*, cf. ἐ-λαχύ-ς; *niu-is* for **nigu-is*, cf. *nix*=**nig-s*, *ningu-o*; accordingly the same process must be assumed in *uīuo* for **uīgu-o*, cf. *uixi*, i.e. **uig-si*, √*uig* (v. §§ 72, 1; 73, 1).

d disappears bef. *v* in *suāu-is* for **suād-uis*, cf. Gk. ἡδύ-ς, Sk. *svādú-s*.

Bef. nasals sometimes *g*, oftener *c*, disappears (*c* may also remain and become *g*, v. c in this section), more rarely without, more often with compensatory lengthening, *c* was evidently softened to *g* before it fell out (v. c), e.g. *stĭ-mulus* (goad), *stĭ-mulo* (I goad), √*stig*, raised a step to *stīg* (*in-stīg-o*, urge), nasalized in *in-stinc-tus* (urged)=**in-sting-tus*, cf. Gk στίχω (prick)=**στιγ-γω*; *ex-ā-men* (swarm of bees, rank) for **ex-ăg-men*, √*ag* in *a-gere* bes. *ag-men*, *teg-men*, *seg-mentum* (*g* is common bef. *n*, e.g. *lig-num*, *dig-nus*, *mag-nus*, etc.); *uā-nus* (empty) fr. **uăc-nus*, cf. *uăc-uos* (empty); *dē-ni* (ten apiece) fr. **dĕc-ni*, cf. *dĕc-em*; *pī-nus* fr. *pĭc-nus*, cf. *pix*, *pĭc-is* (pitch; *pīnus*, on acct. of the vowel, cannot be akin to πεύκ-η, Germ. *vieh-te*, which point to a √*puk*); *nc* disappears thus in *quī-ni* (five apiece) for **quinc-ni*, cf. *quinque* (five).

Before *m*, *c* disappears in *lū(c)-men* (light), where it is doubtful whether the vowel is simple or whether it is raised in the scale, whether fr. **lŭc-men* or **louc-*, **lūc-men*; *cs*, i.e. *x*, disappeared bef. *m* in *sē-mestris* (six-monthly) for **sex-mestris*, prob. also in *tē-mo* (pole) for **tex-mo*, cf. O.H.G. *dīhs-ila*, and Sk. √*takš* (compose, make).

Bef. *m*, *b* disappears, e.g. *glūma* (shell) for **glūb-ma*, cf. *glūb-ere* (pare); *grĕmium* (lap) for **greb-mium*, cf. Sk. *gárbha-* (masc. id.), etc. (Corss. Krit. N. p. 236).

Bef. *l*, *x* has died out in *tē-la* (web), which, however, can only § 77.
be explained as prob. coming fr. **tex-la*, cf. *tex-ere* (weave).

Bef. *c*, *d* and *t* disappear in *hoc* for **hod-c*, **hod-ce*, cf. *quod;
ac* for **at-c*, cf. *atque*.

Bef. sonant consonn. *s* disappears, thus e.g. bef. *n* in *pō-no*
for **pos-no*, cf. *pos-uī; cē-na* for **ces-na*, cf. Umbr. *çes-na; penis*
for **pes-nis*, cf. πέος for **πεσ-ος*, Sk. *pás-as;* in *penna* for earlier
pesna the assimiln. has been kept, *pesna* stands for **pet-na* (v.
c), √*pet*, πετ, Sk. *pat* (fly), cf. *prae-pet-es* (aues; Fest.), O.H.G.
fëd-ara, fëd-ah, Gk. πτ-ίλον, πτε-ρόν (feather, wing), etc.

Bef. *m*, *s* is lost in *rē-mus* (oar), cf. *tri-resmus* (three-oared)
Col. Rostr., *res-mus* stands for **ret-mus*, cf. ἐ-ρετ-μός; *s* is lost
without compensatory lengthening in *Că-mēna* for *Cas-mena*,
√*cas*, cf. *car-men*, Sk. √*ças, çãs* (count, say).

Bef. *n* and *m*, *s* also becomes *r*. v. e.

Bef. *l*, *s* is lost in *corpu-lentus* for **corpus-lentus*, cf. *corpus*,
corpor-is.

Bef. *d*, *s* is lost in, e.g. *iū-dex* for **iūs-dex*, *ī-dem* for **īs-dem*,
dī-duco for **dīs-duco*, etc., but it remains in *trans-dūco, trans-do*,
bes. *trā-dūco, trā-do*, further in cases like *eius-dem, cuius-dam*.

Bef. *b*, also, *s* is lost, e.g. *tene-brae* for *tenĕs-brae*, and the like;
v. post.

Bef. *d*, *r* is lost with compensat. lengthening in *pēd-o, pōd-ex*,
bes. πέρδ-ω, Sk. √*pard*, O.H.G. *farz*, Lith. *perd* (1 sg. pres.
pérdžu=**perd-yu*).

The change of *r* to *s* by assimiln. is well known, e.g. *rūsum,
russum*, bes. *rur-sum, sū-sum* bes. *sur-sum, retrō-sum* bes. *retror-
sum*, etc.

Bef. *sc*, consonn. are lost, prob. only to make pronunciation
simpler and easier; thus in *di-sco* for **dic-sco*, cf. *di-dĭc-i; po-sco*
(where *sc* became fixed, though origl. only in pres., cf. *po-posc-i*),
prob. for **porc-sco*, cf. √*proc, prec*, in *proc-ax, proc-us, prec-or*, cf.
Germ. *frah, frag* (in Goth. *fraih-nan-*, N.H.G. *frag-en*); *mi-sceo*
for **mig-sceo*, cf. μίγ-νυμι (here, too, has the *sc* in Lat. grown
into the root).

§ 77.   Similarly *mis-tus* stands for and bes. *mics-tus, mix-tus,* and this prob. for **misc-tus,* cf. *misc-eo ; tos-tus* for **tors-tus,* cf. *torr-eo* for **tors-eo,* Germ. *durs-t,* Sk. √*tarš* (thirst), i.e. *tars,* to which prob. belongs *tes-ta* (crock, jar) for *ters-ta (lit. ' baked,' ' burnt') ; cf. *terra* (dry land) for **ters-a.*

It is certain that certain groups composed of more consonn. were lightened by the evaporation (ejection) of one of these consonn.

Thus after *r, l,* are lost gutt. *c, g,* when folld. by *t* or *s,* e.g. *sar-tus* for **sarc-tus,* cf. *sarc-io ; tor-tus* for **torc-tus,* cf. *torqu-eo ; ul-tor* for **ulc-tor,* cf. *ulc-iscor ; in-dul-tus* for **in-dulc-tus,* and this for *in-dulg-tus fr. *in-dulg-eo,* and so others ; *sar-si* for **sarc-si,* cf. *sarc-io ; tor-si* for **torc-si,* cf. *torqu-eo ; mul-si, mul-sus,* for **mulg-si,* **mulg-sus,* fr. *mulg-tus,* cf. *mulg-eo ; spar-si* for **sparg-si, spar-sus* for *sparg-sus fr. *sparg-tus,* cf. *sparg-o,* etc. ; *par-simonia* for *parc-simonia fr. **parc-timonia,* like the underlying fm. *par-sus* fr. **parc-tus,* cf. *parc-o ;* thus also *ursus* for *urcsus fr. **urctus,* cf. Gk. ἄρκτος, Sk. *ŕkšas.*

On the other hand, *rcs* was tolerated *in fine,* in *arx, merx.*

Also the combinations *s-br, r-br* are avoided by the evaporation of the *s, r,* bef. *b,* e.g. *mulie-bris* for *mulier-bris (or **mulies-bris) ; fune-bris* for *funes-bris bes. *funer-a, funus ; tene-brae* for **tenes-brae,* **temes-brae,* (§ 75, 2, n.) ; *fe-bris, he-bris,* for **fer-bris,* √*fer* (in *fer-uor,* etc.), origl. *ghar* (§ 73, 1 ; Corss. Krit. Beitr. 204 sqq.; Ebel, Zeitschr. xiv. 78 ; cf. L. Meyer, Comp. Gr. ii. 235, 241). Similarly in above-mentioned *tos-tus* for **tors-tus,* etc.

Quintus for *Quinc-tus* is late, cf. common *Quinc-tius* bes. later *Quin-tius;* the same holds good in *au-tor* for *auc-tor* fr. **aug-tor,* etc. Yet it cannot be doubted that *c* was lost bef. *t* sporadically even at an earlier period of the lang. in such cases as *in-uītus* fr. **in-uic-(i)-tus,* √*uic, uec,* Gk. ϝεκ (ἐκ-ών), Sk. *vaç,* i.e. *vak* (will) : *in-uī-tare* fr. **in-uic-(i)-tare,* √*uic, uec, uoc* (*uoc-are*), Gk. ϝεπ, Sk. *vak,* origl. *vak* (speak), etc. (cf. Corss. Krit. B. p. 4 sqq., and Krit. N. p. 47 sqq. where other views, however, are expressed). Also *Vitoria, Vitorius,* are supported

by inscrr. as by-forms of *Victorius, -a* (Corss. Krit. N. p. 45 § 77.
sqq.). v. another explanation of *inuītare*, etc., in § 39, 2.

b. **Complete assimiln. of following to foregoing
consonn.** This branch of assimiln. is well represented in
Lat.; thus e.g. *t* of superl. termn. *-timu-s* (origl. and Sk.
-tama-s, retained in *op-timus*) is assimild. to *s* in *-is-simus*=
*-is-timus; *is*, the shortest fm. of origl. *-yans*, which is in Lat.
iōs, iōr, ius, is accordingly the compar.-sf. to which the superl.
is added, e.g. *longis-simus* fr. **longis-tumu-s;* so too *t* of *-timus*
becomes assimild. to *r* and *l* in those superll. which are fmd. fr.
an unraised adj.-stem, e.g. *celer-rimus* fr. **celer-timu-s*, **facil-
-limus* fr.* *facil-tumu-s*, etc., unless these superll. stand (as G.
Curt. conjectures in a letter) for **celer-is-timus, *facil-is-timus,
*celerstimus, *facilstimus, *celersimus, *facilsimus.*

s is assimild. to *r* in *torr-eo* for **tors-eo* bes. *tos-tu-m* for
*tors-tu-m, terra for **ters-a*, origl. √*tars* (be dry), as in Germ.
dürr-e bes. *durs-t; fer-rem, uel-lem*, are fr. **fer-sem, *uel-sem*, cf.
ama-rem for **ama-sem, fac-sem*, etc. (cf. Corss. Krit. B. 402 sqq.).

Perh. *y* has become similar to the preceding consonn. in pres.
fmns. with doubled root-termns., as *pello, fallo, curro, mitto*, etc.,
though the combinations *lio, rio, tio*, are ordinary (v. pres.-st.).

v seems assimild. to preceding *l* in *pallor, pallidus*, for **pal-uor,
pal-uidus, cf. O.H.G. *falo, falaw-er, falw-er*, Lith. and f.f. *pálv-as*
(fallow—of deer); *mollis*, prob. fr. **molvis, *moldv-is*,=Sk. *mrdú-s*,
f.f. *mardu-s; sollu-s* (totus) equal to *saluo-s*, Sk. *sárva-s*, Gk.
ὅλος for **ὁλϝος. In these double fms. (*sollus* : *saluos* : : *pello* :
alius) we must prob. recognize traces of a mixture of dialects.

t after *s* becomes assimld. to it, in *censor, census*, √*cens*+sff.
-tor-, -tu-, cf. Osk. *cens-tur, cens-tom = censum*. Moreover,
assimiln. of *t* to foregoing *s* occurs in the many cases where fr.
d, t+t arise (subsequently *st*, cf. 2, Dissimiln.); after short
vowels the doubling is expressed in writing as well, after long
vowels, and after consonn. we find regularly only one *s*; yet we
find by their side spellings such as *fussus, cassus, diuissio, rissus*,
etc.,—which have therefore a good foundation in the lang.,—

§ 77. e.g. *fissus* fr. **fid-tus*, **fis-tus*, √*fid* in *findo*, *fĭd-i*; *gressu-s* fr. **gred-tu-s*, **gres-tu-s*, cf. *grad-ior*; *fossa* fr. **fos-ta*, **fod-ta*, √*fod* in *fod-io*; *passus* fr. **pat-tu-s*, **pas-tu-s*, cf. *pat-ior*; *ēsum* for **essum*, which we might have expected, fr. **ĕd-tu-m*, **es-tu-m*, cf. *ĕd-o*; *clausus* fr. **claud-tu-s*, **claus-tu-s*, cf. *claud-o*; *ūsus* (rarely *ussus*, inscrr.) fr. **ūt-tu-s*, **ūs-tu-s*, cf. *oit-ier*, *ūt-i*; *tonsu-s* fr. **tond-tu-s*, **tons-tu-s*, cf. *tond-eo*; *uicensumus*, *uicēsumus*, fr. **uicent-tumu-s*, **uicens-tumu-s* (unless here, as in *deci-mu-s*, only *mo* was added, in which case the fm. would be **uiginti-mu-s*); *uersus*, *uorsus*, for **uers-tus*, **uors-tus*, fr. **uert-tus*, **uort-tus* (*uert-ere*), etc.   On this Sound-law, cf. Corss. Krit. B. 418 sqq.

c. **Partial assimiln. of foregoing to follg. consonn.**
It is well known that bef. mutes mom. sonant consonn. become mute; e.g. *ac-tus* for **ag-tus*, cf. *ag-o*; *scrip-tus*, *scrip-si*, for **scrib-tus*, **scrib-si*, cf. *scrib-o*, etc.; in *uec-tus* bes. *ueh-o*, origl. *vagh-āmi*, we must assume a representation of origl. *gh* by Lat. *g*: origl. *vagh-ta-s*, Lat. **ueg-to-s*, *uec-tu-s*.   On the other hand, *sec-are*, *salic-em*, stand bes. *seg-mentum*, *salig-nus*, etc.; the sonant consonn. *m*, *n*, here change *c* to son. *g*.

Lab. moment. consonn. pass into their nasals bef. *n*: *som-nus*, *Sam-nium*, for **sop-nus*, **Sab-nium* (cf. *sop-ire*, *Sab-īni*, *Sab-elli*).

The earlier lang. still shows *s* bef. nasals, softened fr. *t*, as *res-mu-s* (*rēmus*) fr. **ret-mu-s* (ἐ-ρετ-μό-ς); *pes-na* (penna) fr. **pet-na* (√*pet*, fly, v. a).

Quadra-ginta bes. *quatri-duo* is peculiar; *t* bef. sonant *r* has become *d*.

From origl. *tr* in Lat. there have arisen sometimes **thr*, *dhr*, *br*, through the aspirating force of the *r* (v. supr. Gk., also Zend), (on *b* as a representative of origl. *dh*, v. § 73, 2), e.g. *consobrinus* (cousin) for **-sosbrinus* (*s* bef. *b* is lost regularly, v. sup.), and this for **sosdhrinus*, **sosthrinus*, **sostrinus*, fr. **sostor--inu-s*, st. **sos-tor-*, usu. **sosor-*, *soror-* (sister); *salūbris* fr. **salus-bris*, and this for **salus-dhris*, **salus-thris*, **salus-tris*, **salut--tris* (*salus*, *salut-is*). Cf. Ebel, Zeitschr. xiv. 78; Kuhn, Zeitschr. xiv. 222, xv. 238.   On the other hand, Cors. Krit. N. p. 186 sqq.

d. Partial assimilation of following to foregoing § 77.
consonants. This takes place esp. in the case of *t*, which,
after nasals and liquids, commonly changes into spir.
s; the same tendency is seen after gutt. (after *c*),—the latter occurs
also in Sk. (v. § 52, 2, n. 2); e.g. *man-sum* for **man-tu-m*
(*man-eo*); in *Leu-cesie*—important on acct. of *eu*, v. § 36 —
(voc.; title of Iuppiter) for **leucetie*, fr. **Leucentie*, cf. *Leucetios*,
Loucetios, for **leucent-ios*, **loucent-ios*, further fmm. fr. **leucent-*,
loucent-, pres. part. act. fr. **leuc-o*, **louc-o*, f.f. *rauk-āmi*, √*luc*,
origl. *ruk* (Corss. Krit. B. 471); *t* has become *s* after origl. *n*,
which afterwards was lost, in the same way; *pul-su-s* for **pul-tu-s*
(*pel-lo*, *pe-pul-i*), *spar-sus* for **spar(g)-tu-s* (*sparg-o*), etc.; but
by their side occur *ten-tu-s* (and *ten-su-s*), *sepul-tu-s* (*sepel-io*),
tor-tu-s for **tor(c)-tu-s*, (*torqu-eo*), etc.; **mac-simu-s* thus is for
*mag-timu-s (*mag-nus*; cf. *op-timu-s*); *fixus*, i.e. *fic-su-s*, for **fig-tu-s*
(*figo*); *noxa*, i.e. **noc-sa*, for **noc-ta* (*noc-eo*), etc., bes. *ac-tu-s* (*ag-o*),
fic-tu-s (√*fig* in *fi-n-g-o*), and many others with retained *t*.

Regularly *t* does not pass into *s* after *n*, when *nt* belongs to
one and the same word-formative particle, e.g. *feru-nt*, *fere-nt-em*,
etc. (yet cf. above-mentioned *Leucesios* for **Leucentios*).

Lapsus for **lap-tu-s*, **lab-tu-s*, is singular (cf. *lab-i*), bes.
scrip-tu-s (*scrib-ere*), cf. Corss. Krit. B. 420 sqq. (Ebel, Zeitschr.
xiv. 245 sqq. here assumes an inserted *s*: **lap-stus*, **man-stum*,
to which *t* was assimild.)

Note.—Yet *mend-ax* belongs prob. to *ment-iri*, according to
the system laid down by Schuchardt, Vocalismus des vulgär-
lateins, Lpz. 1866; cf. however on this point Aufrecht in
Zeitschr. ix. 232; Corss. Krit. B. 117 sqq.

e. Change of *s* to *r* betw. vowels, or betw. vowels
and sonant consonn., also after vowels in termination (in the lang. in question). The sonant consonn. here
change the mute *s* into sonant *r*. The same process takes place,
e.g. in Germ. also (*war*, *wären*, for *was*, *wäsen*, √*was*, cf.
ge-wēs-en, etc.), and in Sk. So, e.g. in *gener-is* (genus) for old
Lat. **genes-os*; *maiores* fr. **maioses*; *erat* fr. **esat*, √*es*, etc.;

§ 77. *ueter-nus* fr. **uetes-nus* (*uetus, ueter-is*) ; *car-men* fr. **cas-men,* cf. Old-Lat. *Cas-mena,* √*cas ; diur-nus, ho-dier-nus,* from an otherwise lost st. **dios-, *dies-*=origl. *divas* (in *dies, diei,* the final *s* of the root has been lost), etc.; *arbor* for earlier *arbos ; amor* fr. **amos, *amo-se,* etc. *In fine* this *r* for *s* is caused through analogy of the other fms. (*arbor-is, amar-is*). Betw. vowels *s* has remained but rarely, e.g. *nasus,* cf. Sk. *nas,* Scl. *nosŭ,* etc., *miser, uasa, posui ;* regularly *s* only remains instead of *ss,* e.g. *casus* for *cassus* fr. **cad-tu-s,* etc. (v. b).

f. Loss of consonn. betw. vowels. Here too we see a kind of assimiln., in that sonant consonn. become thereby similar to the surrounding vowels, and are swallowed up by them, so that only the attendant accent remains.

In the Romance langg. this process is very common (e.g. *ducatus,* It. *ducato,* Sp. *ducado,* Fr. *duché*). The commonest case is the loss of *y* and *v,* as *moneo, monēs,* fr. **moneyo, *moneyis,* f.f. *mānayāmi, mānayasi ; amasti* fr. **amaisti, amauisti ; fluont, fluunt,* fr. *flouont,* etc. Exceptionally *s* has been lost betw. two vowels (Corss. Krit. Beitr. 464 sqq.), thus e.g. in *uēr* (spring) fr. **veser,* cf. Gk. ἔαρ for **Ϝεσαρ,* Lith. *vasarà* (summer), Sk. *vas-antá-s* (spring), O. Bulg. *ves-na ; uīs, uim,* bes. *uires, uirium,* st. *uisi-, uiri-* ; prob. through analogy fr. origl. **divas-* arose a fm. *diēs, diēi,* bes. *ho-dier-nus,* fr. **dives-no-s* ; fr. origl. and Sk. *nábhas-, nūbēs, nūbi-s* ; fr. origl. and Sk. *sadas-* (cf. Gk. ἕδος), *sēdēs, sēdi-s,* and other like forms. Further, loss of origl. *bh,* Lat. *f, b,* has certainly occurred in *ama-ui* for **ama-fui,* etc.; in dat. pl. e.g. *equīs,* f.f. *akva-bhya(m)s* (v. § 73, 3). On the doubtful loss of *c* betw. vowels, cf. § 39, 2; § 77, a, sub fin.; on loss of *h,* cf. § 73, 1.

g. Evident insertion of conson. betw. concurrent consonn. The change fr. *m* to *mp,* for the accommodation of *m* to the follg. *s, t,* is well known ; it occurs in the best MSS. (e.g. in Cod. Medic. Vergili), e.g. *hiem-p-s, sum-p-si, sum-p-tus,* etc. Bef. the *s, t, m* became an audible conclusion, i.e. changed to *mp.*

2. Dissimilation.

t, d, before follg. *t,* change into *s* (as in Zend, Gk., Scl.-Germ.),

e.g. *eques-ter, pedes-ter*, for **equet-ter, *pedet-ter*, cf. *equit-is*, § 77.
pedit-is ; es-t, es-tis, for **ed-t, *ed-tis*, cf. *ed-o ; claus-trum* for
*claud-trum, cf. *claud-o* ; st. *potēs-tāti̇̄- (potestas)* for **potens-tāti-*
fr.**potent-tāti-*, st. *potent- (potens)* +sf. *-tāti-*, etc.
Likewise through the striving after dissimiln. *-āli-s* is interchanged with *-āri-s*; the latter is found in those cases where the
word-st. to which this secondary sf. is added contains an *l*, e.g.
mor-tali-s, but *uolg-ari-s, popul-ari-s, epul-ari-s*.

In the dislike of the immediate succession of two like sounds
is found also the cause of the contraction of two like or similar
consonn., which are separated by only one vowel, into one,
through evanescence of the intervening vowel (cf. Gk. § 68, 2 ;
a similar phenom. in M.H.G. has been mentioned by me in
Kuhn's Zeitschr. x. 160) ; thus *consuētūdo* for **consuēti-tūdo*
(con-suētu-s), st. *aestāti-* for **aestitāti- (aestu-s)*, st. *nūtrīc-* for
nūtrī-trīc- (nutrī-re), *stipendium* for **stipi-pendium (stip-s, stip-is)*,
uenēficus for **uenēni-ficus (uenēnu-m)*, etc. (L. Meyer. Comp. Gr.
i. 281).

INITIAL.   § 78.

In Lat. more than in the other kindred langg., where loss of
initial consonn. occurs in the main only sporadically, initial
consonn. are exposed to evaporation : of two initial consonn.
the former often falls away, yet even one single conson. is found
to disappear bef. a follg. vowel (*c* bef. *u*).

Thus no Lat. word begins with *sn, sm, sr* ; where these combinations origl. occurred initially, the *s* is lost, and only the
second conson. remains, e.g. *nix, niuis*, fr. **snig-s, *snigv-is* (v.
supr. § 72, 1), cf. Zend √*çniž* (snow), O. Bulg. *snĕg-ŭ* (snow),
Lith. *snìg-ti* (snow, v.), *snĕg-as* (snow, n.), Goth. *snaiv-s* (snow) ;
nurus (daughter-in-law) fr. **snurus*, cf. O.H.G. *snur*, Sk. *snušá̆*,
me-mor (mindful) fr. **sme-mor* (cf. *spo-pond-i, ste-ti* for **ste-sti*,
etc.), and this fr. **sme-smor*, as Sk. and origl. √*smar* (bethink ;
on √*flu*=origl. *sru*, v. § 71, 3 n.).

Neither does initial *vr, vl*, occur in Lat., e.g. *laqueus* (noose),
cf. Goth. *vruggō* (sling), **vriggan* (wring, wind); *lacer* (torn),

§ 78. cf. ῥάκος (rag), Aiol. βράκος, i.e. Ϝράκος, Sk. √vraçk, i.e. vrak (tear); radix (root), cf. ῥίζα, Lesb. βρίσδα, i.e. Ϝρίζα, *Ϝριδ-ya, Goth. vaúrts (root), O.H.G. wurza, wurzala, f.f. of root there-fore=vrad, etc.

Bef. f, s has disappeared in fallere (deceive) bes. σφάλλειν, fungus (id.) bes. σφόγγος, funda (sling) bes. σφενδόνη, fides (lyre) bes. σφίδη; on the conjectured loss of s bef. p, v. Corss. Krit. B. 457. More singular, on the other hand, are cases like teg-o (cover) for *steg-o, cf. i-steg-a for *in-steg-a (cover), Gk. στέγ-ω, στέγ-η, bes. τέγ-η, Lith. stógas (roof), in Germ. likewise the s is lost, cf. deck-en, dach; tundo (thump), √tud, bes. Goth. stauta, √stut, but Sk. √tud; taurus (bull), ταῦρος, O. Bulg. turŭ, but Goth. stiur, Sk. sthūra-s; cau-ere (beware) bes. Goth. us-skav-yan (be wakeful), origl. √skav, etc.; bes. freq. initial st, sc. Whilst, inversely, of sc only the s remains in sirpeus (rush—), sirpea, sirpiculus, -la, (junket), sirpare (bind), bes. scirpus (withe), scirpeus, scirpea, etc., cf. O.H.G. scilaf, sciluf, N.H.G. schilf, and perh. in some others (Corss. Krit. B. 31 sqq.). Also in lā-tum for *tlātum, cf. √tol (tollo), init. t is lost. p bef. l has clearly been lost in lien (milt) bes. Sk. plihán-, plīhán, σπλήν; perh. in lanx, lanc-is (dish), bes. πλάξ, πλακ-ός (flat-, plate), O.H.G. flah; whether lae-tus (glad) is for *plai-to-s, and belongs to Sk. √pri (love, cheer), lau in lau-ere, lauare (wash), stands for *plav, and here a causative fmn. of √plu is seen, may seem doubtful (lau belongs prob. to same root as luo, and not to root plu). Upon loss of c bef. l, which is not yet beyond doubt in my opinion, cf. Corss. Krit. B. p. 2 sqq., Krit. N. p. 35 sqq. On the whole there is still considerable doubt and uncertainty in this branch, because we are confined to a few examples.

It is well known that it was not till historic times that men simplified gn into n, as e.g. in nō-sco, nō-tus, nō-men, fr. older gnō-sco, cf. co-gnō-sco, gnō-tus, gnō-men, cf. co-gnō-men; narrare fr. earlier gnā-rigare, from same gnā-rus, where the initial conson. is fully preserved, fr. same root as gnō-sco, origl. gna fr. gan (nosse: cf. γι-γνώ-σκω, Sk. gña, Germ. kan and kna, etc.):

nā-tus for earlier *gnā-tus*, preserved in *co-gnā-tus*, √*gna* fr. *gan* § 78. (gignere), cf. *gen-us.* The same sound-law, by which an initial gutt.+*n* becomes *n*, occurs also in Eng.: the old initials *gn, kn,* are still noticeably written in Eng. of this day, in words like *gnat, gnaw, knowledge,* etc., but *g, k,* are no longer heard. Cf. loss of gutt. bef. nasals medially (§ 77, 1, a).

Similarly at a later period of the lang. *st* was lost before *l* (Corss. Krit. B. 461, cf. 149) in st. *stleiti-, sleiti-, leiti-, līti- (lis,* suit), bes. which we place O.H.G. *strīt,* N.H.G. *streit* (in st.-terminations, it is true, this does not occur in Lat. words), in Inscrr. *slis* is seen, *stl* thus becomes *l* through *sl : stlātu-s, lātu-s* (broad), which is derived from origl, √*star (ster-no, strā-tus,* στορ-έννυμι, etc.)—thus the origl. word means "spread"; *stlocu-s, locu-s* (place), which we refer to Sk. √*sthal,* further fmn. of *stha,* origl. √*sta* (stand), and others whose derivation is not quite clear.

As *suāuis* for **suaduis* (§ 77, 1, a), so *uiginti* for **duiginti,* cf. *duo,* Sk. *dva ;* the dropping away of the *d* occurs nevertheless in Gk. too (εἴκοσι), in Kelt. (Erse *fiche, fichet,* i.e. *uiginti*), in Aryan (Sk. *vīçáti,* Zend *vīçaiti*), and thus dates from the earliest times. If **duiginti* had stood its ground to a later time, **biginti* would have arisen, as *bis* fr. **duis, bellum* fr. *duellum, bonus* fr. *duonus (duonoro ;* Epit. Scip. Barb. f.): here through mutual influence *b* has arisen, as an assimiln. of *d* and *v,* since *d* became assimilated to *v* as regards quality (labial quality), and *v* became like *d* as regards quantity, i.e. became a momentary sonant conson.

Bef. *y, d* is lost in *Iouis,* etc., for **Dyouis,* cf. Old Lat. *Dioue* (Ioui), and Osk. *Diuveí* (Momms. Unterital. Diall. p. 255), Sk. *dyāu-s* (heaven), Gk. Zεύς=*δyευ-ς, etc., √*dyu (=div,* shine). The same loss is seen in *Iuno* for **Diou-no,* fmd. fr. same root (Corss. Krit. N. p. 142).

Even the favourite initial sound *qu* appears simplified to *u* in *uermis* (cf. Germ. *wurm*) for **quermis,* f.f. *karmi-s,* Sk. *krmi-s,* Lith. *kirm-elé* (worm ; but cf. G. Curt. Gr. Et.² p. 485 sqq.) ;

§ 78. so too *v* appears to stand for *gv* in √*uen* (uenire)=**guen* for **ge-n* (§ 77, 1), further fmn. fr. √*ga* (go), by means of *n*. At a very late period arose the loss of init. *c* bef. *u* in several fms. of interrog. pronn., e.g. in *u-bi* for **cu-bi* or **quo-bi*, kept in compd. *ali-cu-bi*, cf. Umbr. *pufe* (*p*=Lat. *c*); *u-nde* for* *cu-nde*, kept in *ali-cu-nde*; *u-ter* for **eu-ter* (compar. fm. st. *cu-*=*quo-*), cf. Osk. *púturus-pid* (i.e. utrique) with *p*=Lat. *e*, Gk. πότερος, earlier Iôn. κότερος, Sk. and f.f. *ka-tarás*.

§ 79.   FINAL.

The Lat. lang., as we have it, generally permits only single consonn. at the end of a word, but also groups of two and even three consonn., viz. nasal or liq.+mutes; mutes, *r*, *l*, *m*, *n*+*s*; *s*+*t*, e.g. *ferunt, hunc, uolt, fert; scrobs, ars* for **art-s*, and so in similar cases (but *uir* for **uirs, quatuor* for **quatuors*, fr. **uiro-s, quatuor-es*), *fers* (fr. *feris*), *puls* for **pult-s* (but *uis* for **uil-s*, f.f. *varsi*, " thou wilt," *sal* for **sal-s*, *s* lost), *hiem(p)s, ferens* for **ferent-s*, and so in such cases (but *nouōs, nouās*, for **nouons, *nouans*); the combinations *rs, ls, ns*, were therefore tolerated in these cases where they stand for *rts, lts, nts*, i.e. when *s* alone =*ss*; *est*; nasal or liq.+mute+*s*, e.g. *hiemps, urbs, arx*, i.e. *arc-s, falx*, i.e. **falcs;* indeed our present final consonn., for by far the greatest part, did not become final until vowels had evaporated, and were not compressed until vowels had been lost. Yet in no case was a doubled conson. tolerated, *in fine*, e.g. *os, fel*, not **oss, *fell*, cf. *oss-is, fell-is*; moreover, the combination of two mom. consonn. was not admissible, e.g. *lac* for **lact*, cf. *lact-is*, and *rd, cor* for **cord*, cf. *cord-is*; where these combinations should have been final, the latter conson. was discarded.

It was not until Lat. became a fixed written language in classical times that the termn. assumed a more definite existence. The earlier national archaic lang. shows in spelling a great indifference towards final consonn. In fact, the consonantal termns. *s, m, t*, important as they are for word-formn., were sometimes expressed in writing, sometimes omitted, which we find to be the case in Umbr. also. This fact proves that in § 79. earlier times (and later also in the unformed branch of the Roman) the final consonn. were heard with difficulty, perh. as in many Romance langg. (e.g. *d* in Span., *t*, *nt*, etc., in Fr.). The correct lang. here introduced a fixed rule, after the pattern of the Gk.; the conson. was now either always written (the rule), or regularly discarded (the exception). A few exx. of the unsettled treatment of the termn. have remained in spelling even as late as the classical period.

We will treat separately of the final consonants, origl. *s*, *m*, *t*, since they are most important for grammar.

s is omitted in writing in the oldest inscrr. in cases like *Tetio, Furio,* n. sg. for *Tetio-s, Furio-s; Corneli, Clodi,* etc., for *Cornelis, Clodis* = *Cornelios, Clodios* (Ritschl, Progr. of 12 March, 1861). Yet in the earliest lang. the loss of final *s* is mainly confined to n. sg. It is well known that even at a later time the poets were wont to neglect final *s* bef. initial consonn , and that the weak pronunciation of final *s* is otherwise attested. The written lang. in most cases decided in favour of the retention of the *s*. Nevertheless the wavering betw. retention and loss of final *s* in 2 p. sg. med. is obvious, e.g. *amabaris, amabare*; further in *magi-s* and *mage, poti-s, pote,* where, at the same time *i* was dulled to *e*.

The loss of *s* was regularly allowed, e.g. in n. pl. masc. of *o*-st., which in the older lang. still shows the *s* here and there, e.g. *heis, magistreis,* etc., bes. *hei, magistrei*; a later fm., as *hi, magistri,* was the one afterwards exclusively fixed upon; the same process takes place in gen. sg. fem. of *a*-stems, e.g. *suaes, dimidiaes,* later *ae* only is found, etc.

Through evaporation of the vowel of the last syll. *s* after *r* is lost, as in *puer, uir, quatuor, acer* (with auxil. vowel bef. *r*), for **pueros, *uiros, *quatuores* (cf. τέσσαρες), *acris*; more rarely this occurs after *l, uigil* for *uigilis, *uigils.*

m, only faintly audible *in fine,* is likewise often unexpressed in earlier monuments of the lang., e.g. *oino, uiro, duonoro* (Epit.

§ 79. Scip.), bes. *pocolom, sacrom*, etc. In popular diall. this faint pronunciation of final *s* remains, as later inscrr. prove; the written lang., however, firmly maintained the letter in spelling. One effect of the weak pronunciation of final *m* must here be noticed, viz. that in verse it was not considered a conson. bef. vowels.

Also final *n* seems to have become only faintly heard, cf. *alioqui* bes. *alioquin* and the like (cf. however, Corss. Krit. B. 272).

Origl. final *t* had in earlier Lat. a weak sound, like a scarcely audible *d*; accordingly it is freq. omitted in writing, e.g. *patre* (Epit. Scip. Barb.) bes. *Gnaiuod*, etc. In classical Lat. *d* for origl. *t* was sometimes retained in writing, thus e.g. in ntr. pronl. decl. e.g. *quo-d*=origl. *ka-t, id*=origl. *i-t*, etc. (the spelling in *t* is rarer in these cases), sometimes completely discarded, as in abl. sg., where *d*=origl. *t* has been retained in archaic Lat. only, but was not written in class. Lat., e.g. *equō-d, equō* =origl. *akvā-t*, Sk. *áçvā-t*; in termn. *-to* of imper. *t* has likewise been lost, e.g. origl. *as-tāt*, Osk. *es-tūd*, Lat. *esto* fr. **es-tōd*. Final *t* in Lat. is not origl., but has become final after vowelloss, and thus remains in class. Lat., whilst archaic Lat. does not show this *t*, e.g. *īt*, f.f. **ei-ti*, origl. *ai-ti; uehit(i), uehunt(i), *uehonti*, origl. *vaghati, vaghanti*, etc., but archaically *dede*= *dedet, dedit*, and even indeed *dedro=dedront, dederunt*.

Thus *nt* also in earlier times and colloquial lang. was barely audible in pronunciation; wherein lies the cause of the double fms. of the later fixed spelling of 3 p. pl. pf., as *fecerunt* (with entire termn. retained) and *fecere* (with lost *nt* and weakened vowel).

The clipping of final consonn. was even more prevalent in Umbr. than in Old Lat.; whilst the Osk. does not show this phenomenon, since there was a generally-received Samnite orthography before the time from which our earliest inscrr. date, and the popular variations in pronunciation were no longer followed in spelling.

STEPHEN AUSTIN AND SONS, PRINTERS, HERTFORD.

For EU product safety concerns, contact us at Calle de José Abascal, 56–1°,
28003 Madrid, Spain or eugpsr@cambridge.org.

www.ingramcontent.com/pod-product-compliance
Ingram Content Group UK Ltd.
Pitfield, Milton Keynes, MK11 3LW, UK
UKHW012343130625
459647UK00009B/495